In his short career of about ten years, Franz Kafka published only a handful of the many stories he had written. Before he died, he asked that his remaining manuscripts be destroyed.

Fortunately, his work was saved, and today, acknowledged as having more influence on modern literature than perhaps any other European writer, Kafka enjoys a posthumous success far greater than any he had ever dreamed of.

For orders other than by individual consumers, Pocket Books grants a discount on the purchase of **10 or more** copies of single titles for special markets or premium use. For further details, please write to the Vice President of Special Markets, Pocket Books, 1230 Avenue of the Americas, 9th Floor, New York, NY 10020-1586.

For information on how individual consumers can place orders, please write to Mail Order Department, Simon & Schuster Inc., 100 Front Street, Riverside, NJ 08075.

THE BASIC
KAFKA

Introduction by Erich Heller

WASHINGTON SQUARE PRESS
PUBLISHED BY POCKET BOOKS

New York   London   Toronto   Sydney   Tokyo   Singapore

Excerpts from the following are reprinted by arrangement
with Schocken Books, Inc.:

THE DIARIES OF FRANZ KAFKA 1910-1913, Max Brod, ed.
Copyright 1948 by Schocken Books, Inc.

THE DIARIES OF FRANZ KAFKA 1914-1923, Max Brod, ed.
Copyright 1949 by Schocken Books, Inc.

LETTERS TO MILENA, Willi Haas, ed. Translated by
Tania and James Stern. Copyright 1953 by
Schocken Books, Inc.

LETTERS TO FELICE, Erich Heller and Jugen Born, eds.
Translated by James Stern and Elizabeth Duckworth.
Copyright © 1967 by Schocken Books, Inc.

LETTERS TO FRIENDS, FAMILY AND EDITORS. Translated
by Richard and Clara Winston. Copyright © 1958 by
Schocken Books, Inc.

A Washington Square Press publication of
POCKET BOOKS, a division of Simon & Schuster Inc.
1230 Avenue of the Americas, New York, NY 10020

Copyright 1946, 1947, 1948, 1949, 1954,
© 1958, 1971 by Schocken Books, Inc.,
Introduction copyright © 1979 by Washington Square Press,
a division of Simon & Schuster Inc.

ISBN: 0-671-53145-X

First Pocket Books printing October 1979

15   14

WASHINGTON SQUARE PRESS and WSP colophon are
registered trademarks of Simon & Schuster Inc.

Printed in the U.S.A.

Grateful acknowledgment is made to Michael Kowal, Associate Professor of English, Queens College, for making the selections from the diaries and letters.

Table of Contents

Introduction

by
Erich Heller

IT WAS A wise decision to include in this anthology of
Franz Kafka's writings not only many of his most
accomplished and most characteristic stories and aphorisms, but also some of the personal and private ut-
terances made in diaries and letters. For once it would
be right to use quotation marks not for marking a
quotation but—as it has become a bad habit—as a
kind of patronizing apology for using dubious and worn-
out words. Indeed, it is doubtful whether the designation
"personal and private" can, in the case of Kafka, truly
set off what was meant to be read only by the diarist
himself or by the recipients of his letters from what
was intended for publication. Was *anything* he wrote
meant for the public? Or *everything*? If his friend and
first editor, Max Brod, had done what in a kind of
informal last will he asked him to do (to destroy all
the unpublished paper on which he had written), what
would have survived would not exceed one modestly
sized volume of disquieting stories, written in a style
that is as unusual as it is exquisite. But one volume,
however stirring, would not have been enough to establish Franz Kafka as the classic of a whole literary
epoch; and every epoch has the classic it deserves.
Perhaps it was the fear of such a prospect, questionable in the widest sense of the word, that accounts for
Kafka's ambiguous and predominantly negative attitude
toward publicity.

Was Max Brod right in tirelessly disobeying his

friend's ostensible wish? Was it not the same wish as that of Josephine in Kafka's story, the greatest singer that had ever emerged from the nation of mice; Josephine who *said* she wanted to be forgotten and thus reach "the height of redemption"? But this is a redemption that comes to Josephine through miscalculation. For one day, having failed in all her efforts to be released from her ordinary work duties as a citizen in reward of her unique artistry, she refuses to sing any more and even goes into hiding in the expectation that she would be discovered and besieged with requests at all costs to sing again. For "what Josephine really wants is not what she puts into words." No, "what she wants is public, unambiguous, permanent recognition of her art. . . ." It would seem that Kafka has succeeded where his last heroine has failed in her bid for fame by withdrawing her art from the world. Strange that Max Brod has never called on Josephine to sanction his strategy to make his friend, seemingly against his will, perform in public after all.

Nonetheless, was not an offense committed by all those who later assiduously collected, edited, and translated into many languages Kafka's thoughts and confessions that fill his personal notebooks, diaries, and correspondence, including even the telegrams, those shorthand documents of protracted agonies, that arrange and then again cancel appointments with what he called life—journeys, for instance, from Prague to Berlin to visit his fiancée Felice Bauer—as irreconcilably opposed to his existence as a writer, a life outside his life? When a graphologist said of him—Felice had shown the man a sample of his handwriting and then reported it to Kafka—that he was interested in literature, he responded with vehement irony. No, he said, he had no literary interests: "I consist of literature and am unable to be anything else." Therefore, the line dividing the "purely personal" from the literary is, with Kafka, more tenuous and elusive than with any other writer, with the exception, perhaps, of Flaubert whom he regarded, within the family of literature, as his next of kin.

Where the art of writing is indistinguishable from living—or what he felt to be his failure in living—there is hardly any room for those indiscretions and violations of privacy that threaten to become a constant feature of the literary-biographical industry. At the beginning of March 1912, at a time when he had published not more than a few short sketches, he entered in his diary the ominous question: "Who is to confirm for me the truth or probability of this, that it is only because of my literary mission* that I am uninterested in all other things and therefore heartless." A few months later he was persuaded that he had fallen in love with Felice, or rather had stumbled into it, and before long she might have been ready to provide that confirmation, not only after the breaking of his two engagements to her. Two years later, in August 1914, he himself endorsed that truth. He was in no need of any confirmation any more. "My talent for portraying my dreamlike inner life has thrust all other matters into the background; my life has dwindled dreadfully, nor will it cease to dwindle," an observation the more remarkable for the fact that the "other matters" were not only his first separation from Felice but also a war that had just been declared and was to acquire the designation "the First World War."

Kafka was not yet twenty-eight and far from having made a name for himself as a writer when, on February 19, 1911, he wrote a sentence in his diary that might be regarded as a symptom of megalomania but betrays a humbler if not less extraordinary state of mind. He was about to go to bed at two o'clock in the morning, obviously after long nocturnal hours at the writing table, inspired hours, it seems, for the inspiration lasted and would prove itself, he thought, beyond whatever it was that he had written during that night; in fact, in everything he produced, and be it merely an arbitrary brief phrase like "He looked out of the window." And of this simple sequence of words

---

* The German is *"literarische Bestimmung."* "Destiny" might be a more fitting translation.

Kafka said: "It already has perfection." No doubt, a great deal of higher nonsense could be written in commenting on this diary entry. The temptation is to be resisted. Suffice it to say that Kafka might just as well have used as an example of inspired prose the two words with which he would soon address the woman in Berlin: "Dearest Felice."

The startling diary remark shows that the moment Kafka put pen to paper—if it was a promising, an inspired, moment—he knew he had exchanged the domain of living for that of art, indeed of alchemy. It was as if he had touched a magic stone that opened the enchanted mountain, enclosing him in the crystalline space within, a shining cave that more often than not revealed itself at closer inspection as a torture chamber. He had not yet seen Felice again after their one short meeting in the Brods' house in Prague, but had begun prodigiously to write to Berlin, declaring his love and his desire to live with her—*and*, as he did during the night of January 14–15, 1913, his need for absolute solitude: "I have often thought that the best mode of life for me would be to sit in the innermost room of a spacious locked cellar with my writing things and a lamp. . . . And how I would write! From what depths I would drag it up! Without effort! For extreme concentration knows no effort. The trouble is that I might not be able to keep it up for long, and at the first failure . . . would be bound to end in a grandiose fit of madness." It is unlikely that there is another love letter in which the lover's imagination, addressing itself to the beloved, at the same time locks the door on her and descends into the lonely cellar, the true abode of his true passion.

Sometime in 1922, two years before his death, Kafka wrote a sentence almost as simple as "He looked out of the window." The sentence ran: "It was very early in the morning, the streets clean and deserted, I was on my way to the station." Perfection? Only because the sentence perfectly succeeds in concealing the magic stone that imperceptibly has been smuggled into the writer's hand. In the next sentence an unusually responsive reader, familiar with Kafka's work, may become aware of slight tremors of the earth beneath those empty streets, one of which would in all probability lead to the station. Still, there is no trace yet of any signpost pointing in the direction of the secret entrance gate to the realm of mystical metaphors. Yet the truth is that we are already watching, without quite knowing it, a traveler in headlong pursuit of an elusive, mysterious goal. The passage continues: "As I compared the tower clock with my watch I realized that it was much later than I had thought and that I had to hurry; the shock of this discovery made me feel uncertain of the way, I wasn't very well acquainted with the town as yet; fortunately, there was a policeman at hand, I ran to him and breathlessly asked him the way."

Perhaps one has had to have some spies in the territory of Kafka's mind and imagination to become instantly distrustful of the material reliability of his watches and clocks, particularly when they show different times. In the same year in which this anecdote was written, Kafka entered in his diary, January 16, 1922, the following observation about two behaviors of time, radically at variance the one with the other; and although it is impossible to relate them exactly to the disagreement between the tower clock and the traveler's own watch, related they undoubtedly are (and who will want to insist on exactitude where even instruments whose sole purpose is to be precise care so little about precision): "The clocks are not in unison; the inner one runs crazily on at a devilish or demonic or in any case inhuman pace, the outer one limps along at its usual speed. What else can happen but that the worlds split apart, and they do split apart, or at least clash in a fearful manner."

The two "times," be it noted, instantly come to stand for two worlds, the external world and the world within. Their not being "in unison" but on the contrary in ferocious disagreement is, ever since *Hamlet*, one of the most persistent calamities of modern persons, incurable patients of the fatal disorder. Three faith healers are customarily sitting at their double bedsides: one, taught in the school of Freud, prescribing psychological adjustment to the irritating circumstances, the second, instructed by Marx, recommending the revolution that would bring those circumstances into accord with the ever frustrated demands of the inner soul, and the third, looking much like Rilke and murmuring "Only within can be world, my love!" There is no doubt that Kafka is the most alienated alien among the swarms of alienation, estranged even from them by the unique nature of his genius. He hardly ever blames his suffering upon the world. No, *he* is, he thinks, the culprit and accepts the judgment that concludes his "trial."

In our anecdote this falling apart of two times and worlds occurs with utter abruptness, and yet the unprepared event seems, in retrospect, to have been in the making throughout the "perfect" sentences that preceded it, and not only because the experienced reader pricks up his ears as soon as Kafka speaks of someone who breathlessly asks the way, even if the question is addressed, in a deserted street, to only a policeman of whom he expects to learn how to get to the station. Among Kafka's aphorisms, published by his editor in the volume *Wedding Preparations* and printed under the heading "Reflections on Sin, Suffering, Hope and the True Way," there is one—and it is one of his most desperate and only very "hesitatingly" hopeful—that says: "There is a goal, but no way; what we call a way is hesitation." It is this "no way" into which the way to the station is suddenly transformed, just as the watch, the tower clock, and the policeman suffer a "metamorphosis," effected by the mere use of language. "Metamorphosis" could serve as a title for many more stories than the one known under that name; and in most instances it would be a transformation considerably subtler than the notorious one in which the salesman Gregor Samsa was changed into a giant insect.

This is how our anecdote of only a few lines ends: "The policeman smiled and said: 'You asking me the way?' 'Yes', I said, 'since I can't find it myself.' 'Give it up! Give it up!' said he, and turned with a sudden jerk, like someone who wants to be left alone with his laughter." "Give it up" is written above the anecdote that now is no longer an anecdote but has become a parable. Max Brod named it thus; Kafka called it "A Commentary." It is a commentary, of course, on nothing less than human life in the perspective of Franz Kafka, and could also serve as a motto to his fragmentary novels *The Trial* and *The Castle*. "Give it up!"—by not completing the novels he appears to have obeyed the injunction, understood both literally and symbolically, if ever he quite knew the difference. In any case, the difference all but vanished as soon as he took up his pen; and it is only a slight exaggeration to say that it did not matter much whether he began to write a novel, a story, a diary note, or a letter. Hence much in his letters is indistinguishable from his literary creations, and most of them enact the devilish or demonic conversation between the watch and the tower clock, the question and the laughter, and above all the dialogue between the real and the symbolic that concludes his masterful reflection "On Parables." It is a most remarkable ending, for it aims at the elimination of the "merely" or "only" with which one partner in the short dialogue tries to reduce the other's belief in the reality of the symbol. What can a parable with its symbolic meaning really do for us, he asks; for when

the sage says: "Go over," he does not mean that we should cross to some actual place, which we could do anyhow if the labor were worth it; he means some fabulous yonder, something unknown to us, something that he cannot designate more precisely either, and therefore cannot help us here in the very least.

At best the wise instruct us, the speaker continues, in the incomprehensibility of the incomprehensible, and nobody needs to learn that. What everybody would be grateful for is advice on how to get through a day of real cares and worries. And Kafka's most wittily pointed rejoinder to this imaginary voice in the imaginary dialogue is: By breaking down the barrier we have erected between our notions of a heavily fenced-in prosaic reality ("the cares we have to struggle with every day") and the realm of the parable, the symbol, which appears, viewed from the angle of the care-ridden and worried and realistic man, as a mere extravagance of the intellectual fancy. For he who inhabits a reality that has been successfully fortified against all symbolic incursions may indeed pride himself, sometimes, on his "real" victories, but "in parable you have lost." For the "symbolic" stone he has rejected in the building of the seemingly quite real house was meant to be the cornerstone of the true edifice. "On Parables," a mere morsel of literature, is yet that piece of writing in which Kafka, effortlessly and perhaps even unawares, comes as close to the spirit of biblical parables as any writer of the twentieth century may get without sacrifice of authenticity.

What is biblical is, above all, Kafka's preoccupation with guilt. "Guilt is never to be doubted," says the officer in the story Kafka wrote after the dissolution of his first engagement to Felice Bauer, "In the Penal Colony" (October 1914). That officer had been appointed judge *and* prosecutor of a soldier horribly done to death for an offense that would be regarded as quite trivial in any sane legal order. The words, spoken in reply to a visitor's reproachful question whether the wretched victim had ever had any chance of defending himself, mark the very center of the moral imagination at work in that story as well as in all of Kafka's novels, and certainly in "The Judgment" and "The Metamorphosis." (Kafka once thought of publishing these two stories together with "In the Penal Colony" in one volume to be called "Punishments," a plan that not only might have resulted in the most crowdedly oppressive book of world literature but also, implicitly, might have made Gregor Samsa of "The Metamorphosis" one of Kafka's sentenced characters.) "Guilt is never to be doubted" and if, in any legal sense, it cannot even be detected, it has to be assumed that it lies hidden under an opaque surface of innocence. In his diary entry of September 30, 1915, Kafka says of the heroes of his two fragmentary novels, *Amerika* and *The Trial:* ". . . the innocent and the guilty, both executed without distinction in the end . . ." With regard to *Amerika,* Kafka never wrote that ending and did most probably change his mind in the course of his work; and Joseph K. of *The Trial* is certainly not, as that diary note will have it, disposed of "with a gentler hand, more pushed aside than struck down." There is nothing gentle about his being stabbed to death in that quarry from which, it seems, nightmares rather than rocks are being cut; but although the execution was, in the first novel, suspended or, in the second, carried out more brutally than the writer anticipated, the absence of definable guilt is what the two books have in common. The innocent and the guilty? How is this? The man who stands and loses his "trial" is, for all we know, not guiltier than the innocent youth in *Amerika.*

In one of Kafka's last letters to Felice (October 1, 1917), during the time of their second engagement but after tuberculosis had been diagnosed and he knew that he would never marry her for "I will never be well again," he said in reply to a question of hers or one that he had asked himself: Had he ever deceived her? No, not intentionally, although it was impossible for him to be entirely truthful. How could he be, with at least two fighters fighting each other in his tubercular breast? But if he had to appear before a tribunal, a human tribunal, he would like to conceal from it the inner combat between the good and evil soul which, to make the confusion worse, change their roles from round to round. Yes, he would like to deceive his judges, "and what's more, without actual deception." Deceiving without deception: three years before, recording in his diary (July 23, 1914) the Berlin family scene when he withdrew from his first engagement to Felice, he called it "the tribunal," seemed to be pleased that they all agreed that "there was nothing, or not much, that could be said against me," and felt himself to be "devilish in my innocence." This is a quotation from "The Judgment," written two years before that family "tribunal," the story in which Kafka made the incomprehensibly enraged father about to pass the sentence of "death by drowning" upon his son: "An innocent child, yes, that you were, truly, but still more truly have you been a devilish human being!" Like much else in the story, it comes as a shock to the reader who searches in vain for any sign of devilishness in what he has come to know about the condemned.

Kafka once said: "Sometimes I feel I understand the Fall of Man better than anyone."

This might have made him into a theologian. Yet he became a writer and, therefore, a psychologist. It was the theologian in him, the mind speaking to perfection the language of parables, who once in the "Reflections on Sin" rehearsed the renunciation that is all but impossible for a writer of his time: "Never again psychology!" And he rejected psychoanalysis with its therapeutic claims as "an impotent error," for "all these so-called illnesses, however sad they may look, are facts of belief, the distressed human being's anchorages in some maternal ground . . . ; thus, it is not surprising that psychoanalysis finds the primal ground of all religions to be precisely the same thing as what causes the individual's 'illnesses' . . ."

Whenever he despaired of the power of literature—the literature that he "was"—to lift "the world into the pure, the true, and the immutable" (as he put it in his diary on September 25, 1917, a few days after he had admonished himself, on September 18: "Tear everything up"), he would curse his writing (the very writing which he said "sustains me") as the "delicious reward" given by the devil for "services rendered." This he said in the extraordinary letter to Max Brod (July 5, 1922), a letter that is itself a "delicious" piece of writing. Indeed, theology and psychology are at the opposite ends of the scale of human understanding, not because the psyche that the psychologist discovers is necessarily different from that of God's children but because the psychological manner of approaching, examining, and treating it is utterly destructive of what "sin, suffering, hope, and the true way" meant after that Fall which Kafka claimed to understand so well. Yet he did, "of course," think of Freud after that tremendous night in which he wrote, between ten o'clock in the evening and six o'clock in the morning (September 22–23, 1912) the story "The Judgment" that proved to him that he was a true writer; and it may well have done so because, disregarding the impenetrable nature of genius, it was for the first time that the theologian in him succeeded in uniting with the psychologist; and the Oedipus complex was on the friendliest terms—if friendliness can ever prevail where everything is hostile—with the Fall of Man.

Seven years, a biblical number, stretch between "The Judgment" and that "Letter to his Father," written in November 1919 and never delivered to the defendant. It is safe to say that no father has ever had a son so aggressive as a prosecutor *and* so effective as the same father's defense attorney, with both the prosecutor and the defense attorney distinguishing themselves as psychologists of the first order. That letter is a superb piece of literature (once again the obliterated borderline between the literary and the epistolary!) and may well be the last psychological document before Kafka's resolution "never again psychology!" Having read it, in the place of the father who never did, the interpreter can hardly resist the temptation to account for the most striking and recurrent theme of Kafka's work, the fearful disproportion between guilt and punishment (the more minute the offense—if it can be seen at all by the naked eye—the more horrible the retribution), and to explain it by going back to the early childhood memory that Kafka remembers in writing the letter. One night the child kept his parents awake by mischievously continuing to cry for water, "partly to be annoying, partly to amuse myself," until his father took him out of bed, carried him onto the *pavlatche* (a long glass-covered veranda that stretches along the court-side of some old Prague houses) and locked him out there for a while in his nightshirt. These two things, Kafka writes, his playfully keeping his parents awake and the terrifying *pavlatche* banishment in the depth of night, he could never causally connect: "Even years afterwards I suffered from the tormenting fancy that the huge man, my father, the ultimate authority, would come almost for no reason at all and take me out of bed in the night and carry me out onto the *pavlatche*. . . ."

"My nature being what it was" is what Kafka circumspectly says in reminding his father of that childhood trauma he inflicted upon the boy. It is a remark that ought to scare away all confidently psychological interpreters of Kafka's works. Had the "nature" of this particular child been different, that humble Prague *pavlatche* would never have become the entrance to the whole godforsaken world into which Adam and Eve, garbed only in their figleaf nightshirts, were driven by "the ultimate authority." They at least knew that they had eaten of the forbidden tree. But their late, very late, descendant Kafka? He had merely inherited the guilt and the curse and came to understand better than anyone the Fall of Man. No other children are on record who made so much of a nocturnal discomfiture. Their "natures" were different and hence their "psychologies."

In bringing Kafka's preoccupation with guilt into the proximity of the Fall of Man, or original sin, we need not enter the wide field or the desert or the labyrinth of those endless theological speculations that the third chapter of Genesis has brought forth throughout the centuries, more often than not tortures of the mind that seem more sinful than the Sin itself. We may even ignore the grand poetic versions of the subject, such as Milton's amorously unbiblical treatment of it, and turn without further ado to Kafka's own mind which, its "nature being what it was," had the closest affinity to what can be deduced from the incredibly simple text of the Bible. He has superbly parodied it in one of his very last and not quite completed stories, "Investigations of a Dog," but parodied it as only one who most intimately knows it—knows it truly "by heart"—can do. And of the biblical account of the Fall it is correct to say that, like Josephine the Singer, it does not say what it means, indeed it cannot say it; and Kafka knows this.

For language is, as it were, a postlapsarian invention;

before the Fall there were no words as we know them; there was only one "subject," *the* Word, which after the Fall, and because of it, we do not know any more, or know only darkly. Therefore, Genesis has to speak in parables when it speaks of the Garden and its first inhabitants. For it was only after they had eaten of the fruit that they knew they were naked and were ashamed, and only after they were driven out that "Adam knew Eve his wife." At this point the *principium individuationis,* the principle of individuation, began to work. Paradoxically (but the idiom of parables cannot but be paradoxical), individuals came into being only when God sent His cherub with the flaming sword to guard the Eastern Gate against any possible invasion of Paradise by individuated beings. Inside the Garden there could never have been any Adam who did not "know" his wife, and no Eve who did not desire Adam. Impossible that there should be Paradise where fully articulated individuals, and be they so undesiring and apparently undesirable as our first ancestors seem to have been before the Fall; before, that is, they arrived, like the very first dogs in the story "Investigations," at "the crossroads." When the prophet Isaiah ecstatically invoked the vision of a future homecoming, he was not less paradoxical in describing the blissful place where "the wolf . . . shall dwell with the lamb, and the leopard shall lie down with the kid. . . ." No, none of these beasts could remain what they are, and do what Isaiah says they would. For a wolf that does not feed on lambs must have ceased to be a wolf, and the leopard would have to change more than its spots before leaving the kid in peace. "Even in those days wonders did not openly walk the street for anyone to seize, but all the same, dogs—I cannot put it in any other way—had not yet become so doggish as today." Nonetheless, says Kafka in his "Investigations of a Dog," they must have already become doggish enough in their souls to enjoy dogs' lives. This is why the forefathers of our dogs did not turn back in time to cease being dogs although "they could still literally see the crossroads" after they had strayed quite a way from the blissful state in which there were no dogs yet, not even the very little ones that would need laps to sit on: there were no laps either—

"Sometimes I feel I understand the Fall of Man better than anyone."

Georg Bendemann, the unheroic hero of "The Judgment"—Georg has as many letters as Franz, and Bende as many as Kafka, with the vowels in the same place, as the author explains in his letter of June 2, 1913, to Felice Bauer to whom he has dedicated the story. Georg Bendemann, then, has to die for, as it were, appropriating to himself the "mann," the manliness to assert himself a little more forcefully as an individual standing up to his father, the "ultimate authority." This, and nothing else, is his guilt. For he was an "innocent child," and "yet a devilish human being" because far back in time, if time there was, his forebears had been persuaded by the serpentine ambassador of Evil to disrupt the harmony of the all-oneness and, in abandoning it, become the individual Adam and Eve, the parents of Cain.

Of course, this is not all that there is to the story "The Judgment." It is not for nothing that the name of Freud occurred to Kafka as he lay in bed in the morning after the night of writing it. Much later, in 1920, he said in a letter to Milena that during that night the "wound" opened for the first time. The nature of the wound? No doubt father and woman. But the mighty terror of the father's hostility is *too* terrifying ever to yield to Freud's analysis. He is the embodiment of "the ultimate authority," an exceedingly capricious one, and because of his unfathomably nightmarish unpredictability the story is "somewhat wild and meaningless," as Kafka said of it in his letter to Felice; and half a year later on June 2, 1913, he again spoke of "her" story, asking whether she could "discover any meaning" in it, "some straightforward, coherent meaning that one could follow?" On August 14, 1913, he was able to extract some sense from it after all. This is what his diary entry of that day says: "I am indirectly in her debt for the story. But Georg goes to pieces because of his fiancée," a finding that, had he come upon it earlier, would have made a sad mockery of the dedication.

True, the shadowy girl in "The Judgment" bears a name that, as Kafka on June 2, 1913 claimed he discovered only after he had written it, has a certain relationship to hers. Frieda Brandenfeld has the same initials as Felice Bauer, Frieda (peace) is related to the "happiness" that is in "Felice," "Branden" is the first part of Brandenburg, the Mark Brandenburg, with Berlin as its capital, and "feld" (field) is what belongs to "Bauer" (farmer or peasant). Still, in "The Judgment" it is certainly not she, or she only "indirectly," who brings about Georg Bendemann's death; his father's demonic rejection of the engagement does that. The father sees in it the assertion of his son's self, much in the manner of the "ultimate authority" in Genesis regarding the sin of His creature. If He did not intervene in time, the man would "become as one of us," and, who knows, might even "cover up" the creator Himself. " 'No!' cried his father . . . , threw the blankets off with a strength that sent them all flying in a moment and sprang erect in bed." Whereupon he passes the sentence of death upon the son, not without having, in the craziest of authoritarian maneuvers, appropriated to himself the son's friend in Russia, the only other possession of Georg's self. This friend, moreover, is only the *alter ego* of Kafka himself; like Kafka, a German-speaking Jew in a Czech city, he is a foreigner in another country, a country that happens to be given the name of Russia, but may well represent a domain with which the practical business father maintains, as it were, no diplomatic relations, a country possibly made up, like Kafka himself, of literature, where the sickly friend, estranged even from his fellow foreigners, resigns himself to "becoming a permanent bachelor," "wears himself out to no purpose," and tells "incredible stories" of priests cutting crosses in blood into the palms of their hands.

The fiancée is in the eyes of the father a mere object of Georg's disreputable sensuality: "Because she lifted her skirts like this, the nasty creature, you made up to her, and in order to make free with her undisturbed you have disgraced your mother's memory, betrayed your friend, and stuck your father into bed so that he can't move. But he can move, or can't he?" It is a most remarkable anticipation in 1912 of what, according to the "Letter to his Father" of 1919, the old man said about Kafka's next engagement: "She probably put on some specially chosen blouse, the thing these Prague Jewesses are good at, and straightaway, of course, you made up your mind to marry her. And what's more, as fast as possible, in a week, tomorrow, today." Deprived of friend and fiancée, and utterly defeated in his attempts to assert his selfhood, he plunges, innocently devilish or devilishly innocent, into the river, the fluid element that is both the originator of individual shapes as it is the medium of their dissolution.

This is how the wound opened and proved deadly in the night of "The Judgment." "Poor boy," Kafka would write in the story "A Country Doctor" of 1916–17, "poor boy, you were past helping. I had discovered your great wound; this blossom in your side was destroying you." The wound was in the boy's right side, "near the hip," in the place where Adam's wound might have been after the removal of his rib, the fatal initiation of the Fall. But just as intimately as he understood the Fall, Kafka, strangely enough, understood something else: that it was immensely desirable to accept resolutely and even joyfully the fallen state of man. He was unable to accomplish this. In the "Letter to his Father" he blamed him for having stood between his son and that "good life," for having very badly failed in preparing him for it, namely for "marrying, founding a family, accepting all the children that come, supporting them in this insecure world and even guiding them a little. . . ." He was convinced—or so he said to his father—that this was "the utmost a human being can succeed in doing at all." And he was fond of quoting what Flaubert, his fellow-victim, as he believed, of the demon of literature, said after a visit to his niece's friends in the country, a family working hard and diligently raising their children: *"Ils sont dans le vrai,"* they live in the truth.

"In the truth" and "the utmost a human being can succeed in doing at all"—in the heart, as it were, of man's fallen state. And yet at the same time Kafka would wish to attain through his writing that happiness that lies in lifting the world "into the pure, the true, and the immutable"—the realm, that is, of a truth quite different from that "utmost" of the "Letter" or that "*vrai*" of the family idyll that so impressed Flaubert. No, "the pure, the true, and the immutable" are of a world of which Kafka once said, in the "Reflections on Sin," that it is the only real world, so much so that there was no other world beside it: ". . . what we call the world of the senses, is the Evil in the spiritual world." And yet, again and again, he—indeed desperately—tried to "take the side of the world" because "one must not cheat anyone, not even the world of its victory." And when, in that series of "Reflections," he wrote that the "state in which we are is sinful, irrespective of guilt," he gave as the reason for our sinfulness not only that we have eaten of the Tree of Knowledge, but also that "we have not yet eaten of the Tree of Life." And the "Tree of Life" he meant is surely not the other tree in Eden that the Lord felt He had to protect from so ambitious a creature as man, intent upon himself becoming God, but, on the contrary, stands for that "utmost" a human being can achieve by being fully alive in *this* world.

This profound spiritual ambiguity is the source of the impenetrable darkness of many of Kafka's stories; and yet his language moves in that darkness as if it were the brightness of a bright noonday. Is it, the reader is compelled to ask, the "spiritual world" that the writer affirms in his stories or that "world of the senses" that is nothing but "the Evil in the spiritual world," and yet at the same time ("the clocks are not in unison") life as lived under the Tree of Life, life *"dans le vrai"*? Look at "The Metamorphosis," "this exceptionally repulsive story," as Kafka described it on November 24, 1912 to Felice. "The Evil in the spiritual world" could hardly be represented more conspicuously than through the insect into which an innocent commercial traveler by the name of Gregor Samsa ("Samsa" has as many letters as Kafka, with the a's in the same places) finds himself transformed upon waking up one morning.

Then there comes that moving moment in the story when a ray, or rather a sound, of the "only real" world, the world of the spirit, penetrates into the room inhabited by the abhorrent creature: His sister plays the violin, and while the family and their lodgers are bored, Gregor feels that the beautiful music was opening the way before him "to the unknown nourishment he craved." Only just before, hearing the sound next door of mealtime "masticating teeth," Gregor had sadly said to himself: "I'm hungry enough, . . . but not for that kind of food." It is a perfect representation of the two worlds, and for the time being there can be no doubt which of the two is affirmed, which rejected. Yet when the corpse of the insect had been got rid of by the charwoman, the family, relieved of the intolerable burden, go for a walk in the warm sunshine; and out there "it struck both Mr. and Mrs. Samsa, . . . as they became aware of their daughter's increasing vivacity, that in spite of all the sorrow of recent times, . . . she had bloomed into a pretty girl with a good figure. . . . Soon it would be time to find a good husband for her." Can the slightest trace of negation be detected in the last sentence of the story when at the end of their tram journey "the pretty girl springs to her feet . . . and stretches her young body"? *Joie de vivre:* the warmth of the sun, the beauty of the countryside, the attractiveness of the girl. Who would be foolish enough to crave for an unknown nourishment? The Tree of Life bears ample fruit for the hungry.

The theme and the ambiguity are the same in a much shorter and surpassingly successful story, written ten years later, in 1922: "The Hunger Artist." Just before he dies, the hunger artist gives away his secret. He *had* to fast, he couldn't help it. " 'What a fellow you are,' said the overseer, 'and why can't you help it?' 'Because,' said the hunger artist . . . 'I couldn't find the food I liked. If I had found it, believe me, I should have made no fuss and stuffed myself like you or anyone else.' These were his last words. . . ." " 'Well, clear this out now!' said the overseer," and the cage of the hunger artist was soon occupied by a young panther. He did not even mind his imprisonment because his noble body, furnished almost to the bursting point with all that is needed, seemed to carry freedom around with it too, "somewhere in his jaws it seemed to lurk. . . ." "What we call the senses, is the Evil in the spiritual world. . . ." Can thoughts of Evil be thought in the sight of this noble, sensuous creature? Is he who died from his contempt for the food of this world praiseworthy? Ambiguity has never been considered an elemental force; it is precisely this in the stories of Franz Kafka.

Chronology

(Titles of published books italicized)

1883   Born in Prague, July 3, son of Hermann (1852–1931) and Julie (née Löwy, 1856–1934). His father is the son of a butcher from a Bohemian village who settles as a quite successful merchant in Prague. His wife's ancestry includes several piously learned men.

1889–93   Elementary school at Fleischmarkt, Prague.

1889, 1890, 1892   Birth of sisters Elli, Valli, Ottla. Two younger brothers died in infancy.

1893–1901   German Gymnasium, Prague: friendship with Oskar Pollak. Family resides in Zeltnergasse.

ca. 1899–1900   Reads Spinoza, Darwin, Nietzsche. Friendship with Hugo Bergmann, the philosopher who later became Director of the Hebrew University Library in Jerusalem.

1899–1903   Early writings (destroyed).

1901–06   Study of German literature, then law at German University, Prague; partly in Munich.

1902	Vacation in the country, in Schelesen and Triesch, with his favorite uncle Dr. Siegfried Löwy (the country doctor). Meets Max Brod, the writer, critic, literary editor of *Prager Tagblatt*; friendship with the philosopher Felix Weltsch and the blind writer Oskar Baum.
1903	Working on a novel *The Child and the City* (lost).
1903–04	Writes "Description of a Struggle."
1905–06	Summers in Zuckmantel. Love affair with an unknown woman.
1906	Works in a Prague law office. June: Receives degree of *doctor juris* at German University, Prague. From October: One year's internship in the law courts.
1907–08	Writes "Wedding Preparations in the Country" (fragments of a novel).
1907	October: Position in Prague with Assicurazioni Generali, an Italian insurance company. Family moves to Niklas-Strasse.
1908	Position at the semigovernmental Workers' Accident Insurance Institute (until retirement, July, 1922). The friendship with Max Brod has become very close. Writes "On Mandatory Insurance in the Construction Industry."
1909	Publication of eight prose pieces—parts of the later volume *Betrachtung*—in the Munich literary journal *Hyperion*. September: At Riva and Brescia with Max and Otto Brod. Writes "The Aeroplanes at Brescia."

1910	Member of circle of intellectuals (Mrs. Berta Fanta). March: Publication of five prose pieces in Prague German newspaper *Bohemia*. May: Beginning of the *Diaries* (quarto notebooks; last entry: June 12, 1923). Yiddish theatre company from Eastern Europe performs in Prague. October: Paris, with Max and Otto Brod. December: Berlin.
1911	January–February: Business trip to Friedland and Reichenberg. Summer: Zurich, Lugano, Milan, Paris with Max Brod. Plans to write a novel with Brod, "Richard and Samuel." In a sanatorium in Erlenbach near Zurich. Travel diaries. Writes "Measures to Prevent Accidents (in Factories and Farms)" and "Worker's Accident Insurance and Management."
1911–12	Winter: Becomes deeply interested in the Yiddish theatre company. Friendship with Yiddish actor Isak Löwy; study of Jewish folklore; beginning of a sketch on Löwy.
1911–14	Working on *Amerika* (main parts written 1911–12).
1912	Studies Judaism (works by H. Graetz, M. I. Pines). February: Gives lecture on the Yiddish language. July: Weimar with Max Brod, then alone in the Harz Mountains (Sanatorium Just). Meets the publishers Ernst Rowohlt and Kurt Wolff, at that time joint managers of Rowohlt Verlag. August 13: Meets Felice Bauer, a secretarial assistant in a Berlin business firm and relation of the Brods, in the house of Max Brod's father in Prague. August 14: Manuscript of *Betrachtung (Meditation)* sent to the publisher. September 20: Beginning of correspondence with Felice Bauer. September 22–23: Writes "The Judgment." September–October: Writes "The

Stoker" (or "The Man Who Disappeared") which later became first chapter of *Amerika*. October 1912 to February 1913: Gap in the diaries. November: Writes "The Metamorphosis."

1913   January: Publication of *Betrachtung (Meditation)*. February 1913 to July 1914: Lacuna in productivity. Easter: First visit to Felice Bauer in Berlin. Spring: Publication of *The Judgment*. May: Publication of "The Stoker." September: Journey to Vienna, Venice, Riva, on the shore of Lake Garda in North Italy. At Riva, friendship with "the Swiss girl." November: Meeting with Grete Bloch, a secretarial assistant employed most of the time in Berlin, close friend of Felice Bauer. Beginning of correspondence with her.

1914   Easter: In Berlin. April 12: Engagement to Felice Bauer in Berlin. July 12: Engagement broken. Summer: Writes "Memoirs of the Kalda Railroad." Hellerau, Lübeck. Marienlyst on the Baltic with his friend Ernst Weiss, the physician and writer who, born in Moravia, lived in Berlin. October: Writes "In the Penal Colony." Autumn: Begins writing *The Trial*. Winter: Writes "Before the Law" (part of *The Trial*).

1915   January: Renewed meeting with Felice Bauer (in Bodenbach). Continues working on *The Trial*. Receives Fontane Prize for "The Stoker." February: Moves from parents' home into rented rooms. Bilekgasse and Langegasse. Journey to Hungary with sister Elli. November: Publication of *The Metamorphosis*. December (and January 1916): Writes "The Village Schoolmaster" ("The Giant Mole").

1916	July: Meeting with Felice Bauer in Marienbad. August 20: Draws up a list of reasons for and against marriage. Writes stories, later collected in *A Country Doctor*. Winter: K. moves to Alchemists' Lane in the Castle district of Prague.
1917	First half: Writes "The Hunter Gracchus." Learns Hebrew. Spring: Writes "The Great Wall of China." July: Second engagement to Felice Bauer. August: Begins coughing blood. September 4: Diagnosis of tuberculosis. Moves in with sister Ottla in Zürau. September 12: Leave of absence from office. November 10: Diary entries break off. End of December: Breaking of second engagement to Felice Bauer. Autumn and winter: Writes aphorisms (octavo notebooks).
1918	January to June: Zürau. Reads Kierkegaard. Spring: Continues writing aphorisms. Prague, Turnau. November: Schelesen. Meets Julie Wohryzek, daughter of a synagogue custodian. A project for "The Society of Poor Workers."
1919	January 10: Resumes diary. Schelesen. Spring: Again in Prague. Felice Bauer married. Engagement to Julie Wohryzek, broken November 1919. May: Publication of *In the Penal Colony*. Fall: Publication of *A Country Doctor*. November: Writes "Letter to His Father." Winter: Writes "He," a collection of aphorisms.
1920	January 1920 to October 15, 1921: Gap in diaries. Sick leave from Workers' Accident Insurance Institute. End of March: Meets Gustav Janouch. Meran. Meets Milena Jesenká-Pollak, Czech writer, living as a married woman in Vienna. Correspondence. Sum-

	mer and autumn: Prague. Writes stories. December: Tatra Mountains (Matliary). Meets Robert Klopstock who is to become his friend and physician.
1921	October 15: Note in diary that all his diaries are being given to Milena. Until September: Tatra Mountains sanatorium; then Prague.
1921–24	Writes stories, later included in the volume *A Hunger Artist*.
1922	January to September: Writes *The Castle*. February: Prague. Spring: Writes "A Hunger Artist." May: Last meeting with Milena. End of June to September: In Planá on the Luschnitz with sister Ottla. Prague. Summer: Writes "Investigations of a Dog."
1923	Prague. July: In Müritz with sister Elli, in a vacation camp of the Berlin Jewish People's Home, meets Dora Dymant (Diamant), daughter of Jewish-Orthodox parents from Poland. Prague, Schelesen. End of September: With Dora Dymant in Berlin-Zehlendorf. Later moves, with Dora, to Grunewaldstrasse. Attends lectures at the Berlin Academy (Hochschule) for Jewish Studies. Winter: Writes "The Burrow." K. and Dora move to Berlin-Zehlendorf. Sends *A Hunger Artist* to publisher.
1924	Spring: Writes "Josephine the Singer, or the Mouse Folk." Brought as a patient from Berlin to Prague. April 10: To Wiener Wald Sanatorium, Professor Hajek's clinic in Vienna; then sanatorium in Kierling, near Vienna, accompanied by Dora Dymant and Robert Klopstock. June 3: Death in Kierling: burial June 11 in the Jewish cemetery in Prague-Straschnitz. Publication of *A Hunger Artist*.

1942	Death of K.'s sister Ottla in Auschwitz. The other two sisters also perished in German concentration camps.
1944	Death of Grete Bloch at the hands of National Socialists. Death of Milena in a German concentration camp.
1952	August: Death of Dora Dymant in London.
1960	Death of Felice Bauer.

THE BASIC
KAFKA

THE METAMORPHOSIS

I

As GREGOR SAMSA awoke one morning from uneasy
dreams he found himself transformed in his bed into a
gigantic insect. He was lying on his hard, as it were
armor-plated, back and when he lifted his head a little
he could see his dome-like brown belly divided into stiff
arched segments on top of which the bed quilt could
hardly keep in position and was about to slide off completely. His numerous legs, which were pitifully thin
compared to the rest of his bulk, waved helplessly before his eyes.

What has happened to me? he thought. It was no
dream. His room, a regular human bedroom, only rather
too small, lay quiet between the four familiar walls.
Above the table on which a collection of cloth samples
was unpacked and spread out—Samsa was a commercial traveler—hung the picture which he had recently
cut out of an illustrated magazine and put into a pretty
gilt frame. It showed a lady, with a fur cap on and a fur
stole, sitting upright and holding out to the spectator a
huge fur muff into which the whole of her forearm had
vanished!

Gregor's eyes turned next to the window, and the
overcast sky—one could hear rain drops beating on the
window gutter—made him quite melancholy. What
about sleeping a little longer and forgetting all this nonsense, he thought, but it could not be done, for he was

accustomed to sleep on his right side and in his present condition he could not turn himself over. However violently he forced himself towards his right side he always rolled on to his back again. He tried it at least a hundred times, shutting his eyes to keep from seeing his struggling legs, and only desisted when he began to feel in his side a faint dull ache he had never experienced before.

Oh God, he thought, what an exhausting job I've picked on! Traveling about day in, day out. It's much more irritating work than doing the actual business in the office, and on top of that there's the trouble of constant traveling, of worrying about train connections, the bed and irregular meals, casual acquaintances that are always new and never become intimate friends. The devil take it all! He felt a slight itching up on his belly; slowly pushed himself on his back nearer to the top of the bed so that he could lift his head more easily; identified the itching place which was surrounded by many small white spots the nature of which he could not understand and made to touch it with a leg, but drew the leg back immediately, for the contact made a cold shiver run through him.

He slid down again into his former position. This getting up early, he thought, makes one quite stupid. A man needs his sleep. Other commercials live like harem women. For instance, when I come back to the hotel of a morning to write up the orders I've got, these others are only sitting down to breakfast. Let me just try that with my chief; I'd be sacked on the spot. Anyhow, that might be quite a good thing for me, who can tell? If I didn't have to hold my hand because of my parents I'd have given notice long ago, I'd have gone to the chief and told him exactly what I think of him. That would knock him endways from his desk! It's a queer way of doing, too, this sitting on high at a desk and talking down to employees, especially when they have to come quite near because the chief is hard of hearing. Well, there's still hope; once I've saved enough money to pay back my parents' debts to him—that should take another five or six years—I'll do it without fail. I'll cut

2

myself completely loose then. For the moment, though, I'd better get up, since my train goes at five.

He looked at the alarm clock ticking on the chest. Heavenly Father! he thought. It was half-past six o'clock and the hands were quietly moving on, it was even past the half-hour, it was getting on toward a quarter to seven. Had the alarm clock not gone off? From the bed one could see that it had been properly set for four o'clock; of course it must have gone off. Yes, but was it possible to sleep quietly through that ear-splitting noise? Well, he had not slept quietly, yet apparently all the more soundly for that. But what was he to do now? The next train went at seven o'clock; to catch that he would need to hurry like mad and his samples weren't even packed up, and he himself wasn't feeling particularly fresh and active. And even if he did catch the train he wouldn't avoid a row with the chief, since the firm's porter would have been waiting for the five o'clock train and would have long since reported his failure to turn up. The porter was a creature of the chief's, spineless and stupid. Well, supposing he were to say he was sick? But that would be most unpleasant and would look suspicious, since during his five years' employment he had not been ill once. The chief himself would be sure to come with the sick-insurance doctor, would reproach his parents with their son's laziness and would cut all excuses short by referring to the insurance doctor, who of course regarded all mankind as perfectly healthy malingerers. And would he be so far wrong on this occasion? Gregor really felt quite well, apart from a drowsiness that was utterly superfluous after such a long sleep, and he was even unusually hungry.

As all this was running through his mind at top speed without his being able to decide to leave his bed—the alarm clock had just struck a quarter to seven—there came a cautious tap at the door behind the head of his bed. "Gregor," said a voice—it was his mother's—"it's a quarter to seven. Hadn't you a train to catch?" That gentle voice! Gregor had a shock as he heard his own voice answering hers, unmistakably his own voice, it was true, but with a persistent horrible twittering squeak

3

behind it like an undertone, that left the words in their clear shape only for the first moment and then rose up reverberating round them to destroy their sense, so that one could not be sure one had heard them rightly. Gregor wanted to answer at length and explain everything, but in the circumstances he confined himself to saying: "Yes, yes, thank you, Mother, I'm getting up now." The wooden door between them must have kept the change in his voice from being noticeable outside, for his mother contented herself with this statement and shuffled away. Yet this brief exchange of words had made the other members of the family aware that Gregor was still in the house, as they had not expected, and at one of the side doors his father was already knocking, gently, yet with his fist. "Gregor, Gregor," he called, "what's the matter with you?" And after a little while he called again in a deeper voice: "Gregor! Gregor!" At the other side door his sister was saying in a low, plaintive tone: "Gregor? Aren't you well? Are you needing anything?" He answered them both at once: "I'm just ready," and did his best to make his voice sound as normal as possible by enunciating the words very clearly and leaving long pauses between them. So his father went back to his breakfast, but his sister whispered: "Gregor, open the door, do." However, he was not thinking of opening the door, and felt thankful for the prudent habit he had acquired in traveling of locking all doors during the night, even at home.

His immediate intention was to get up quietly without being disturbed, to put on his clothes and above all eat his breakfast, and only then to consider what else was to be done, since in bed, he was well aware, his meditations would come to no sensible conclusion. He remembered that often enough in bed he had felt small aches and pains, probably caused by awkward postures, which had proved purely imaginary once he got up, and he looked forward eagerly to seeing this morning's delusions gradually fall away. That the change in his voice was nothing but the precursor of a severe chill, a standing ailment of commercial travelers, he had not the least possible doubt.

To get rid of the quilt was quite easy; he had only to inflate himself a little and it fell off by itself. But the next move was difficult, especially because he was so uncommonly broad. He would have needed arms and hands to hoist himself up; instead he had only the numerous little legs which never stopped waving in all directions and which he could not control in the least. When he tried to bend one of them it was the first to stretch itself straight; and did he succeed at last in making it do what he wanted, all the other legs meanwhile waved the more wildly in a high degree of unpleasant agitation. "But what's the use of lying idle in bed," said Gregor to himself.

He thought that he might get out of bed with the lower part of his body first, but this lower part, which he had not yet seen and of which he could form no clear conception, proved too difficult to move; it shifted so slowly; and when finally, almost wild with annoyance, he gathered his forces together and thrust out recklessly, he had miscalculated the direction and bumped heavily against the lower end of the bed, and the stinging pain he felt informed him that precisely this lower part of his body was at the moment probably the most sensitive.

So he tried to get the top part of himself out first, and cautiously moved his head towards the edge of the bed. That proved easy enough, and despite its breadth and mass the bulk of his body at last slowly followed the movement of his head. Still, when he finally got his head free over the edge of the bed he felt too scared to go on advancing, for after all if he let himself fall in this way it would take a miracle to keep his head from being injured. And at all costs he must not lose consciousness now, precisely now; he would rather stay in bed.

But when after a repetition of the same efforts he lay in his former position again, sighing, and watched his little legs struggling against each other more wildly than ever, if that were possible, and saw no way of bringing any order into this arbitrary confusion, he told himself again that it was impossible to stay in bed and that the most sensible course was to risk everything for the smallest hope of getting away from it. At the same time he did not forget meanwhile to remind himself that cool reflection, the coolest possible, was much better than desperate resolves. In such moments he focused his eyes as sharply as possible on the window, but, unfortunately, the prospect of the morning fog, which muffled even the other side of the narrow street, brought him little encouragement and comfort. "Seven o'clock already," he said to himself when the alarm clock chimed again, "seven o'clock already and still such a thick fog." And for a little while he lay quiet, breathing lightly, as if perhaps expecting such complete repose to restore all things to their real and normal condition.

But then he said to himself: "Before it strikes a quarter past seven I must be quite out of this bed, without fail. Anyhow, by that time someone will have come from the office to ask for me, since it opens before seven." And he set himself to rocking his whole body at once in a regular rhythm, with the idea of swinging it out of the bed. If he tipped himself out in that way he could keep his head from injury by lifting it at an acute angle when he fell. His back seemed to be hard and was not likely to suffer from a fall on the carpet. His biggest worry was the loud crash he would not be able to help making, which would probably cause anxiety, if not terror, behind all the doors. Still, he must take the risk.

When he was already half out of the bed—the new method was more a game than an effort, for he needed only to hitch himself across by rocking to and fro—it struck him how simple it would be if he could get help. Two strong people—he thought of his father and the servant girl—would be amply sufficient; they would only have to thrust their arms under his convex back, lever him out of the bed, bend down with their burden and then be patient enough to let him turn himself right over on to the floor, where it was to be hoped his legs would then find their proper function. Well, ignoring the fact that the doors were all locked, ought he really to call for help? In spite of his misery he could not suppress a smile at the very idea of it.

He had got so far that he could barely keep his equilibrium when he rocked himself strongly, and he would have to nerve himself very soon for the final decision since in five minutes' time it would be a quarter past seven—when the front door bell rang. "That's someone from the office," he said to himself, and grew almost rigid, while his little legs only jigged about all the faster. For a moment everything stayed quiet. "They're not going to open the door," said Gregor to himself, catching at some kind of irrational hope. But then of course the servant girl went as usual to the door with her heavy tread and opened it. Gregor needed only to hear the first good morning of the visitor to know immediately who it was—the chief clerk himself. What a fate, to be condemned to work for a firm where the smallest omission at once gave rise to the gravest suspicion! Were all employees in a body nothing but scoundrels, was there not among them one single loyal devoted man who, had he wasted only an hour or so of the firm's time in a morning, was so tormented by conscience as to be driven out of his mind and actually incapable of leaving his bed? Wouldn't it really have been sufficient to send an apprentice to inquire—if any inquiry were necessary at all—did the chief clerk himself have to come and thus indicate to the entire family, an innocent family, that this suspicious circumstance could be investigated by no one less versed in affairs than himself? And more through the agitation caused by these reflections than through any act of will Gregor swung himself out of bed with all his strength. There was a loud thump, but it was not really a crash. His fall was broken to some extent by the carpet, his back, too, was less stiff than he thought, and so there was merely a dull thud, not so very startling. Only he had not lifted his head carefully enough and had hit it; he turned it and rubbed it on the carpet in pain and irritation.

"That was something falling down in there," said the chief clerk in the next room to the left. Gregor tried to suppose to himself that something like what had happened to him today might some day happen to the chief clerk; one really could not deny that it was possible. But as if in brusque reply to this supposition the chief clerk took a couple of firm steps in the next-door room and his patent leather boots creaked. From the right-hand room his sister was whispering to inform him of the situation: "Gregor, the chief clerk's here." "I know," muttered Gregor to himself; but he didn't dare to make his voice loud enough for his sister to hear it.

"Gregor," said his father now from the left-hand room, "the chief clerk has come and wants to know why you didn't catch the early train. We don't know what to say to him. Besides, he wants to talk to you in person. So open the door, please. He will be good enough to excuse the untidiness of your room." "Good morning, Mr. Samsa," the chief clerk was calling amiably meanwhile. "He's not well," said his mother to the visitor, while his father was still speaking through the door, "he's not well, sir, believe me. What else would make him miss a train! The boy thinks about nothing but his work. It makes me almost cross the way he never goes out in the evenings; he's been here the last eight days and has stayed at home every single evening. He just sits there quietly at the table reading a news-paper or looking through railway timetables. The only amusement he gets is doing fretwork. For instance, he spent two or three evenings cutting out a little picture frame; you would be surprised to see how pretty it is; it's hanging in his room; you'll see it in a minute when Gregor opens the door. I must say I'm glad you've come, sir; we should never have got him to unlock the door by ourselves; he's so obstinate; and I'm sure he's unwell, though he wouldn't have it to be so this morn-ing." "I'm just coming," said Gregor slowly and care-fully, not moving an inch for fear of losing one word of the conversation. "I can't think of any other explana-tion, madam," said the chief clerk, "I hope it's nothing serious. Although on the other hand I must say that we men of business—fortunately or unfortunately—very often simply have to ignore any slight indisposition, since business must be attended to." "Well, can the chief clerk come in now?" asked Gregor's father impa-tiently, again knocking on the door. "No," said Gregor. In the left-hand room a painful silence followed this refusal, in the right-hand room his sister began to sob.

Why didn't his sister join the others? She was probably newly out of bed and hadn't even begun to put on her clothes yet. Well, why was she crying? Because he wouldn't get up and let the chief clerk in, because he was in danger of losing his job, and because the chief would begin dunning his parents again for the old debts? Surely these were things one didn't need to worry about for the present. Gregor was still at home and not in the least thinking of deserting the family. At the moment, true, he was lying on the carpet and no one who knew the condition he was in could seriously expect him to admit the chief clerk. But for such a small discourtesy, which could plausibly be explained away somehow later on, Gregor could hardly be dismissed on the spot. And it seemed to Gregor that it would be much more sensible to leave him in peace for the present than to trouble him with tears and entreaties. Still, of course, their uncertainty bewildered them all and excused their behavior.

"Mr. Samsa," the chief clerk called now in a louder voice, "what's the matter with you? Here you are, barricading yourself in your room, giving only 'yes' and 'no' for answers, causing your parents a lot of unnecessary trouble and neglecting—I mention this only in passing—neglecting your business duties in an incredible fashion. I am speaking here in the name of your parents and of your chief, and I beg you quite seriously to give me an immediate and precise explanation. You amaze me, you amaze me. I thought you were a quiet, dependable person, and now all at once you seem bent on making a disgraceful exhibition of yourself. The chief did hint to me early this morning a possible explanation for your disappearance—with reference to the cash payments that were entrusted to you recently—but I almost pledged my solemn word of honor that this could not be so. But now that I see how incredibly obstinate you are, I no longer have the slightest desire to take your part at all. And your position in the firm is not so unassailable. I came with the intention of telling you all this in private, but since you are wasting my time so needlessly I don't see why your parents shouldn't

9

hear it too. For some time past your work has been most unsatisfactory; this is not the season of the year for a business boom, of course, we admit that, but a season of the year for doing no business at all, that does not exist, Mr. Samsa, must not exist."

"But, sir," cried Gregor, beside himself and in his agitation forgetting everything else, "I'm just going to open the door this very minute. A slight illness, an attack of giddiness, has kept me from getting up. I'm still lying in bed. But I feel all right again. I'm getting out of bed now. Just give me a moment or two longer! I'm not quite so well as I thought. But I'm all right, really. How a thing like that can suddenly strike one down! Only last night I was quite well, my parents can tell you, or rather I did have a slight presentiment. I must have showed some sign of it. Why didn't I report it at the office! But one always thinks that an indisposition can be got over without staying in the house. Oh sir, do spare my parents! All that you're reproaching me with now has no foundation; no one has ever said a word to me about it. Perhaps you haven't looked at the last orders I sent in. Anyhow, I can still catch the eight o'clock train, I'm much the better for my few hours' rest. Don't let me detain you here, sir; I'll be attending to business very soon, and do be good enough to tell the chief so and to make my excuses to him!"

And while all this was tumbling out pell-mell and Gregor hardly knew what he was saying, he had reached the chest quite easily, perhaps because of the practice he had had in bed, and was now trying to lever himself upright by means of it. He meant actually to open the door, actually to show himself and speak to the chief clerk; he was eager to find out what the others, after all their insistence, would say at the sight of him. If they were horrified then the responsibility was no longer his and he could stay quiet. But if they took it calmly, then he had no reason either to be upset, and could really get to the station for the eight o'clock train if he hurried. At first he slipped down a few times from the polished surface of the chest, but at length with a last heave he stood upright; he paid no more attention to the pains in the lower part of his body, however they smarted. Then he let himself fall against the back of a near-by chair, and clung with his little legs to the edges of it. That brought him into control of himself again and he stopped speaking, for now he could listen to what the chief clerk was saying.

"Did you understand a word of it?" the chief clerk was asking; "surely he can't be trying to make fools of us?" "Oh dear," cried his mother, in tears, "perhaps he's terribly ill and we're tormenting him. Grete! Grete!" she called out then. "Yes Mother?" called his sister from the other side. They were calling to each other across Gregor's room. "You must go this minute for the doctor. Gregor is ill. Go for the doctor, quick. Did you hear how he was speaking?" "That was no human voice," said the chief clerk in a voice noticeably low beside the shrillness of the mother's. "Anna! Anna!" his father was calling through the hall to the kitchen, clapping his hands, "get a locksmith at once!" And the two girls were already running through the hall with a swish of skirts —how could his sister have got dressed so quickly?— and were tearing the front door open. There was no sound of its closing again; they had evidently left it open, as one does in houses where some great misfortune has happened.

But Gregor was now much calmer. The words he uttered were no longer understandable, apparently, although they seemed clear enough to him, even clearer than before, perhaps because his ear had grown accustomed to the sound of them. Yet at any rate people now believed that something was wrong with him, and were ready to help him. The positive certainty with which these first measures had been taken comforted him. He felt himself drawn once more into the human circle and hoped for great and remarkable results from both the doctor and the locksmith, without really distinguishing precisely between them. To make his voice as clear as possible for the decisive conversation that was now imminent he coughed a little, as quietly as he could, of course, since this noise too might not sound like a human cough for all he was able to judge. In the next room meanwhile there was complete silence. Perhaps his parents were sitting at the table with the chief clerk, whispering, perhaps they were all leaning against the door and listening.

Slowly Gregor pushed the chair towards the door, then let go of it, caught hold of the door for support—the soles at the end of his little legs were somewhat sticky—and rested against it for a moment after his efforts. Then he set himself to turning the key in the lock with his mouth. It seemed, unhappily, that he hadn't really any teeth—what could he grip the key with?—but on the other hand his jaws were certainly very strong; with their help he did manage to set the key in motion, heedless of the fact that he was undoubtedly damaging them somewhere, since a brown fluid issued from his mouth, flowed over the key and dripped on the floor. "Just listen to that," said the chief clerk next door; "he's turning the key." That was a great encouragement to Gregor; but they should all have shouted encouragement to him, his father and mother too: "Go on, Gregor," they should have called out, "keep going, hold on to that key!" And in the belief that they were all following his efforts intently, he clenched his jaws recklessly on the key with all the force at his command. As the turning of the key progressed he circled round the lock, holding on now only with his mouth, pushing on the key, as required, or pulling it down again with all the weight of his body. The louder click of the finally yielding lock literally quickened Gregor. With a deep breath of relief he said to himself: "So I didn't need the locksmith," and laid his head on the handle to open the door wide.

Since he had to pull the door towards him, he was still invisible when it was really wide open. He had to edge himself slowly round the near half of the double door, and to do it very carefully if he was not to fall plump upon his back just on the threshold. He was still carrying out this difficult manoeuvre, with no time to observe anything else, when he heard the chief clerk utter a loud "Oh!"—it sounded like a gust of wind—and now he could see the man, standing as he was nearest

12

to the door, clapping one hand before his open mouth and slowly backing away as if driven by some invisible steady pressure. His mother—in spite of the chief clerk's being there her hair was still undone and sticking up in all directions—first clasped her hands and looked at his father, then took two steps towards Gregor and fell on the floor among her outspread skirts, her face quite hidden on her breast. His father knotted his fist with a fierce expression on his face as if he meant to knock Gregor back into his room, then looked uncertainly round the living room, covered his eyes with his hands and wept till his great chest heaved.

Gregor did not go now into the living room, but leaned against the inside of the firmly shut wing of the door, so that only half his body was visible and his head above it bending sideways to look at the others. The light had meanwhile strengthened; on the other side of the street one could see clearly a section of the endlessly long, dark gray building opposite—it was a hospital—abruptly punctuated by its row of regular windows; the rain was still falling, but only in large singly discernible and literally singly splashing drops. The breakfast dishes were set out on the table lavishly, for breakfast was the most important meal of the day to Gregor's father, who lingered it out for hours over various newspapers. Right opposite Gregor on the wall hung a photograph of himself on military service, as a lieutenant, hand on sword, a carefree smile on his face, inviting one to respect his uniform and military bearing. The door leading to the hall was open, and one could see that the front door stood open too, showing the landing beyond and the beginning of the stairs going down.

"Well," said Gregor, knowing perfectly that he was the only one who had retained any composure, "I'll put my clothes on at once, pack up my samples and start off. Will you only let me go? You see, sir, I'm not obstinate, and I'm willing to work; traveling is a hard life, but I couldn't live without it. Where are you going, sir? To the office? Yes? Will you give a true account of all this? One can be temporarily incapacitated, but that's

13

just the moment for remembering former services and bearing in mind that later on, when the incapacity has been got over, one will certainly work with all the more industry and concentration. I'm loyally bound to serve the chief, you know that very well. Besides, I have to provide for my parents and my sister. I'm in great difficulties, but I'll get out of them again. Don't make things any worse for me than they are. Stand up for me in the firm. Travelers are not popular there, I know. People think they earn sacks of money and just have a good time. A prejudice there's no particular reason for revising. But you, sir, have a more comprehensive view of affairs than the rest of the staff, yes, let me tell you in confidence, a more comprehensive view than the chief himself, who, being the owner, lets his judgment easily be swayed against one of his employees. And you know very well that the traveler, who is never seen in the office almost the whole year round, can so easily fall a victim to gossip and ill luck and unfounded complaints, which he mostly knows nothing about, except when he comes back exhausted from his rounds, and only then suffers in person from their evil consequences, which he can no longer trace back to the original causes. Sir, sir, don't go away without a word to me to show that you think me in the right at least to some extent!"

But at Gregor's very first words the chief clerk had already backed away and only stared at him with parted lips over one twitching shoulder. And while Gregor was speaking he did not stand still one moment but stole away towards the door, without taking his eyes off Gregor, yet only an inch at a time, as if obeying some secret injunction to leave the room. He was already at the hall, and the suddenness with which he took his last step out of the living room would have made one believe he had burned the sole of his foot. Once in the hall he stretched his right arm before him towards the staircase, as if some supernatural power were waiting there to deliver him.

Gregor perceived that the chief clerk must on no account be allowed to go away in this frame of mind if his position in the firm were not to be endangered to the

14

utmost. His parents did not understand this so well; they had convinced themselves in the course of years that Gregor was settled for life in this firm, and besides they were so preoccupied with their immediate troubles that all foresight had forsaken them. Yet Gregor had this foresight. The chief clerk must be detained, soothed, persuaded and finally won over; the whole future of Gregor and his family depended on it! If only his sister had been there! She was intelligent; she had begun to cry while Gregor was still lying quietly on his back. And no doubt the chief clerk, so partial to ladies, would have been guided by her; she would have shut the door of the flat and in the hall talked him out of his horror. But she was not there, and Gregor would have to handle the situation himself. And without remembering that he was still unaware what powers of movement he possessed, without even remembering that his words in all possibility, indeed in all likelihood, would again be unintelligible, he let go the wing of the door, pushed himself through the opening, started to walk towards the chief clerk, who was already ridiculously clinging with both hands to the railing on the landing; but immediately, as he was feeling for a support, he fell down with a little cry upon all his numerous legs. Hardly was he down when he experienced for the first time this morning a sense of physical comfort; his legs had firm ground under them; they were completely obedient, as he noted with joy; they even strove to carry him forward in whatever direction he chose; and he was inclined to believe that a final relief from all his sufferings was at hand. But in the same moment as he found himself on the floor, rocking with suppressed eagerness to move, not far from his mother, indeed just in front of her, she, who had seemed so completely crushed, sprang all at once to her feet, her arms and fingers outspread, cried: "Help, for God's sake, help!" bent her head down as if to see Gregor better, yet on the contrary kept backing senselessly away; had quite forgotten that the laden table stood behind her; sat upon it hastily, as if in absence of mind, when she bumped into it; and seemed

15

altogether unaware that the big coffee pot beside her was upset and pouring coffee in a flood over the carpet.

"Mother, Mother," said Gregor in a low voice, and looked up at her. The chief clerk, for the moment, had quite slipped from his mind; instead, he could not resist snapping his jaws together at the sight of the streaming coffee. That made his mother scream again, she fled from the table and fell into the arms of his father, who hastened to catch her. But Gregor had now no time to spare for his parents; the chief clerk was already on the stairs; with his chin on the banisters he was taking one last backward look. Gregor made a spring, to be as sure as possible of overtaking him; the chief clerk must have divined his intention, for he leaped down several steps and vanished; he was still yelling "Ugh!" and it echoed through the whole staircase.

Unfortunately, the flight of the chief clerk seemed completely to upset Gregor's father, who had remained relatively calm until now, for instead of running after the man himself, or at least not hindering Gregor in his pursuit, he seized in his right hand the walking stick which the chief clerk had left behind on a chair, together with a hat and greatcoat, snatched in his left hand a large newspaper from the table and began stamping his feet and flourishing the stick and the newspaper to drive Gregor back into his room. No entreaty of Gregor's availed, indeed no entreaty was even understood, however humbly he bent his head his father only stamped on the floor the more loudly. Behind his father his mother had torn open a window, despite the cold weather, and was leaning far out of it with her face in her hands. A strong draught set in from the street to the staircase, the window curtains blew in, the newspapers on the table fluttered, stray pages whisked over the floor. Pitilessly Gregor's father drove him back, hissing and crying "Shoo!" like a savage. But Gregor was quite unpracticed in walking backwards, it really was a slow business. If he only had a chance to turn round he could get back to his room at once, but he was afraid of exasperating his father by the slowness of such a rotation and at any moment the stick in his father's hand might hit him a fatal blow on the back or on the head. In the end, however, nothing else was left for him to do since to his horror he observed that in moving backwards he could not even control the direction he took; and so, keeping an anxious eye on his father all the time over his shoulder, he began to turn round as quickly as he could, which was in reality very slowly. Perhaps his father noted his good intentions, for he did not interfere except every now and then to help him in the manoeuvre from a distance with the point of the stick. If only he would have stopped making that unbearable hissing noise! It made Gregor quite lose his head. He had turned almost completely round when the hissing noise so distracted him that he even turned a little the wrong way again. But when at last his head was fortunately right in front of the doorway, it appeared that his body was too broad simply to get through the opening. His father, of course, in his present mood was far from thinking of such a thing as opening the other half of the door, to let Gregor have enough space. He had merely the fixed idea of driving Gregor back into his room as quickly as possible. He would never have suffered Gregor to make the circumstantial preparations for standing up on end and perhaps slipping his way through the door. Maybe he was now making more noise than ever to urge Gregor forward, as if no obstacle impeded him; to Gregor, anyhow, the noise in his rear sounded no longer like the voice of one single father; this was really no joke, and Gregor thrust himself—come what might—into the doorway. One side of his body rose up, he was tilted at an angle in the doorway, his flank was quite bruised, horrid blotches stained the white door, soon he was stuck fast and, left to himself, could not have moved at all, his legs on one side fluttered trembling in the air, those on the other were crushed painfully to the floor—when from behind his father gave him a strong push which was literally a deliverance and he flew far into the room, bleeding freely. The door was slammed behind him with the stick, and then at last there was silence.

II

NOT UNTIL IT was twilight did Gregor awake out of a deep sleep, more like a swoon than a sleep. He would certainly have waked up of his own accord not much later, for he felt himself sufficiently rested and well-slept, but it seemed to him as if a fleeting step and a cautious shutting of the door leading into the hall had aroused him. The electric lights in the street cast a pale sheen here and there on the ceiling and the upper surfaces of the furniture, but down below, where he lay, it was dark. Slowly, awkwardly trying out his feelers, which he now first learned to appreciate, he pushed his way to the door to see what had been happening there. His left side felt like one single long, unpleasantly tense scar, and he had actually to limp on his two rows of legs. One little leg, moreover, had been severely damaged in the course of that morning's events—it was almost a miracle that only one had been damaged—and trailed uselessly behind him.

He had reached the door before he discovered what had really drawn him to it: the smell of food. For there stood a basin filled with fresh milk in which floated little sops of white bread. He could almost have laughed with joy, since he was now still hungrier than in the morning, and he dipped his head almost over the eyes straight into the milk. But soon in disappointment he withdrew it again; not only did he find it difficult to feed because of his tender left side—and he could only feed with the palpitating collaboration of his whole body —he did not like the milk either, although milk had been his favorite drink and that was certainly why his sister had set it there for him, indeed it was almost with repulsion that he turned away from the basin and crawled back to the middle of the room.

He could see through the crack of the door that the gas was turned on in the living room, but while usually at this time his father made a habit of reading the afternoon newspaper in a loud voice to his mother and occasionally to his sister as well, not a sound was now to be heard. Well, perhaps his father had recently given up this habit of reading aloud, which his sister had mentioned so often in conversation and in her letters. But there was the same silence all around, although the flat was certainly not empty of occupants. "What a quiet life our family has been leading," said Gregor to himself, and as he sat there motionless staring into the darkness he felt great pride in the fact that he had been able to provide such a life for his parents and sister in such a fine flat. But what if all the quiet, the comfort, the contentment were now to end in horror? To keep himself from being lost in such thoughts Gregor took refuge in movement and crawled up and down the room.

Once during the long evening one of the side doors was opened a little and quickly shut again, later the other side door too; someone had apparently wanted to come in and then thought better of it. Gregor now stationed himself immediately before the living room door, determined to persuade any hesitating visitor to come in or at least to discover who it might be; but the door was not opened again and he waited in vain. In the early morning, when the doors were locked, they had all wanted to come in; now that he had opened one door and the other had apparently been opened during the day, no one came in and even the keys were on the other side of the doors.

It was late at night before the gas went out in the living room, and Gregor could easily tell that his parents and his sister had all stayed awake until then, for he could clearly hear the three of them stealing away on tiptoe. No one was likely to visit him, not until the morning, that was certain; so he had plenty of time to meditate at his leisure on how he was to arrange his life afresh. But the lofty, empty room in which he had to lie flat on the floor filled him with an apprehension he could not account for, since it had been his very own room for the past five years—and with a half-unconscious action, not without a slight feeling of shame, he scuttled under the sofa, where he felt comfortable at once, although his back was a little cramped and he could not lift his head up, and his only regret was that his body was too broad to get the whole of it under the sofa.

He stayed there all night, spending the time partly in a light slumber, from which his hunger kept waking him up with a start, and partly in worrying and sketching vague hopes, which all led to the same conclusion, that he must lie low for the present and, by exercising patience and the utmost consideration, help the family to bear the inconvenience he was bound to cause them in his present condition.

Very early in the morning, it was still almost night, Gregor had the chance to test the strength of his new resolutions, for his sister, nearly fully dressed, opened the door from the hall and peered in. She did not see him at once, yet when she caught sight of him under the sofa—well, he had to be somewhere, he couldn't have flown away, could he?—she was so startled that without being able to help it she slammed the door shut again. But as if regretting her behavior she opened the door again immediately and came in on tiptoe, as if she were visiting an invalid or even a stranger. Gregor had pushed his head forward to the very edge of the sofa and watched her. Would she notice that he had left the milk standing, and not for lack of hunger, and would she bring in some other kind of food more to his taste? If she did not do it of her own accord, he would rather starve than draw her attention to the fact, although he felt a wild impulse to dart out from under the sofa, throw himself at her feet and beg her for something to eat. But his sister at once noticed, with surprise, that the basin was still full, except for a little milk that had been spilt all around it, she lifted it immediately, not with her bare hands, true, but with a cloth and carried it away. Gregor was wildly curious to know what she would bring instead, and made various speculations about it. Yet what she actually did next, in the goodness of her heart, he could never have guessed at. To find out what he liked she brought him a whole selection of food, all set out on an old newspaper. There were old, half-decayed vegetables, bones from last night's supper covered with a white sauce that had thickened; some raisins and almonds; a piece of cheese that Gregor would have called uneatable two days ago; a dry roll of bread, a buttered roll, and a roll both buttered and salted. Besides all·that, she set down again the same basin, into which she had poured some water, and which was apparently to be reserved for his exclusive use. And with fine tact, knowing that Gregor would not eat in her presence, she withdrew quickly and even turned the key, to let him understand that he could take his ease as much as he liked. Gregor's legs all whizzed towards the food. His wounds must have healed completely, moreover, for he felt no disability, which amazed him and made him reflect how more than a month ago he had cut one finger a little with a knife and had still suffered pain from the wound only the day before yesterday. Am I less sensitive now? he thought, and sucked greedily at the cheese, which above all the other edibles attracted him at once and strongly. One after another and with tears of satisfaction in his eyes he quickly devoured the cheese, the vegetables and the sauce; the fresh food, on the other hand, had no charms for him, he could not even stand the smell of it and actually dragged away to some little distance the things he could eat. He had long finished his meal and was only lying lazily on the same spot when his sister turned the key slowly as a sign for him to retreat. That roused him at once, although he was nearly asleep, and he hurried under the sofa again. But it took considerable self-control for him to stay under the sofa, even for the short time his sister was in the room, since the large meal had swollen his body somewhat and he was so cramped he could hardly breathe. Slight attacks of breathlessness afflicted him and his eyes were starting a little out of his head as he watched his unsuspecting sister sweeping together with a broom not only the remains of what he had eaten but even the things he had not touched, as if these were now of no use to anyone, and hastily shoveling it all into a bucket, which she covered with a wooden lid and carried away. Hardly had she turned her back when Gregor came from under the sofa and stretched and puffed himself out.

21

In this manner Gregor was fed, once in the early morning while his parents and the servant girl were still asleep, and a second time after they had all had their midday dinner, for then his parents took a short nap and the servant girl could be sent out on some errand or other by his sister. Not that they would have wanted him to starve, of course, but perhaps they could not have borne to know more about his feeding than from hearsay, perhaps too his sister wanted to spare them such little anxieties wherever possible, since they had quite enough to bear as it was.

Under what pretext the doctor and the locksmith had been got rid of on that first morning Gregor could not discover, for since what he said was not understood by the others it never struck any of them, not even his sister, that he could understand what they said, and so whenever his sister came into his room he had to content himself with hearing her utter only a sigh now and then and an occasional appeal to the saints. Later on, when she had got a little used to the situation—of course she could never get completely used to it—she sometimes threw out a remark which was kindly meant or could be so interpreted. "Well, he liked his dinner today," she would say when Gregor had made a good clearance of his food; and when he had not eaten, which gradually happened more and more often, she would say almost sadly: "Everything's been left standing again."

But although Gregor could get no news directly, he overheard a lot from the neighboring rooms, and as soon as voices were audible, he would run to the door of the room concerned and press his whole body against it. In the first few days especially there was no conversation that did not refer to him somehow, even if only indirectly. For two whole days there were family consultations at every mealtime about what should be done; but also between meals the same subject was discussed, for there were always at least two members of the family at home, since no one wanted to be alone in the flat and to leave it quite empty was unthinkable. And on the very first of these days the household cook—it was not quite clear what and how much she knew of the situation—

went down on her knees to his mother and begged leave to go, and when she departed, a quarter of an hour later, gave thanks for her dismissal with tears in her eyes as if for the greatest benefit that could have been conferred on her, and without any prompting swore a solemn oath that she would never say a single word to anyone about what had happened.

Now Gregor's sister had to cook too, helping her mother; true, the cooking did not amount to much, for they ate scarcely anything. Gregor was always hearing one of the family vainly urging another to eat and getting no answer but: "Thanks, I've had all I want," or something similar. Perhaps they drank nothing either. Time and again his sister kept asking his father if he wouldn't like some beer and offered kindly to go and fetch it herself, and when he made no answer suggested that she could ask the concierge to fetch it, so that he need feel no sense of obligation, but then a round "No" came from his father and no more was said about it.

In the course of that very first day Gregor's father explained the family's financial position and prospects to both his mother and his sister. Now and then he rose from the table to get some voucher or memorandum out of the small safe he had rescued from the collapse of his business five years earlier. One could hear him opening the complicated lock and rustling papers out and shutting it again. This statement made by his father was the first cheerful information Gregor had heard since his imprisonment. He had been of the opinion that nothing at all was left over from his father's business, at least his father had never said anything to the contrary, and of course he had not asked him directly. At that time Gregor's sole desire was to do his utmost to help the family to forget as soon as possible the catastrophe which had overwhelmed the business and thrown them all into a state of complete despair. And so he had set to work with unusual ardor and almost overnight had become a commercial traveler instead of a little clerk, with of course much greater chances of earning money, and his success was immediately translated into good round coin which he could lay on the table for his amazed and happy family. These had been fine times, and they had never recurred, at least not with the same sense of glory, although later on Gregor had earned so much money that he was able to meet the expenses of the whole household and did so. They had simply got used to it, both the family and Gregor; the money was gratefully accepted and gladly given, but there was no special uprush of warm feeling. With his sister alone had he remained intimate, and it was a secret plan of his that she, who loved music, unlike himself, and could play movingly on the violin, should be sent next year to study at the Conservatorium, despite the great expense that would entail, which must be made up in some other way. During his brief visits home the Conservatorium was often mentioned in the talks he had with his sister, but always merely as a beautiful dream which could never come true, and his parents discouraged even these innocent references to it; yet Gregor had made up his mind firmly about it and meant to announce the fact with due solemnity on Christmas Day.

Such were the thoughts, completely futile in his present condition, that went through his head as he stood clinging upright to the door and listening. Sometimes out of sheer weariness he had to give up listening and let his head fall negligently against the door, but he always had to pull himself together again at once, for even the slight sound his head made was audible next door and brought all conversation to a stop. "What can he be doing now?" his father would say after a while, obviously turning towards the door, and only then would the interrupted conversation gradually be set going again.

Gregor was now informed as amply as he could wish —for his father tended to repeat himself in his explanations, partly because it was a long time since he had handled such matters and partly because his mother could not always grasp things at once—that a certain amount of investments, a very small amount it was true, had survived the wreck of their fortunes and had even increased a little because the dividends had not been touched meanwhile. And besides that, the money Gregor brought home every month—he had kept only a few dollars for himself—had never been quite used up and now amounted to a small capital sum. Behind the door Gregor nodded his head eagerly, rejoiced at this evidence of unexpected thrift and foresight. True, he could really have paid off some more of his father's debts to the chief with this extra money, and so brought much nearer the day on which he could quit his job, but doubtless it was better the way his father had arranged it.

Yet this capital was by no means sufficient to let the family live on the interest of it; for one year, perhaps, or at the most two, they could live on the principal, that was all. It was simply a sum that ought not to be touched and should be kept for a rainy day; money for living expenses would have to be earned. Now his father was still hale enough but an old man, and he had done no work for the past five years and could not be expected to do much; during these five years, the first years of leisure in his laborious though unsuccessful life, he had grown rather fat and become sluggish. And Gregor's old mother, how was she to earn a living with her asthma, which troubled her even when she walked through the flat and kept her lying on a sofa every other day panting for breath beside an open window? And was his sister to earn her bread, she who was still a child of seventeen and whose life hitherto had been so pleasant, consisting as it did in dressing herself nicely, sleeping long, helping in the housekeeping, going out to a few modest entertainments and above all playing the violin? At first whenever the need for earning money was mentioned Gregor let go his hold on the door and threw himself down on the cool leather sofa beside it, he felt so hot with shame and grief.

Often he just lay there the long nights through without sleeping at all, scrabbling for hours on the leather. Or he nerved himself to the great effort of pushing an armchair to the window, then crawled up over the window sill and, braced against the chair, leaned against the window panes, obviously in some recollection of the sense of freedom that looking out of a window always used to give him. For in reality day by day things that

25

were even a little way off were growing dimmer to his sight; the hospital across the street, which he used to execrate for being all too often before his eyes, was now quite beyond his range of vision, and if he had not known that he lived in Charlotte Street, a quiet street but still a city street, he might have believed that his window gave on a desert waste where gray sky and gray land blended indistinguishably into each other. His quick-witted sister only needed to observe twice that the armchair stood by the window; after that whenever she had tidied the room she always pushed the chair back to the same place at the window and even left the inner casements open.

If he could have spoken to her and thanked her for all she had to do for him, he could have borne her ministrations better; as it was, they oppressed him. She certainly tried to make as light as possible of whatever was disagreeable in her task, and as time went on she succeeded, of course, more and more, but time brought more enlightenment to Gregor too. The very way she came in distressed him. Hardly was she in the room when she rushed to the window, without even taking time to shut the door, careful as she was usually to shield the sight of Gregor's room from the others, and as if she were almost suffocating tore the casements open with hasty fingers, standing then in the open draught for a while even in the bitterest cold and drawing deep breaths. This noisy scurry of hers upset Gregor twice a day; he would crouch trembling under the sofa all the time, knowing quite well that she would certainly have spared him such a disturbance had she found it at all possible to stay in his presence without opening the window.

On one occasion, about a month after Gregor's metamorphosis, when there was surely no reason for her to be still startled at his appearance, she came a little earlier than usual and found him gazing out of the window, quite motionless, and thus well placed to look like a bogey. Gregor would not have been surprised had she not come in at all, for she could not immediately open the window while he was there, but not only did she retreat, she jumped back as if in alarm and banged the door shut; a stranger might well have thought that he had been lying in wait for her there meaning to bite her. Of course he hid himself under the sofa at once, but he had to wait until midday before she came again, and she seemed more ill at ease than usual. This made him realize how repulsive the sight of him still was to her, and that it was bound to go on being repulsive, and what an effort it must cost her not to run away even from the sight of the small portion of his body that stuck out from under the sofa. In order to spare her that, therefore, one day he carried a sheet on his back to the sofa—it cost him four hours' labor—and arranged it there in such a way as to hide him completely, so that even if she were to bend down she could not see him. Had she considered the sheet unnecessary, she would certainly have stripped it off the sofa again, for it was clear enough that this curtaining and confining of himself was not likely to conduce to Gregor's comfort, but she left it where it was, and Gregor even fancied that he caught a thankful glance from her eye when he lifted the sheet carefully a very little with his head to see how she was taking the new arrangement.

For the first fortnight his parents could not bring themselves to the point of entering his room, and he often heard them expressing their appreciation of his sister's activities, whereas formerly they had frequently scolded her for being as they thought a somewhat useless daughter. But now, both of them often waited outside the door, his father and his mother, while his sister tidied his room, and as soon as she came out she had to tell them exactly how things were in the room, what Gregor had eaten, how he had conducted himself this time and whether there was not perhaps some slight improvement in his condition. His mother, moreover, began relatively soon to want to visit him, but his father and sister dissuaded her at first with arguments which Gregor listened to very attentively and altogether approved. Later, however, she had to be held back by main force, and when she cried out: "Do let me in to

Gregor, he is my unfortunate son! Can't you understand that I must go to him?" Gregor thought that it might be well to have her come in, not every day, of course, but perhaps once a week; she understood things, after all, much better than his sister, who was only a child despite the efforts she was making and had perhaps taken on so difficult a task merely out of childish thoughtlessness.

Gregor's desire to see his mother was soon fulfilled. During the daytime he did not want to show himself at the window, out of consideration for his parents, but he could not crawl very far around the few square yards of floor space he had, nor could he bear lying quietly at rest all during the night, while he was fast losing any interest he had ever taken in food, so that for mere recreation he had formed the habit of crawling crisscross over the walls and ceiling. He especially enjoyed hanging suspended from the ceiling; it was much better than lying on the floor; one could breathe more freely; one's body swung and rocked lightly; and in the almost blissful absorption induced by this suspension it could happen to his own surprise that he let go and fell plump on the floor. Yet he now had his body much better under control than formerly, and even such a big fall did him no harm. His sister at once remarked the new distraction Gregor had found for himself—he left traces behind him of the sticky stuff on his soles wherever he crawled—and she got the idea in her head of giving him as wide a field as possible to crawl in and of removing the pieces of furniture that hindered him, above all the chest of drawers and the writing desk. But that was more than she could manage all by herself; she did not dare ask her father to help her; and as for the servant girl, a young creature of sixteen who had had the courage to stay on after the cook's departure, she could not be asked to help, for she had begged as an especial favor that she might keep the kitchen door locked and open it only on a definite summons; so there was nothing left but to apply to her mother at an hour when her father was out. And the old lady did come, with exclamations of joyful eagerness, which, however, died away at the door of Gregor's room. Gregor's sister, of course, went in first, to see that everything was in order before letting his mother enter. In great haste Gregor pulled the sheet lower and rucked it more in folds so that it really looked as if it had been thrown accidentally over the sofa. And this time he did not peer out from under it; he renounced the pleasure of seeing his mother on this occasion and was only glad that she had come at all. "Come in, he's out of sight," said his sister, obviously leading her mother in by the hand. Gregor could now hear the two women struggling to shift the heavy old chest from its place, and his sister claiming the greater part of the labor for herself, without listening to the admonitions of her mother who feared she might overstrain herself. It took a long time. After at least a quarter of an hour's tugging his mother objected that the chest had better be left where it was, for in the first place it was too heavy and could never be got out before his father came home, and standing in the middle of the room like that it would only hamper Gregor's movements, while in the second place it was not at all certain that removing the furniture would be doing a service to Gregor. She was inclined to think to the contrary; the sight of the naked walls made her own heart heavy, and why shouldn't Gregor have the same feeling, considering that he had been used to his furniture for so long and might feel forlorn without it. "And doesn't it look," she concluded in a low voice—in fact she had been almost whispering all the time as if to avoid letting Gregor, whose exact whereabouts she did not know, hear even the tones of her voice, for she was convinced that he could not understand her words—"doesn't it look as if we were showing him, by taking away his furniture, that we have given up hope of his ever getting better and are just leaving him coldly to himself? I think it would be best to keep his room exactly as it has always been, so that when he comes back to us he will find everything unchanged and be able all the more easily to forget what has happened in between."

On hearing these words from his mother Gregor realized that the lack of all direct human speech for the past two months together with the monotony of family life must have confused his mind, otherwise he could not account for the fact that he had quite earnestly looked forward to having his room emptied of furnishing. Did he really want his warm room, so comfortably fitted with old family furniture, to be turned into a naked den in which he would certainly be able to crawl unhampered in all directions but at the price of shedding simultaneously all recollection of his human background? He had indeed been so near the brink of forgetfulness that only the voice of his mother, which he had not heard for so long, had drawn him back from it. Nothing should be taken out of his room; everything must stay as it was; he could not dispense with the good influence of the furniture on his state of mind; and even if the furniture did hamper him in his senseless crawling round and round, that was no drawback but a great advantage.

Unfortunately his sister was of the contrary opinion; she had grown accustomed, and not without reason, to consider herself an expert in Gregor's affairs as against her parents, and so her mother's advice was now enough to make her determined on the removal not only of the chest and the writing desk, which had been her first intention, but of all the furniture except the indispensable sofa. This determination was not, of course, merely the outcome of childish recalcitrance and of the self-confidence she had recently developed so unexpectedly and at such cost; she had in fact perceived that Gregor needed a lot of space to crawl about in, while on the other hand he never used the furniture at all, so far as could be seen. Another factor might have been also the enthusiastic temperament of an adolescent girl, which seeks to indulge itself on every opportunity and which now tempted Grete to exaggerate the horror of her brother's circumstances in order that she might do all the more for him. In a room where Gregor lorded it all alone over empty walls no one save herself was likely ever to set foot.

And so she was not to be moved from her resolve

30

by her mother, who seemed moreover to be ill at ease in Gregor's room and therefore unsure of herself, was soon reduced to silence and helped her daughter as best she could to push the chest outside. Now, Gregor could do without the chest, if need be, but the writing desk he must retain. As soon as the two women had got the chest out of his room, groaning as they pushed it, Gregor stuck his head out from under the sofa to see how he might intervene as kindly and cautiously as possible. But as bad luck would have it, his mother was the first to return, leaving Grete clasping the chest in the room next door where she was trying to shift it all by herself, without of course moving it from the spot. His mother however was not accustomed to the sight of him, it might sicken her and so in alarm Gregor backed quickly to the other end of the sofa, yet could not prevent the sheet from swaying a little in front. That was enough to put her on the alert. She paused, stood still for a moment and then went back to Grete.

Although Gregor kept reassuring himself that nothing out of the way was happening, but only a few bits of furniture were being changed round, he soon had to admit that all this trotting to and fro of the two women, their little ejaculations and the scraping of furniture along the floor affected him like a vast disturbance coming from all sides at once, and however much he tucked in his head and legs and cowered to the very floor he was bound to confess that he would not be able to stand it for long. They were clearing his room out; taking away everything he loved; the chest in which he kept his fret saw and other tools was already dragged off; they were now loosening the writing desk which had almost sunk into the floor, the desk at which he had done all his homework when he was at the commercial academy, at the grammar school before that, and, yes, even at the primary school—he had no more time to waste in weighing the good intentions of the two women, whose existence he had by now almost forgotten, for they were so exhausted that they were laboring in silence and nothing could be heard but the heavy scuffling of their feet.

And so he rushed out—the women were just leaning against the writing desk in the next room to give themselves a breather—and four times changed his direction, since he really did not know what to rescue first, then on the wall opposite, which was already otherwise cleared, he was struck by the picture of the lady muffled in so much fur and quickly crawled up to it and pressed himself to the glass, which was a good surface to hold on to and comforted his hot belly. This picture at least, which was entirely hidden beneath him, was going to be removed by nobody. He turned his head towards the door of the living room so as to observe the women when they came back.

They had not allowed themselves much of a rest and were already coming; Grete had twined her arm round her mother and was almost supporting her. "Well, what shall we take now?" said Grete, looking round. Her eyes met Gregor's from the wall. She kept her composure, presumably because of her mother, bent her head down to her mother, to keep her from looking up, and said, although in a fluttering, unpremeditated voice: "Come, hadn't we better go back to the living room for a moment?" Her intentions were clear enough to Gregor, she wanted to bestow her mother in safety and then chase him down from the wall. Well, just let her try it! He clung to his picture and would not give it up. He would rather fly in Grete's face.

But Grete's words had succeeded in disquieting her mother, who took a step to one side, caught sight of the huge brown mass on the flowered wallpaper, and before she was really conscious that what she saw was Gregor screamed in a loud, hoarse voice: "Oh God, oh God!" fell with outspread arms over the sofa as if giving up and did not move. "Gregor!" cried his sister, shaking her fist and glaring at him. This was the first time she had directly addressed him since his metamorphosis. She ran into the next room for some aromatic essence with which to rouse her mother from her fainting fit. Gregor wanted to help too—there was still time to rescue the picture—but he was stuck fast to the glass and had to tear himself loose; he then ran after his sister into the next room as if he could advise her, as he used to do; but then had to stand helplessly behind her; she meanwhile searched among various small bottles and when she turned round started in alarm at the sight of him; one bottle fell on the floor and broke; a splinter of glass cut Gregor's face and some kind of corrosive medicine splashed him; without pausing a moment longer Grete gathered up all the bottles she could carry and ran to her mother with them; she banged the door shut with her foot. Gregor was now cut off from his mother, who was perhaps nearly dying because of him; he dared not open the door for fear of frightening away his sister, who had to stay with her mother; there was nothing he could do but wait; and harassed by self-reproach and worry he began now to crawl to and fro, over everything, walls, furniture and ceiling, and finally in his despair, when the whole room seemed to be reeling round him, fell down on to the middle of the big table.

A little while elapsed, Gregor was still lying there feebly and all around was quiet, perhaps that was a good omen. Then the doorbell rang. The servant girl was of course locked in her kitchen, and Grete would have to open the door. It was his father. "What's been happening?" were his first words; Grete's face must have told him everything. Grete answered in a muffled voice, apparently hiding her head on his breast: "Mother has been fainting, but she's better now. Gregor's broken loose." "Just what I expected," said his father, "just what I've been telling you, but you women would never listen." It was clear to Gregor that his father had taken the worst interpretation of Grete's all too brief statement and was assuming that Gregor had been guilty of some violent act. Therefore Gregor must now try to propitiate his father, since he had neither time nor means for an explanation. And so he fled to the door of his own room and crouched against it, to let his father see as soon as he came in from the hall that his son had the good intention of getting back into his room immediately and that it was not necessary to drive

33

him there, but that if only the door were opened he would disappear at once.

Yet his father was not in the mood to perceive such fine distinctions. "Ah!" he cried as soon as he appeared, in a tone which sounded at once angry and exultant. Gregor drew his head back from the door and lifted it to look at his father. Truly, this was not the father he had imagined to himself; admittedly he had been too absorbed of late in his new recreation of crawling over the ceiling to take the same interest as before in what was happening elsewhere in the flat, and he ought really to be prepared for some changes. And yet, and yet, could that be his father? The man who used to lie wearily sunk in bed whenever Gregor set out on a business journey; who welcomed him back of an evening lying in a long chair in a dressing gown; who could not really rise to his feet but only lifted his arms in greeting, and on the rare occasions when he did go out with his family, on one or two Sundays a year and on high holidays, walked between Gregor and his mother, who were slow walkers anyhow, even more slowly than they did, muffled in his old greatcoat, shuffling laboriously forward with the help of his crook-handled stick which he set down most cautiously at every step and, whenever he wanted to say anything, nearly always came to a full stop and gathered his escort around him? Now he was standing there in fine shape; dressed in a smart blue uniform with gold buttons, such as bank messengers wear; his strong double chin bulged over the stiff high collar of his jacket; from under his bushy eyebrows his black eyes darted fresh and penetrating glances; his onetime tangled white hair had been combed flat on either side of a shining and carefully exact parting. He pitched his cap, which bore a gold monogram, probably the badge of some bank, in a wide sweep across the whole room on to a sofa and with the tailends of his jacket thrown back, his hands in his trouser pockets, advanced with a grim visage towards Gregor. Likely enough he did not himself know what he meant to do; at any rate he lifted his feet uncommonly high, and Gregor was dumbfounded at the enormous size of his shoe soles. But Gregor could not risk standing up to him, aware as he had been from the very first day of his new life that his father believed only the severest measures suitable for dealing with him, And so he ran before his father, stopping when he stopped and scuttling forward again when his father made any kind of move. In this way they circled the room several times without anything decisive happening, indeed the whole operation did not even look like a pursuit because it was carried out so slowly. And so Gregor did not leave the floor, for he feared that his father might take as a piece of peculiar wickedness any excursion of his over the walls or the ceiling. All the same, he could not stay this course much longer, for while his father took one step he had to carry out a whole series of movements. He was already beginning to feel breathless, just as in his former life his lungs had not been very dependable. As he was staggering along, trying to concentrate his energy on running, hardly keeping his eyes open; in his dazed state never even thinking of any other escape than simply going forward; and having almost forgotten that the walls were free to him, which in this room were well provided with finely carved pieces of furniture full of knobs and crevices—suddenly something lightly flung landed close behind him and rolled before him. It was an apple; a second apple followed immediately; Gregor came to a stop in alarm; there was no point in running on, for his father was determined to bombard him. He had filled his pockets with fruit from the dish on the sideboard and was now shying apple after apple, without taking particularly good aim for the moment. The small red apples rolled about the floor as if magnetized and cannoned into each other. An apple thrown without much force grazed Gregor's back and glanced off harmlessly. But another following immediately landed right on his back and sank in; Gregor wanted to drag himself forward, as if this startling, incredible pain could be left behind him; but he felt as if nailed to the spot and flattened himself out in a complete derangement of all his senses. With his last conscious look he saw the door of his room being torn open and his mother rushing out ahead of his screaming sister, in her underbodice, for her daughter had loosened her clothing to let her breathe more freely and recover from her swoon; he saw his mother rushing towards his father, leaving one after another behind her on the floor her loosened petticoats, stumbling over her petticoats straight to his father and embracing him, in complete union with him—but here Gregor's sight began to fail—with her hands clasped round his father's neck as she begged for her son's life.

III

THE SERIOUS INJURY done to Gregor, which disabled him for more than a month—the apple went on sticking in his body as a visible reminder, since no one ventured to remove it—seemed to have made even his father recollect that Gregor was a member of the family, despite his present unfortunate and repulsive shape, and ought not to be treated as an enemy, that, on the contrary, family duty required the suppression of disgust and the exercise of patience, nothing but patience.

And although his injury had impaired, probably forever, his powers of movement, and for the time being it took him long, long minutes to creep across his room like an old invalid—there was no question now of crawling up the wall—yet in his own opinion he was sufficiently compensated for this worsening of his condition by the fact that towards evening the living-room door, which he used to watch intently for an hour or two beforehand, was always thrown open, so that lying in the darkness of his room, invisible to the family, he could see them all at the lamp-lit table and listen to their talk, by general consent as it were, very different from his earlier eavesdropping.

True, their intercourse lacked the lively character of former times, which he had always called to mind with a certain wistfulness in the small hotel bedrooms where he had been wont to throw himself down, tired out, on damp bedding. They were now mostly very silent. Soon after supper his father would fall asleep in his armchair; his mother and sister would admonish each other to be silent; his mother, bending low over the lamp, stitched at fine sewing for an underwear firm; his sister, who had taken a job as a salesgirl, was learning shorthand and French in the evenings on the chance of bettering herself. Sometimes his father woke up, and as if quite unaware that he had been sleeping said to his mother: "What a lot of sewing you're doing today!" and at once fell asleep again, while the two women exchanged a tired smile.

With a kind of mulishness his father persisted in keeping his uniform on even in the house; his dressing gown hung uselessly on its peg and he slept fully dressed where he sat, as if he were ready for service at any moment and even here only at the beck and call of his superior. As a result, his uniform, which was not brand-new to start with, began to look dirty, despite all the loving care of the mother and sister to keep it clean, and Gregor often spent whole evenings gazing at the many greasy spots on the garment, gleaming with gold buttons always in a high state of polish, in which the old man sat sleeping in extreme discomfort and yet quite peacefully.

As soon as the clock struck ten his mother tried to rouse his father with gentle words and to persuade him after that to get into bed, for sitting there he could not have a proper sleep and that was what he needed most, since he had to go on duty at six. But with the mulishness that had obsessed him since he became a bank messenger he always insisted on staying longer at the table, although he regularly fell asleep again and in the end only with the greatest trouble could be got out of his armchair and into his bed. However insistently Gregor's mother and sister kept urging him with gentle reminders, he would go on slowly shaking his head for a quarter of an hour, keeping his eyes shut, and refuse to get to his feet. The mother plucked at his sleeve, whispering endearments in his ear, the sister left her lessons to come to her mother's help, but Gregor's father was not to be caught. He would only sink down deeper in his chair. Not until the two women hoisted him up by the armpits did he open his eyes and look at them both, one after the other, usually with the remark: "This is a life. This is the peace and quiet of my old age." And leaning on the two of them he would heave himself up, with difficulty, as if he were a great burden to himself, suffer them to lead him as far as the door and then wave them off and go on alone, while the mother abandoned her needlework and the sister her pen in order to run after him and help him farther.

Who could find time, in this overworked and tired-out family, to bother about Gregor more than was absolutely needful? The household was reduced more and more; the servant girl was turned off; a gigantic bony charwoman with white hair flying round her head came in morning and evening to do the rough work; everything else was done by Gregor's mother, as well as great piles of sewing. Even various family ornaments, which his mother and sister used to wear with pride at parties and celebrations, had to be sold, as Gregor discovered of an evening from hearing them all discuss the prices obtained. But what they lamented most was the fact that they could not leave the flat which was much too big for their present circumstances, because they could not think of any way to shift Gregor. Yet Gregor saw well enough that consideration for him was not the main difficulty preventing the removal, for they could have easily shifted him in some suitable box with a few air holes in it; what really kept them from moving into another flat was rather their own complete hopelessness and the belief that they had been singled out for a misfortune such as had never happened to any of their relations or acquaintances. They fulfilled to the uttermost all that the world demands of poor people, the father fetched breakfast for the small clerks in the bank, the mother devoted her energy to making underwear for strangers, the sister trotted to and fro behind the counter at the behest of customers, but more than this they had not the strength to do. And the wound in Gregor's back began to nag at him afresh when his mother and sister, after getting his father into bed, came back again, left their work lying, drew close to each other and sat cheek by cheek; then his mother, pointing towards his room, said: "Shut that door now, Grete," and he was left again in darkness, while next door the women mingled their tears or perhaps sat dry-eyed staring at the table.

Gregor hardly slept at all by night or by day. He was often haunted by the idea that next time the door opened he would take the family's affairs in hand again just as he used to do; once more, after this long interval, there appeared in his thoughts the figures of the chief and the chief clerk, the commercial travelers and the apprentices, the porter who was so dull-witted, two or three friends in other firms, a chambermaid in one of the rural hotels, a sweet and fleeting memory, a cashier in a milliner's shop, whom he had wooed earnestly but too slowly—they all appeared, together with strangers or people he had quite forgotten, but instead of helping him and his family they were one and all unapproachable and he was glad when they vanished. At other times he would not be in the mood to bother about his family, he was only filled with rage at the way they were neglecting him, and although he had no clear idea of what he might care to eat he would make plans for getting into the larder to take the food that was after all his due, even if he were not hungry. His sister no longer took thought to bring him what might especially please him, but in the morning and at noon before she went to business hurriedly pushed into his room with her foot any food that was available, and in the evening cleared it out again with one sweep of the broom, heedless of whether it had been merely tasted, or—as most frequently happened—left untouched. The cleaning of his room, which she now did always in the evenings, could not have been more hastily done. Streaks of dirt stretched along the walls, here and there lay balls of dust and filth. At first Gregor used to station himself in some particularly filthy corner when his sister arrived, in order to reproach her with it, so to speak. But he could have sat there for weeks without getting her to make any improvement; she could see the dirt as well as he did, but she had simply made up her mind to leave it alone. And yet, with a touchiness that was new to her, which seemed anyhow to have infected the whole family, she jealously guarded her claim to be the sole caretaker of Gregor's room. His mother once subjected his room to a thorough cleaning, which was achieved only by means of several buckets of water —all this dampness of course upset Gregor too and he lay widespread, sulky and motionless on the sofa— but she was well punished for it. Hardly had his sister noticed the changed aspect of his room that evening than she rushed in high dudgeon into the living room and, despite the imploringly raised hands of her mother, burst into a storm of weeping, while her parents—her father had of course been startled out of his chair— looked on at first in helpless amazement; then they too began to go into action; the father reproached the mother on his right for not having left the cleaning of Gregor's room to his sister; shrieked at the sister on his left that never again was she to be allowed to clean Gregor's room; while the mother tried to pull the father into his bedroom, since he was beyond himself with agitation; the sister, shaken with sobs, then beat upon the table with her small fists; and Gregor hissed loudly with rage because not one of them thought of shutting the door to spare him such a spectacle and so much noise.

Still, even if the sister, exhausted by her daily work, had grown tired of looking after Gregor as she did formerly, there was no need for his mother's intervention or for Gregor's being neglected at all. The charwoman was there. This old widow, whose strong bony frame had enabled her to survive the worst a long life could offer, by no means recoiled from Gregor. Without being in the least curious she had once by chance opened the door of his room and at the sight of Gregor, who, taken by surprise, began to rush to and fro although no one was chasing him, merely stood there with her arms folded. From that time she never failed to open his door a little for a moment, morning and evening, to have a look at him. At first she even used to call him to her, with words which apparently she took to be friendly, such as: "Come along, then, you old dung beetle!" or "Look at the old dung beetle, then!" To such allocutions Gregor made no answer, but stayed motionless where he was, as if the door had never been opened. Instead of being allowed to disturb him so senselessly whenever the whim took her, she should rather have been ordered to clean out his room daily, that charwoman! Once, early in the morning—heavy rain was lashing on the windowpanes, perhaps a sign that spring was on the way—Gregor was so exasperated when she began addressing him again that he ran at her, as if to attack her, although slowly and feebly enough. But the charwoman instead of showing fright merely lifted high a chair that happened to be beside the door, and as she stood there with her mouth wide open it was clear that she meant to shut it only when she brought the chair down on Gregor's back. "So you're not coming any nearer?" she asked, as Gregor turned away again, and quietly put the chair back into the corner.

Gregor was now eating hardly anything. Only when he happened to pass the food laid out for him did he take a bit of something in his mouth as a pastime, kept it there for an hour at a time and usually spat it out again. At first he thought it was chagrin over the state of his room that prevented him from eating, yet he soon got used to the various changes in his room. It had become a habit in the family to push into his room things there was no room for elsewhere, and there were plenty of these now, since one of the rooms had been let to three lodgers. These serious gentlemen—all three of them with full beards, as Gregor once observed through a crack in the door—had a passion for order, not only in their own room but, since they were now members of the household, in all its arrangements, especially in the kitchen. Superfluous, not to say dirty, objects they could not bear. Besides, they had brought with them most of the furnishings they needed. For this reason many things could be dispensed with that it was no use trying to sell but that should not be thrown away either. All of them found their way into Gregor's room. The ash can likewise and the kitchen garbage can. Anything that was not needed for the moment was simply flung into Gregor's room by the charwoman, who did everything in a hurry; fortunately Gregor usually saw only the object, whatever it was, and the hand that held it. Perhaps she intended to take the things away again as time and opportunity offered, or to collect them until she could throw them all out in a heap, but in fact they just lay wherever she happened to throw them, except when Gregor pushed his way through the junk heap and shifted it somewhat, at first out of necessity, because he had not room enough to crawl, but later with increasing enjoyment, although after such excursions, being sad and weary to death, he would lie motionless for hours. And since the lodgers often ate their supper at home in the common living room, the living-room door stayed shut many an evening, yet Gregor reconciled himself quite easily to the shutting of the door, for often enough on evenings when it was opened he had disregarded it entirely and lain in the darkest corner of his room, quite unnoticed by the family. But on one occasion the charwoman left the door open a little and it stayed ajar even when the lodgers came in for supper and the lamp was lit. They set themselves at the top end of the table where formerly Gregor and his father and mother had eaten their meals, unfolded their napkins and took knife and fork in hand. At once his mother appeared in the other doorway with a dish of meat and close behind her his sister with a dish of potatoes piled high. The food steamed with a thick vapor. The lodgers bent over the food set before them as if to scrutinize it before eating, in fact the man in the middle, who seemed to pass for an authority with the other two, cut a piece of meat as it lay on the dish, obviously to discover if it were tender or should be sent back to the kitchen. He showed satisfaction, and Gregor's mother and sister, who had been watching anxiously, breathed freely and began to smile.

The family itself took its meals in the kitchen. None the less, Gregor's father came into the living room before going into the kitchen and with one prolonged bow, cap in hand, made a round of the table. The lodgers all stood up and murmured something in their beards. When they were alone again they ate their food in almost complete silence. It seemed remarkable to Gregor that among the various noises coming from the table he could always distinguish the sound of their masticating teeth, as if this were a sign to Gregor that one needed teeth in order to eat, and that with toothless jaws even of the finest make one could do nothing. "I'm hungry enough," said Gregor sadly to himself, "but not for that kind of food. How these lodgers are stuffing themselves, and here am I dying of starvation!"

On that very evening—during the whole of his time there Gregor could not remember ever having heard the violin—the sound of violin-playing came from the kitchen. The lodgers had already finished their supper, the one in the middle had brought out a newspaper and given the other two a page apiece, and now they were leaning back at ease reading and smoking. When the violin began to play they pricked up their ears, got to their feet, and went on tiptoe to the hall door where they stood huddled together. Their movements must have been heard in the kitchen, for Gregor's father called out: "Is the violin-playing disturbing you, gentlemen? It can be stopped at once." "On the contrary," said the middle lodger, "could not Fräulein Samsa come and play in this room, beside us, where it is much more convenient and comfortable?" "Oh certainly," cried Gregor's father, as if he were the violin-player. The lodgers came back into the living room and waited. Presently Gregor's father arrived with the music stand, his mother carrying the music and his sister with the violin. His sister quietly made everything ready to start playing; his parents, who had never let rooms before and so had an exaggerated idea of the courtesy due to lodgers, did not venture to sit down on their own chairs; his father leaned against the door, the right hand thrust between two buttons of his livery coat, which was formally buttoned up; but his mother was offered a chair by one of the lodgers and, since she left the chair just where he had happened to put it, sat down in a corner to one side.

Gregor's sister began to play; the father and mother, from either side, intently watched the movements of her hands. Gregor, attracted by the playing, ventured to move forward a little until his head was actually inside the living room. He felt hardly any surprise at his growing lack of consideration for the others; there had been a time when he prided himself on being considerate. And yet just on this occasion he had more reason than ever to hide himself, since owing to the amount of dust which lay thick in his room and rose into the air at the slightest movement, he too was covered with dust; fluff and hair and remnants of food trailed with him, caught on his back and along his sides; his indifference to everything was much too great for him to turn on his back and scrape himself clean on the carpet, as once he had done several times a day. And in spite of his condition, no shame deterred him from advancing a little over the spotless floor of the living room.

To be sure, no one was aware of him. The family was entirely absorbed in the violin-playing; the lodgers, however, who first of all had stationed themselves, hands in pockets, much too close behind the music stand so that they could all have read the music, which must have bothered his sister, had soon retreated to the window, half-whispering with downbent heads, and stayed there while his father turned an anxious eye on them. Indeed, they were making it more than obvious that they had been disappointed in their expectation of hearing good or enjoyable violin-playing, that they had had more than enough of the performance and only out of courtesy suffered a continued disturbance of their peace. From the way they all kept blowing the smoke of their cigars high in the air through nose and mouth one could divine their irritation. And yet Gregor's sister was playing so beautifully. Her face leaned sideways, intently and sadly her eyes followed the notes of music. Gregor crawled a little farther forward and lowered his head to the ground so that it might be possible for his eyes to meet hers. Was he an animal, that music had such an

44

effect upon him? He felt as if the way were opening before him to the unknown nourishment he craved. He was determined to push forward till he reached his sister, to pull at her skirt and so let her know that she was to come into his room with her violin, for no one here appreciated her playing as he would appreciate it. He would never let her out of his room, at least, not so long as he lived; his frightful appearance would become, for the first time, useful to him; he would watch all the doors of his room at once and spit at intruders; but his sister should need no constraint, she should stay with him of her own free will; she should sit beside him on the sofa, bend down her ear to him and hear him confide that he had had the firm intention of sending her to the Conservatorium, and that, but for his mishap, last Christmas—surely Christmas was long past?—he would have announced it to everybody without allowing a single objection. After this confession his sister would be so touched that she would burst into tears, and Gregor would then raise himself to her shoulder and kiss her on the neck, which, now that she went to business, she kept free of any ribbon or collar.

"Mr. Samsa!" cried the middle lodger, to Gregor's father, and pointed, without wasting any more words, at Gregor, now working himself slowly forwards. The violin fell silent, the middle lodger first smiled to his friends with a shake of the head and then looked at Gregor again. Instead of driving Gregor out, his father seemed to think it more needful to begin by soothing down the lodgers, although they were not at all agitated and apparently found Gregor more entertaining than the violin-playing. He hurried towards them and, spreading out his arms, tried to urge them back into their own room and at the same time to block their view of Gregor. They now began to be really a little angry, one could not tell whether because of the old man's behavior or because it had just dawned on them that all unwittingly they had such a neighbor as Gregor next door. They demanded explanations of his father, they waved their arms like him, tugged uneasily at their beards, and only with reluctance backed towards their room. Meanwhile Gregor's sister, who stood there as if lost when her playing was so abruptly broken off, came to life again, pulled herself together all at once after standing for a while holding violin and bow in nervelessly hanging hands and staring at her music, pushed her violin into the lap of her mother, who was still sitting in her chair fighting asthmatically for breath, and ran into the lodgers' room to which they were now being shepherded by her father rather more quickly than before. One could see the pillows and blankets on the beds flying under her accustomed fingers and being laid in order. Before the lodgers had actually reached their room she had finished making the beds and slipped out.

The old man seemed once more to be so possessed by his mulish self-assertiveness that he was forgetting all the respect he should show to his lodgers. He kept driving them on and driving them on until in the very door of the bedroom the middle lodger stamped his foot loudly on the floor and so brought him to a halt. "I beg to announce," said the lodger, lifting one hand and looking also at Gregor's mother and sister, "that because of the disgusting conditions prevailing in this household and family"—here he spat on the floor with emphatic brevity—"I give you notice on the spot. Naturally I won't pay you a penny for the days I have lived here, on the contrary I shall consider bringing an action for damages against you, based on claims—believe me—that will be easily susceptible of proof." He ceased and stared straight in front of him, as if he expected something. In fact his two friends at once rushed into the breach with these words: "And we too give notice on the spot." On that he seized the door-handle and shut the door with a slam.

Gregor's father, groping with his hands, staggered forward and fell into his chair; it looked as if he were stretching himself there for his ordinary evening nap, but the marked jerkings of his head, which was as if uncontrollable, showed that he was far from asleep. Gregor had simply stayed quietly all the time on the spot where the lodgers had espied him. Disappointment at the failure of his plan, perhaps also the weakness arising from extreme hunger, made it impossible for him to move. He feared, with a fair degree of certainty, that at any moment the general tension would discharge itself in a combined attack upon him, and he lay waiting. He did not react even to the noise made by the violin as it fell off his mother's lap from under her trembling fingers and gave out a resonant note.

"My dear parents," said his sister, slapping her hand on the table by way of introduction, "things can't go on like this. Perhaps you don't realize that, but I do. I won't utter my brother's name in the presence of this creature, and so all I say is: we must try to get rid of it. We've tried to look after it and to put up with it as far as is humanly possible, and I don't think anyone could reproach us in the slightest."

"She is more than right," said Gregor's father to himself. His mother, who was still choking for lack of breath, began to cough hollowly into her hand with a wild look in her eyes.

His sister rushed over to her and held her forehead. His father's thoughts seemed to have lost their vagueness at Grete's words, he sat more upright, fingering his service cap that lay among the plates still lying on the table from the lodgers' supper, and from time to time looked at the still form of Gregor.

"We must try to get rid of it," his sister now said explicitly to her father, since her mother was coughing too much to hear a word, "it will be the death of both of you, I can see that coming. When one has to work as hard as we do, all of us, one can't stand this continual torment at home on top of it. At least I can't stand it any longer." And she burst into such a passion of sobbing that her tears dropped on her mother's face, where she wiped them off mechanically.

"My dear," said the old man sympathetically, and with evident understanding, "but what can we do?"

Gregor's sister merely shrugged her shoulders to indicate the feeling of helplessness that had now overmastered her during her weeping fit, in contrast to her former confidence.

"If he could understand us," said her father, half

47

questioningly; Grete, still sobbing, vehemently waved a hand to show how unthinkable that was.

"If he could understand us," repeated the old man, shutting his eyes to consider his daughter's conviction that understanding was impossible, "then perhaps we might come to some agreement with him. But as it is—"

"He must go," cried Gregor's sister, "that's the only solution, Father. You must just try to get rid of the idea that this is Gregor. The fact that we've believed it for so long is the root of all our trouble. But how can it be Gregor? If this were Gregor, he would have realized long ago that human beings can't live with such a creature, and he'd have gone away on his own accord. Then we wouldn't have any brother, but we'd be able to go on living and keep his memory in honor. As it is, this creature persecutes us, drives away our lodgers, obviously wants the whole apartment to himself and would have us all sleep in the gutter. Just look, Father," she shrieked all at once, "he's at it again!" And in an access of panic that was quite incomprehensible to Gregor she even quitted her mother, literally thrusting the chair from her as if she would rather sacrifice her mother than stay so near to Gregor, and rushed behind her father, who also rose up, being simply upset by her agitation, and half-spread his arms out as if to protect her.

Yet Gregor had not the slightest intention of frightening anyone, far less his sister. He had only begun to turn round in order to crawl back to his room, but it was certainly a startling operation to watch, since because of his disabled condition he could not execute the difficult turning movements except by lifting his head and then bracing it against the floor over and over again. He paused and looked round. His good intentions seemed to have been recognized; the alarm had only been momentary. Now they were all watching him in melancholy silence. His mother lay in her chair, her legs stiffly outstretched and pressed together, her eyes almost closing for sheer weariness; his father and his sister were sitting beside each other, his sister's arm around the old man's neck.

Perhaps I can go on turning round now, thought Gregor, and began his labors again. He could not stop himself from panting with the effort, and had to pause now and then to take breath. Nor did anyone harass him, he was left entirely to himself. When he had completed the turn-round he began at once to crawl straight back. He was amazed at the distance separating him from his room and could not understand how in his weak state he had managed to accomplish the same journey so recently, almost without remarking it. Intent on crawling as fast as possible, he barely noticed that not a single word, not an ejaculation from his family, interfered with his progress. Only when he was already in the doorway did he turn his head round, not completely, for his neck muscles were getting stiff, but enough to see that nothing had changed behind him except that his sister had risen to her feet. His last glance fell on his mother, who was not quite overcome by sleep.

Hardly was he well inside his room when the door was hastily pushed shut, bolted and locked. The sudden noise in his rear startled him so much that his little legs gave beneath him. It was his sister who had shown such haste. She had been standing ready waiting and had made a light spring forward, Gregor had not even heard her coming, and she cried "At last!" to her parents as she turned the key in the lock.

"And what now?" said Gregor to himself, looking round in the darkness. Soon he made the discovery that he was now unable to stir a limb. This did not surprise him, rather it seemed unnatural that he should ever actually have been able to move on these feeble little legs. Otherwise he felt relatively comfortable. True, his whole body was aching, but it seemed that the pain was gradually growing less and would finally pass away. The rotting apple in his back and the inflamed area around it, all covered with soft dust, already hardly troubled him. He thought of his family with tenderness and love. The decision that he must disappear was one that he held to even more strongly than his sister, if that were possible. In this state of vacant and peaceful meditation he remained until the tower clock struck three in the morning. The first broadening of light in the world outside the window entered his consciousness once more. Then his head sank to the floor of its own accord and from his nostrils came the last faint flicker of his breath.

When the charwoman arrived early in the morning—what between her strength and her impatience she slammed all the doors so loudly, never mind how often she had been begged not to do so, that no one in the whole apartment could enjoy any quiet sleep after her arrival—she noticed nothing unusual as she took her customary peep into Gregor's room. She thought he was lying motionless on purpose, pretending to be in the sulks; she credited him with every kind of intelligence. Since she happened to have the long-handled broom in her hand she tried to tickle him up with it from the doorway. When that too produced no reaction she felt provoked and poked at him a little harder, and only when she had pushed him along the floor without meeting any resistance was her attention aroused. It did not take her long to establish the truth of the matter, and her eyes widened, she let out a whistle, yet did not waste much time over it but tore open the door of the Samsas' bedroom and yelled into the darkness at the top of her voice: "Just look at this, it's dead; it's lying here dead and done for!"

Mr. and Mrs. Samsa started up in their double bed and before they realized the nature of the charwoman's announcement had some difficulty in overcoming the shock of it. But then they got out of bed quickly, one on either side, Mr. Samsa throwing a blanket over his shoulders, Mrs. Samsa in nothing but her nightgown; in this array they entered Gregor's room. Meanwhile the door of the living room opened, too, where Grete had been sleeping since the advent of the lodgers; she was completely dressed as if she had not been to bed, which seemed to be confirmed also by the paleness of her face. "Dead?" said Mrs. Samsa, looking questioningly at the charwoman, although she could have investigated for herself, and the fact was obvious enough

50

without investigation. "I should say so," said the charwoman, proving her words by pushing Gregor's corpse a long way to one side with her broomstick. Mrs. Samsa made a movement as if to stop her, but checked it. "Well," said Mr. Samsa, "now thanks be to God." He crossed himself, and the three women followed his example. Grete, whose eyes never left the corpse, said: "Just see how thin he was. It's such a long time since he's eaten anything. The food came out again just as it went in." Indeed, Gregor's body was completely flat and dry, as could only now be seen when it was no longer supported by the legs and nothing prevented one from looking closely at it.

"Come in beside us, Grete, for a little while," said Mrs. Samsa with a tremulous smile, and Grete, not without looking back at the corpse, followed her parents into their bedroom. The charwoman shut the door and opened the window wide. Although it was so early in the morning a certain softness was perceptible in the fresh air. After all, it was already the end of March.

The three lodgers emerged from their room and were surprised to see no breakfast; they had been forgotten. "Where's our breakfast?" said the middle lodger peevishly to the charwoman. But she put her finger to her lips and hastily, without a word, indicated by gestures that they should go into Gregor's room. They did so and stood, their hands in the pockets of their somewhat shabby coats, around Gregor's corpse in the room where it was now fully light.

At that the door of the Samsas' bedroom opened and Mr. Samsa appeared in his uniform, his wife on one arm, his daughter on the other. They all looked a little as if they had been crying; from time to time Grete hid her face on her father's arm.

"Leave my house at once!" said Mr. Samsa, and pointed to the door without disengaging himself from the women. "What do you mean by that?" said the middle lodger, taken somewhat aback, with a feeble smile. The two others put their hands behind them and kept rubbing them together, as if in gleeful expectation of a fine set-to in which they were bound to come off

51

the winners. "I mean just what I say," answered Mr. Samsa, and advanced in a straight line with his two companions towards the lodger. He stood his ground at first quietly, looking at the floor as if his thoughts were taking a new pattern in his head. "Then let us go, by all means," he said, and looked up at Mr. Samsa as if in a sudden access of humility he were expecting some renewed sanction for this decision. Mr. Samsa merely nodded briefly once or twice with meaning eyes. Upon that the lodger really did go with long strides into the hall, his two friends had been listening and had quite stopped rubbing their hands for some moments and now went scuttling after him as if afraid that Mr. Samsa might get into the hall before them and cut them off from their leader. In the hall they all three took their hats from the rack, their sticks from the umbrella stand, bowed in silence and quitted the apartment. With a suspiciousness which proved quite unfounded Mr. Samsa and the two women followed them out to the landing; leaning over the banister they watched the three figures slowly but surely going down the long stairs, vanishing from sight at a certain turn of the staircase on every floor and coming into view again after a moment or so; the more they dwindled, the more the Samsa family's interest in them dwindled, and when a butcher's boy met them and passed them on the stairs coming up proudly with a tray on his head, Mr. Samsa and the two women soon left the landing and as if a burden had been lifted from them went back into their apartment.

They decided to spend this day in resting and going for a stroll; they had not only deserved such a respite from work, but absolutely needed it. And so they sat down at the table and wrote three notes of excuse, Mr. Samsa to his board of management, Mrs. Samsa to her employer and Grete to the head of her firm. While they were writing, the charwoman came in to say that she was going now, since her morning's work was finished. At first they only nodded without looking up, but as she kept hovering there they eyed her irritably. "Well?" said Mr. Samsa. The charwoman stood grinning in the doorway as if she had good news to impart to the family but meant not to say a word unless properly questioned. The small ostrich feather standing upright on her hat, which had annoyed Mr. Samsa ever since she was engaged, was waving gaily in all directions. "Well, what is it then?" asked Mrs. Samsa, who obtained more respect from the charwoman than the others. "Oh," said the charwoman, giggling so amiably that she could not at once continue, "just this, you don't need to bother about how to get rid of the thing next door. It's been seen to already." Mrs. Samsa and Grete bent over their letters again, as if preoccupied; Mr. Samsa, who perceived that she was eager to begin describing it all in detail, stopped her with a decisive hand. But since she was not allowed to tell her story, she remembered the great hurry she was in, being obviously deeply huffed: "Bye, everybody," she said, whirling off violently, and departed with a frightful slamming of doors.

"She'll be given notice tonight," said Mr. Samsa, but neither from his wife nor his daughter did he get any answer, for the charwoman seemed to have shattered again the composure they had barely achieved. They rose, went to the window and stayed there, clasping each other tight. Mr. Samsa turned in his chair to look at them and quietly observed them for a little. Then he called out: "Come along, now, do. Let bygones be bygones. And you might have some consideration for me." The two of them complied at once, hastened to him, caressed him and quickly finished their letters.

Then they all three left the apartment together, which was more than they had done for months, and went by tram into the open country outside the town. The tram, in which they were the only passengers, was filled with warm sunshine. Leaning comfortably back in their seats they canvassed their prospects for the future, and it appeared on closer inspection that these were not at all bad, for the jobs they had got, which so far they had never really discussed with each other, were all three admirable and likely to lead to better things later on. The greatest immediate improvement in their condition would of course arise from moving to another house; they wanted to take a smaller and cheaper but also better situated and more easily run apartment than the one they had, which Gregor had selected. While they were thus conversing, it struck both Mr. and Mrs. Samsa, almost at the same moment, as they became aware of their daughter's increasing vivacity, that in spite of all the sorrow of recent times, which had made her cheeks pale, she had bloomed into a pretty girl with a good figure. They grew quieter and half unconsciously exchanged glances of complete agreement, having come to the conclusion that it would soon be time to find a good husband for her. And it was like a confirmation of their new dreams and excellent intentions that at the end of their journey their daughter sprang to her feet first and stretched her young body.

THE JUDGMENT

It was a Sunday morning in the very height of spring. Georg Bendemann, a young merchant, was sitting in his own room on the first floor of one of a long row of small, ramshackle houses stretching beside the river which were scarcely distinguishable from each other except in height and coloring. He had just finished a letter to an old friend of his who was now living abroad, had put it into its envelope in a slow and dreamy fashion, and with his elbows propped on the writing table was gazing out of the window at the river, the bridge and the hills on the farther bank with their tender green.

He was thinking about his friend, who had actually run away to Russia some years before, being dissatisfied with his prospects at home. Now he was carrying on a business in St. Petersburg, which had flourished to begin with but had long been going downhill, as he always complained on his increasingly rare visits. So he was wearing himself out to no purpose in a foreign country, the unfamiliar full beard he wore did not quite conceal the face Georg had known so well since childhood, and his skin was growing so yellow as to indicate some latent disease. By his own account he had no regular connection with the colony of his fellow countrymen out there and almost no social intercourse with Russian families, so that he was resigning himself to becoming a permanent bachelor.

What could one write to such a man, who had obviously run off the rails, a man one could be sorry for but could not help. Should one advise him to come home, to transplant himself and take up his old friendships again —there was nothing to hinder him—and in general to rely on the help of his friends? But that was as good as telling him, and the more kindly the more offensively, that all his efforts hitherto had miscarried, that he should finally give up, come back home, and be gaped at by everyone as a returned prodigal, that only his friends knew what was what and that he himself was just a big child who should do what his successful and home-keeping friends prescribed. And was it certain, besides, that all the pain one would have to inflict on him would achieve its object? Perhaps it would not even be possible to get him to come home at all—he said himself that he was now out of touch with commerce in his native country—and then he would still be left an alien in a foreign land embittered by his friends' advice and more than ever estranged from them. But if he did follow their advice and then didn't fit in at home—not out of malice, of course, but through force of circumstances—couldn't get on with his friends or without them, felt humiliated, couldn't be said to have either friends or a country of his own any longer, wouldn't it have been better for him to stay abroad just as he was? Taking all this into account, how could one be sure that he would make a success of life at home?

For such reasons, supposing one wanted to keep up correspondence with him, one could not send him any real news such as could frankly be told to the most distant acquaintance. It was more than three years since his last visit, and for this he offered the lame excuse that the political situation in Russia was too uncertain, which apparently would not permit even the briefest absence of a small businessman while it allowed hundreds of thousands of Russians to travel peacefully abroad. But during these three years Georg's own position in life had changed a lot. Two years ago his mother had died, since when he and his father had shared the household together, and his friend had of course been informed of that and had expressed his sympathy in a letter phrased so dryly that the grief caused by such an event, one had to conclude, could not be realized in a distant country. Since that time, however, Georg had applied himself with greater determination to the business as well as to everything else.

Perhaps during his mother's lifetime his father's insistence on having everything his own way in the business had hindered him from developing any real activity of his own, perhaps since her death his father had become less aggressive, although he was still active in the business, perhaps it was mostly due to an accidental run of good fortune—which was very probable indeed—but at any rate during those two years the business had developed in a most unexpected way, the staff had had to be doubled, the turnover was five times as great, no doubt about it, farther progress lay just ahead.

But Georg's friend had no inkling of this improvement. In earlier years, perhaps for the last time in that letter of condolence, he had tried to persuade Georg to emigrate to Russia and had enlarged upon the prospects of success for precisely Georg's branch of trade. The figures quoted were microscopic by comparison with the range of Georg's present operations. Yet he shrank from letting his friend know about his business success, and if he were to do it now retrospectively that certainly would look peculiar.

So Georg confined himself to giving his friend unimportant items of gossip such as rise at random in the memory when one is idly thinking things over on a quiet Sunday. All he desired was to leave undisturbed the idea of the home town which his friend must have built up to his own content during the long interval. And so it happened to Georg that three times in three fairly widely separated letters he had told his friend about the engagement of an unimportant man to an equally unimportant girl, until indeed, quite contrary to his intentions, his friend began to show some interest in this notable event.

Yet Georg preferred to write about things like these rather than to confess that he himself had got engaged a month ago to a Fräulein Frieda Brandenfeld, a girl from a well-to-do family. He often discussed this friend of his with his fiancée and the peculiar relationship that had developed between them in their correspondence. "So he won't be coming to our wedding," said she, "and yet I have a right to get to know all your friends." "I don't want to trouble him," answered Georg, "don't misunderstand me, he would probably come, at least I think so, but he would feel that his hand had been forced and he would be hurt, perhaps he would envy me and certainly he'd be discontented and without being able to do anything about his discontent he'd have to go away again alone. Alone—do you know what that means?" "Yes, but may he not hear about our wedding in some other fashion?" "I can't prevent that, of course, but it's unlikely, considering the way he lives." "Since your friends are like that, Georg, you shouldn't ever have got engaged at all." "Well, we're both to blame for that; but I wouldn't have it any other way now." And when, breathing quickly under his kisses, she still brought out: "All the same, I do feel upset," he thought it could not really involve him in trouble were he to send the news to his friend. "That's the kind of man I am and he'll just have to take me as I am," he said to himself, "I can't cut myself to another pattern that might make a more suitable friend for him."

And in fact he did inform his friend, in the long letter he had been writing that Sunday morning, about his engagement, with these words: "I have saved my best news to the end. I have got engaged to a Fräulein Frieda Brandenfeld, a girl from a well-to-do family, who only came to live here a long time after you went away, so that you're hardly likely to know her. There will be time to tell you more about her later, for today let me just say that I am very happy and as between you and me the only difference in our relationship is that instead of a quite ordinary kind of friend you will now have in me a happy friend. Besides that, you will acquire in my fiancée, who sends her warm greetings and will soon write you herself, a genuine friend of the opposite sex, which is not without importance to a bachelor. I know that there are many reasons why you can't come to see us, but would not my wedding be precisely the right occasion for giving all obstacles the go-by? Still, however that may be, do just as seems good to you without regarding any interests but your own."

With this letter in his hand Georg had been sitting a long time at the writing table, his face turned towards the window. He had barely acknowledged, with an absent smile, a greeting waved to him from the street by a passing acquaintance.

At last he put the letter in his pocket and went out of his room across a small lobby into his father's room, which he had not entered for months. There was in fact no need for him to enter it, since he saw his father daily at business and they took their midday meal together at an eating house; in the evening, it was true, each did as he pleased, yet even then, unless Georg—as mostly happened—went out with friends or, more recently, visited his fiancée, they always sat for a while, each with his newspaper, in their common sitting room.

It surprised Georg how dark his father's room was even on this sunny morning. So it was overshadowed as much as that by the high wall on the other side of the narrow courtyard. His father was sitting by the window in a corner hung with various mementoes of Georg's dead mother, reading a newspaper which he held to one side before his eyes in an attempt to overcome a defect of vision. On the table stood the remains of his breakfast, not much of which seemed to have been eaten.

"Ah, Georg," said his father, rising at once to meet him. His heavy dressing gown swung open as he walked and the skirts of it fluttered round him.—"My father is still a giant of a man," said Georg to himself.

"It's unbearably dark here," he said aloud.

"Yes, it's dark enough," answered his father.

"And you've shut the window, too?"

"I prefer it like that."

"Well, it's quite warm outside," said Georg, as if continuing his previous remark, and sat down.

His father cleared away the breakfast dishes and set them on a chest.

"I really only wanted to tell you," went on Georg, who had been vacantly following the old man's movements, "that I am now sending the news of my engagement to St. Petersburg." He drew the letter a little way from his pocket and let it drop back again.

"To St. Petersburg?" asked his father.

"To my friend there," said Georg, trying to meet his father's eye.—In business hours he's quite different, he was thinking, how solidly he sits here with his arms crossed.

"Oh yes. To your friend," said his father, with peculiar emphasis.

"Well, you know, Father, that I wanted not to tell him about my engagement at first. Out of consideration for him, that was the only reason. You know yourself he's a difficult man. I said to myself that someone else might tell him about my engagement, although he's such a solitary creature that that was hardly likely—I couldn't prevent that—but I wasn't ever going to tell him myself."

"And now you've changed your mind?" asked his father, laying his enormous newspaper on the window sill and on top of it his spectacles, which he covered with one hand.

"Yes, I've been thinking it over. If he's a good friend of mine, I said to myself, my being happily engaged should make him happy too. And so I wouldn't put off telling him any longer. But before I posted the letter I wanted to let you know."

"Georg," said his father, lengthening his toothless mouth, "listen to me! You've come to me about this business, to talk it over with me. No doubt that does you honor. But it's nothing, it's worse than nothing, if you don't tell me the whole truth. I don't want to stir up matters that shouldn't be mentioned here. Since the death of our dear mother certain things have been done that aren't right. Maybe the time will come for mentioning them, and maybe sooner than we think. There's many a thing in the business I'm not aware of, maybe it's not done behind my back—I'm not going to say that it's done behind my back—I'm not equal to things any longer, my memory's failing, I haven't an eye for so many things any longer. That's the course of nature in the first place, and in the second place the death of our dear mother hit me harder than it did you.—But since we're talking about it, about this letter, I beg you, Georg, don't deceive me. It's a trivial affair, it's hardly worth mentioning, so don't deceive me. Do you really have this friend in St. Petersburg?"

Georg rose in embarrassment. "Never mind my friends. A thousand friends wouldn't make up to me for my father. Do you know what I think? You're not taking enough care of yourself. But old age must be taken care of. I can't do without you in the business, you know that very well, but if the business is going to undermine your health, I'm ready to close it down tomorrow forever. And that won't do. We'll have to make a change in your way of living. But a radical change. You sit here in the dark, and in the sitting room you would have plenty of light. You just take a bite of breakfast instead of properly keeping up your strength. You sit by a closed window, and the air would be so good for you. No, Father! I'll get the doctor to come, and we'll follow his orders. We'll change your room, you can move into the front room and I'll move in here.

You won't notice the change, all your things will be moved with you. But there's time for all that later, I'll put you to bed now for a little, I'm sure you need to rest. Come, I'll help you to take off your things, you'll see I can do it. Or if you would rather go into the front room at once, you can lie down in my bed for the present. That would be the most sensible thing."

Georg stood close beside his father, who had let his head with its unkempt white hair sink on his chest.

"Georg," said his father in a low voice, without moving.

Georg knelt down at once beside his father, in the old man's weary face he saw the pupils, over-large, fixedly looking at him from the corners of the eyes.

"You have no friend in St. Petersburg. You've always been a leg-puller and you haven't even shrunk from pulling my leg. How could you have a friend out there! I can't believe it."

"Just think back a bit, Father," said Georg, lifting his father from the chair and slipping off his dressing gown as he stood feebly enough, "it'll soon be three years since my friend came to see us last. I remember that you used not to like him very much. At least twice I kept you from seeing him, although he was actually sitting with me in my room. I could quite well understand your dislike of him, my friend has his peculiarities. But then, later, you got on with him very well. I was proud because you listened to him and nodded and asked him questions. If you think back you're bound to remember. He used to tell us the most incredible stories of the Russian Revolution. For instance, when he was on a business trip to Kiev and ran into a riot, and saw a priest on a balcony who cut a broad cross in blood on the palm of his hand and held the hand up and appealed to the mob. You've told that story yourself once or twice since."

Meanwhile Georg had succeeded in lowering his father down again and carefully taking off the woollen drawers he wore over his linen underpants and his socks. The not particularly clean appearance of this underwear made him reproach himself for having been neglectful.

It should have certainly been his duty to see that his father had clean changes of underwear. He had not yet explicitly discussed with his bride-to-be what arrangements should be made for his father in the future, for they had both of them silently taken it for granted that the old man would go on living alone in the old house. But now he made a quick, firm decision to take him into his own future establishment. It almost looked, on closer inspection, as if the care he meant to lavish there on his father might come too late.

He carried his father to bed in his arms. It gave him a dreadful feeling to notice that while he took the few steps towards the bed the old man on his breast was playing with his watch chain. He could not lay him down on the bed for a moment, so firmly did he hang on to the watch chain.

But as soon as he was laid in bed, all seemed well. He covered himself up and even drew the blankets farther than usual over his shoulders. He looked up at Georg with a not unfriendly eye.

"You begin to remember my friend, don't you?" asked Georg, giving him an encouraging nod.

"Am I well covered up now?" asked his father, as if he were not able to see whether his feet were properly tucked in or not.

"So you find it snug in bed already," said Georg, and tucked the blankets more closely round him.

"Am I well covered up?" asked the father once more, seeming to be strangely intent upon the answer.

"Don't worry, you're well covered up."

"No!" cried his father, cutting short the answer, threw the blankets off with a strength that sent them all flying in a moment and sprang erect in bed. Only one hand lightly touched the ceiling to steady him.

"You wanted to cover me up, I know, my young sprig, but I'm far from being covered up yet. And even if this is the last strength I have, it's enough for you, too much for you. Of course I know your friend. He would have been a son after my own heart. That's why you've been playing him false all these years. Why else? Do you think I haven't been sorry for him? And that's why you had to lock yourself up in your office—the Chief is busy, mustn't be disturbed—just so that you could write your lying little letters to Russia. But thank goodness a father doesn't need to be taught how to see through his son. And now that you thought you'd got him down, so far down that you could set your bottom on him and sit on him and he wouldn't move, then my fine son makes up his mind to get married!"

Georg stared at the bogey conjured up by his father. His friend in St. Petersburg, whom his father suddenly knew too well, touched his imagination as never before. Lost in the vastness of Russia he saw him. At the door of an empty, plundered warehouse he saw him. Among the wreckage of his showcases, the slashed remnants of his wares, the falling gas brackets, he was just standing up. Why did he have to go so far away!

"But attend to me!" cried his father, and Georg, almost distracted, ran towards the bed to take everything in, yet came to a stop halfway.

"Because she lifted up her skirts," his father began to flute, "because she lifted her skirts like this, the nasty creature," and mimicking her he lifted his shirt so high that one could see the scar on his thigh from his war wound, "because she lifted her skirts like this and this you made up to her, and in order to make free with her undisturbed you have disgraced your mother's memory, betrayed your friend and stuck your father into bed so that he can't move. But he can move, or can't he?"

And he stood up quite unsupported and kicked his legs out. His insight made him radiant.

Georg shrank into a corner, as far away from his father as possible. A long time ago he had firmly made up his mind to watch closely every least movement so that he should not be surprised by any indirect attack, a pounce from behind or above. At this moment he recalled this long-forgotten resolve and forgot it again, like a man drawing a short thread through the eye of a needle.

"But your friend hasn't been betrayed after all!" cried his father, emphasizing the point with stabs of his forefinger. "I've been representing him here on the spot."

"You comedian!" Georg could not resist the retort, realized at once the harm done and, his eyes starting in his head, bit his tongue back, only too late, till the pain made his knees give.

"Yes, of course I've been playing a comedy! A comedy! That's a good expression! What other comfort was left to a poor old widower? Tell me—and while you're answering me be you still my living son—what else was left to me, in my back room, plagued by a disloyal staff, old to the marrow of my bones? And my son strutting through the world, finishing off deals that I had prepared for him, bursting with triumphant glee and stalking away from his father with the closed face of a respectable businessman! Do you think I didn't love you, I, from whom you are sprung?"

Now he'll lean forward, thought Georg, what if he topples and smashes himself! These words went hissing through his mind.

His father leaned forward but did not topple. Since Georg did not come any nearer, as he had expected, he straightened himself again.

"Stay where you are, I don't need you! You think you have strength enough to come over here and that you're only hanging back of your own accord. Don't be too sure! I am still much the stronger of us two. All by myself I might have had to give way, but your mother has given me so much of her strength that I've established a fine connection with your friend and I have your customers here in my pocket!"

"He has pockets even in his shirt!" said Georg to himself, and believed that with this remark he could make him an impossible figure for all the world. Only for a moment did he think so, since he kept on forgetting everything.

"Just take your bride on your arm and try getting in my way! I'll sweep her from your very side, you don't know how!"

Georg made a grimace of disbelief. His father only nodded, confirming the truth of his words, towards Georg's corner.

"How you amused me today, coming to ask me if you

should tell your friend about your engagement. He knows it already, you stupid boy, he knows it all! I've been writing to him, for you forgot to take my writing things away from me. That's why he hasn't been here for years, he knows everything a hundred times better than you do yourself, in his left hand he crumples your letters unopened while in his right hand he holds up my letters to read through!"

In his enthusiasm he waved his arm over his head. "He knows everything a thousand times better!" he cried.

"Ten thousand times!" said Georg, to make fun of his father, but in his very mouth the words turned into deadly earnest.

"For years I've been waiting for you to come with some such question! Do you think I concern myself with anything else? Do you think I read my newspapers? Look!" and he threw Georg a newspaper sheet which he had somehow taken to bed with him. An old newspaper, with a name entirely unknown to Georg.

"How long a time you've taken to grow up! Your mother had to die, she couldn't see the happy day, your friend is going to pieces in Russia, even three years ago he was yellow enough to be thrown away, and as for me, you see what condition I'm in. You have eyes in your head for that!"

"So you've been lying in wait for me!" cried Georg.

His father said pityingly, in an offhand manner: "I suppose you wanted to say that sooner. But now it doesn't matter." And in a louder voice: "So now you know what else there was in the world besides yourself, till now you've known only about yourself! An innocent child, yes, that you were, truly, but still more truly have you been a devilish human being!—And therefore take note: I sentence you now to death by drowning!"

Georg felt himself urged from the room, the crash with which his father fell on the bed behind him was still in his ears as he fled. On the staircase, which he rushed down as if its steps were an inclined plane, he ran into his charwoman on her way up to do the morning cleaning of the room. "Jesus!" she cried, and covered her face with her apron, but he was already gone. Out of the front door he rushed, across the roadway, driven towards the water. Already he was grasping at the railings as a starving man clutches food. He swung himself over, like the distinguished gymnast he had once been in his youth, to his parents' pride. With weakening grip he was still holding on when he spied between the railings a motor-bus coming which would easily cover the noise of his fall, called in a low voice: "Dear parents, I have always loved you, all the same," and let himself drop.

At this moment an unending stream of traffic was just going over the bridge.

THE GREAT WALL OF CHINA

THE GREAT WALL of China was finished off at its northernmost corner. From the southeast and the southwest it came up in two sections that finally converged there. This principle of piecemeal construction was also applied on a smaller scale by both of the two great armies of labor, the eastern and the western. It was done in this way: gangs of some twenty workers were formed who had to accomplish a length, say, of five hundred yards of wall, while a similar gang built another stretch of the same length to meet the first. But after the junction had been made the construction of the wall was not carried on from the point, let us say, where this thousand yards ended; instead the two groups of workers were transferred to begin building again in quite different neighborhoods. Naturally in this way many great gaps were left, which were only filled in gradually and bit by bit, some, indeed, not till after the official announcement that the wall was finished. In fact it is said that there are gaps which have never been filled in at all, an assertion, however, which is probably merely one of the many legends to which the building of the wall gave rise, and which cannot be verified, at least by any single man with his own eyes and judgment, on account of the extent of the structure.

Now on first thoughts one might conceive that it would have been more advantageous in every way to build the wall continuously, or at least continuously within the two main divisions. After all, the wall was intended, as was universally proclaimed and known, to be a protection against the peoples of the north. But how can a wall protect if it is not a continuous structure? Not only can such a wall not protect, but what there is of it is in perpetual danger. These blocks of wall left standing in deserted regions could be easily pulled down again and again by the nomads, especially as these tribes, rendered apprehensive by the building operations, kept changing their encampments with incredible rapidity, like locusts, and so perhaps had a better general view of the progress of the wall than we, the builders. Nevertheless the task of construction probably could not have been carried out in any other way. To understand this we must take into account the following: the wall was to be a protection for centuries; accordingly, the most scrupulous care in the building, the application of the architectural wisdom of all known ages and peoples, an unremitting sense of personal responsibility in the builders were indispensable prerequisites for the work. True, for the more purely manual tasks ignorant day laborers from the populace, men, women and children who offered their services for good money, could be employed; but for the supervision even of every four day laborers an expert versed in the art of building was required, a man who was capable of entering into and feeling with all his heart what was involved. And the higher the task, the greater the responsibility. And such men were actually to be had, if not indeed so abundantly as the work of construction could have absorbed, yet in great numbers.

For the work had not been undertaken without thought. Fifty years before the first stone was laid the art of architecture, and especially that of masonry, had been proclaimed as the most important branch of knowledge throughout the whole area of a China that was to be walled around, and all other arts gained recognition only insofar as they had reference to it. I can still remember quite well us standing as small children, scarcely sure on our feet, in our teacher's garden, and being ordered to build a sort of wall out of pebbles; and then the teacher, girding up his robe, ran full tilt against the wall, of course knocking it down, and scolded us so terribly for the shoddiness of our work that we ran weeping in all directions to our parents. A trivial incident, but significant of the spirit of the time.

I was lucky inasmuch as the building of the wall was just beginning when, at twenty, I had passed the last examination of the lowest school. I say lucky, for many who before my time had achieved the highest degree of culture available to them could find nothing year after year to do with their knowledge, and drifted uselessly about with the most splendid architectural plans in their heads, and sank by thousands into hopelessness. But those who finally came to be employed in the work as supervisors, even though it might be of the lowest rank, were truly worthy of their task. They were masons who had reflected much, and did not cease to reflect, on the building of the wall, men who with the first stone they sank in the ground felt themselves a part of the wall. Masons of that kind, of course, had not only a desire to perform their work in the most thorough manner, but were also impatient to see the wall finished in its complete perfection. Day laborers have not this impatience, for they look only to their wages, and the higher supervisors, indeed even the supervisors of middle rank, could see enough of the manifold growth of the construction to keep their spirits confident and high. But to encourage the subordinate supervisors, intellectually so vastly superior to their apparently petty tasks, other measures must be taken. One could not, for instance, expect them to lay one stone on another for months or even years on end, in an uninhabited mountainous region, hundreds of miles from their homes; the hopelessness of such hard toil, which yet could not reach completion even in the longest lifetime, would have cast them into despair and above all made them less capable for the work. It was for this reason that the system of piecemeal building was decided on. Five hundred yards could be accomplished in about five years; by that time, however, the supervisors were as a rule quite exhausted and had lost all faith in themselves, in the wall, in the world. Accordingly, while they were still exalted by the jubilant celebrations marking the completion of the thousand yards of wall, they were sent far, far away, saw on their journey finished sections of the wall rising here and there, came past the quarters of the high command and were presented with badges of honor, heard the rejoicings of new armies of labor streaming past from the depths of the land, saw forests being cut down to become supports for the wall, saw mountains being hewn into stones for the wall, heard at the holy shrines hymns rising in which the pious prayed for the completion of the wall. All this assuaged their impatience. The quiet life of their homes, where they rested some time, strengthened them; the humble credulity with which their reports were listened to, the confidence with which the simple and peaceful burgher believed in the eventual completion of the wall, all this filled their hearts with a new buoyancy. Like eternally hopeful children they then said farewell to their homes; the desire once more to labor on the wall of the nation became irresistible. They set off earlier than they needed; half the village accompanied them for long distances. Groups of people with banners and streamers waving were on all the roads; never before had they seen how great and rich and beautiful and worthy of love their country was. Every fellow country-man was a brother for whom one was building a wall of protection, and who would return lifelong thanks for it with all he had and did. Unity! Unity! Shoulder to shoulder, a ring of brothers, a current of blood no longer confined within the narrow circulation of one body, but sweetly rolling and yet ever returning throughout the endless leagues of China.

Thus, then, the system of piecemeal construction becomes comprehensible; but there were still other reasons for it as well. Nor is there anything odd in my pausing over this question for so long; it is one of the crucial problems in the whole building of the wall, unimportant as it may appear at first glance. If I am to convey and make understandable the ideas and feelings of that time I cannot go deeply enough into this very question.

First, then, it must be said that in those days things were achieved scarcely inferior to the construction of the Tower of Babel, although as regards divine approval, at least according to human reckoning, strongly at variance with that work. I say this because during the early days of building a scholar wrote a book in which he drew the comparison in the most exhaustive way. In it he tried to prove that the Tower of Babel failed to reach its goal, not because of the reasons universally advanced, or at least that among those recognized reasons the most important of all was not to be found. His proofs were drawn not merely from written documents and reports; he also claimed to have made inquiries on the spot, and to have discovered that the tower failed and was bound to fail because of the weakness of the foundation. In this respect at any rate our age was vastly superior to that ancient one. Almost every educated man of our time was a mason by profession and infallible in the matter of laying foundations. That, however, was not what our scholar was concerned to prove; for he maintained that the Great Wall alone would provide for the first time in the history of mankind a secure foundation for a new Tower of Babel. First the wall, therefore, and then the tower. His book was in everybody's hands at that time, but I admit that even today I cannot quite make out how he conceived this tower. How could the wall, which did not form even a circle, but only a sort of quarter- or half-circle, provide the foundation for a tower? That could obviously be meant only in a spiritual sense. But in that case why build the actual wall, which after all was something concrete, the result of the lifelong labor of multitudes of people? And why were there in the book plans, somewhat nebulous plans, it must be admitted, of the tower, and proposals worked out in detail for mobilizing the people's energies for the stupendous new work?

There were many wild ideas in people's heads at that time—this scholar's book is only one example—perhaps simply because so many were trying to join forces as far as they could for the achievement of a single aim. Human nature, essentially changeable, unstable as the dust, can endure no restraint; if it binds itself it soon begins to tear madly at its bonds, until it rends everything asunder, the wall, the bonds and its very self.

It is possible that these very considerations, which militated against the building of the wall at all, were not left out of account by the high command when the system of piecemeal construction was decided on. We—and here I speak in the name of many people—did not really know ourselves until we had carefully scrutinized the decrees of the high command, when we discovered that without the high command neither our book learning nor our human understanding would have sufficed for the humble tasks which we performed in the great whole. In the office of the command—where it was and who sat there no one whom I have asked knew then or knows now—in that office one may be certain that all human thoughts and desires revolved in a circle, and all human aims and fulfillments in a countercircle. And through the window the reflected splendors of divine worlds fell on the hands of the leaders as they traced their plans.

And for that reason the incorruptible observer must hold that the command, if it had seriously desired it, could also have overcome those difficulties which prevented a system of continuous construction. There remains, therefore, nothing but the conclusion that the command deliberately chose the system of piecemeal construction. But the piecemeal construction was only a makeshift and therefore inexpedient. Remains the conclusion that the command willed something inexpedient. Strange conclusion! True, and yet in one respect it has much to be said for it. One can perhaps safely discuss it now. In those days many people, and among them the best, had a secret maxim which ran: Try with all your might to comprehend the decrees of the high command, but only up to a certain point; then avoid further meditation. A very wise maxim, which moreover was elaborated in a parable that was later often quoted: Avoid further meditation, but not because it might be harmful; it is not at all certain that it would be harmful. What is harmful or not harmful has nothing to do with the question. Consider rather the river in spring. It rises until it grows mightier and nourishes more richly the soil on the long stretch of its banks, still maintaining its own course until it reaches the sea, where it is all the more welcome because it is a worthier ally. Thus far may you urge your meditations on the decrees of the high command. But after that the river overflows its banks, loses outline and shape, slows down the speed of its current, tries to ignore its destiny by forming little seas in the interior of the land, damages the fields, and yet cannot maintain itself for long in its new expanse, but must run back between its banks again, must even dry up wretchedly in the hot season that presently follows. Thus far may you not urge your meditations on the decrees of the high command.

Now though this parable may have had extraordinary point and force during the building of the wall, it has at most only a restricted relevance for my present essay. My inquiry is purely historical; no lightning flashes any longer from the long since vanished thunderclouds, and so I may venture to seek for an explanation of the system of piecemeal construction which goes farther than the one that contented people then. The limits which my capacity for thought imposes upon me are narrow enough, but the province to be traversed here is infinite.

Against whom was the Great Wall to serve as a protection? Against the people of the north. Now, I come from the southeast of China. No northern people can menace us there. We read of them in the books of the ancients; the cruelties they commit in accordance with their nature make us sigh in our peaceful arbors. The faithful representations of the artist show us these faces of the damned, their gaping mouths, their jaws furnished with great pointed teeth, their half-shut eyes that already seem to be seeking out the victim which their jaws will rend and devour. When our children are unruly we show them these pictures, and at once they fly weeping into our arms. But nothing more than that do we know about these northerners. We have not seen them, and if we remain in our villages we shall never see them, even if on their wild horses they should ride as hard as they can straight towards us—the land is too vast and would not let them reach us, they would end their course in the empty air.

Why, then, since that is so, did we leave our homes, the stream with its bridges, our mothers and fathers, our weeping wives, our children who needed our care, and depart for the distant city to be trained there, while our thoughts journeyed still farther away to the wall in the north? Why? A question for the high command. Our leaders know us. They, absorbed in gigantic anxieties, know of us, know our petty pursuits, see us sitting together in our humble huts, and approve or disapprove the evening prayer which the father of the house recites in the midst of his family. And if I may be allowed to express such ideas about the high command, then I must say that in my opinion the high command has existed from old time, and was not assembled, say, like a gathering of mandarins summoned hastily to discuss somebody's fine dream in a conference as hastily terminated, so that that very evening the people are drummed out of their beds to carry out what has been decided, even if it should be nothing but an illumination in honor of a god who may have shown great favor to their masters the day before, only to drive them into some dark corner with cudgel blows tomorrow, almost before the illuminations have died down. Far rather do I believe that the high command has existed from all eternity, and the decision to build the wall likewise. Unwitting peoples of the north, who imagined they were the cause of it! Honest, unwitting Emperor, who imagined he decreed it! We builders of the wall know that it was not so and hold our tongues.

During the building of the wall and ever since to this very day I have occupied myself almost exclusively with the comparative history of races—there are certain questions which one can probe to the marrow, as it were, only by this method—and I have discovered that we Chinese possess certain folk and political institutions that are unique in their clarity, others again unique in their obscurity. The desire to trace the cause of these phenomena, especially the latter, has always intrigued me and intrigues me still, and the building of the wall is itself essentially involved with these problems.

Now one of the most obscure of our institutions is that of the empire itself. In Peking, naturally, at the imperial court, there is some clarity to be found on this subject, though even that is more illusive than real. Also the teachers of political law and history in the schools of higher learning claim to be exactly informed on these matters, and to be capable of passing on their knowledge to their students. The farther one descends among the lower schools the more, naturally enough, does one find teachers' and pupils' doubts of their own knowledge vanishing, and superficial culture mounting sky-high around a few precepts that have been drilled into people's minds for centuries, precepts which, though they have lost nothing of their eternal truth, remain eternally invisible in this fog of confusion.

But it is precisely this question of the empire which in my opinion the common people should be asked to answer, since after all they are the empire's final support. Here, I must confess, I can only speak once more for my native place. Except for the nature gods, and their ritual which fills the whole year in such beautiful and rich alternation, we think only about the Emperor. But not about the present one; or rather we would think about the present one if we knew who he was or knew anything definite about him. True—and it is the sole curiosity that fills us—we are always trying to get information on this subject, but, strange as it may sound, it is almost impossible to discover anything, either from pilgrims, though they have wandered through much of our land, or from near or distant villages, or from sailors, though they have navigated not only our little stream, but also the sacred rivers. One hears a great many things, true, but can gather nothing definite.

So vast is our land that no fable could do justice to its vastness, the heavens can scarcely span it—and Peking is only a dot in it, and the imperial palace less than a dot. The Emperor as such, on the other hand, is mighty throughout all the hierarchies of the world: admitted. But the existent Emperor, a man like us, lies much like us on a couch which is of generous proportions, perhaps, and yet very possibly may be quite narrow and short. Like us he sometimes stretches himself and when he is very tired yawns with his delicately cut mouth. But how should we know anything about that—thousands of miles away in the south—almost on the borders of the Tibetan Highlands? And besides, any tidings, even if they did reach us, would arrive far too late, would have become obsolete long before they reached us. The Emperor is always surrounded by a brilliant and yet ambiguous throng of nobles and courtiers—malice and enmity in the guise of servants and friends—who form a counterweight to the imperial power and perpetually labor to unseat the ruler from his place with poisoned arrows. The Empire is immortal, but the Emperor himself totters and falls from his throne, yes, whole dynasties sink in the end and breathe their last in one death rattle. Of these struggles and sufferings the people will never know; like tardy arrivals, like strangers in a city, they stand at the end of some densely thronged sidestreet peacefully munching the food they have brought with them, while far away in front, in the market square at the heart of the city, the execution of their ruler is proceeding.

There is a parable that describes this situation very well: The Emperor, so it runs, has sent a message to you, the humble subject, the insignificant shadow cowering in the remotest distance before the imperial sun; the Emperor from his deathbed has sent a message to you alone. He has commanded the messenger to kneel down by the bed, and has whispered the message to him; so much store did he lay on it that he ordered the messenger to whisper it back into his ear again. Then by a nod of the head he has confirmed that it is right. Yes, before the assembled spectators of his death —all the obstructing walls have been broken down, and on the spacious and loftily mounting open staircases stand in a ring the great princes of the Empire—before all these he has delivered his message. The messenger immediately sets out on his journey; a powerful, an indefatigable man; now pushing with his right arm, now with his left, he cleaves a way for himself through the throng; if he encounters resistance he points to his breast, where the symbol of the sun glitters; the way is made easier for him than it would be for any other man. But the multitudes are so vast; their numbers have no end. If he could reach the open fields how fast he would fly, and soon doubtless you would hear the welcome hammering of his fists on your door. But instead how vainly does he wear out his strength; still he is only making his way through the chambers of the innermost palace; never will he get to the end of them; and if he succeeded in that nothing would be gained; he must next fight his way down the stair; and if he succeeded in that nothing would be gained; the courts would still have to be crossed; and after the courts the second outer palace; and once more stairs and courts; and once more another palace; and so on for thousands of years; and if at last he should burst through the outermost gate—but never, never can that happen—the imperial capital would lie before him, the center of the world, crammed to bursting with its own sediment. Nobody could fight his way through here even with a message from a dead man. But you sit at your window when evening falls and dream it to yourself.

Just so, as hopelessly and as hopefully, do our people regard the Emperor. They do not know what Emperor is reigning, and there exist doubts regarding even the name of the dynasty. In school a great deal is taught about the dynasties with the dates of succession, but the universal uncertainty in this matter is so great that even the best scholars are drawn into it. Long-dead emperors are set on the throne in our villages, and one that only lives on in song recently had a proclamation of his read out by the priest before the altar. Battles that are old history are new to us, and one's neighbor rushes in with a jubilant face to tell the news. The wives of the emperors, pampered and overweening, seduced from noble custom by wily courtiers, swelling with ambition, vehement in their greed, uncontrollable in their lust, practice their abominations ever anew. The more deeply they are buried in time the more glaring are the colors in which their deeds are painted, and with a loud cry of woe our village eventually hears how an Empress drank her husband's blood in long draughts thousands of years ago.

Thus, then, do our people deal with departed emperors, but the living ruler they confuse among the dead. If once, only once in a man's lifetime, an imperial official on his tour of the provinces should arrive by chance at our village, make certain announcements in the name of the government, scrutinize the tax lists, examine the school children, inquire of the priest regarding our doings and affairs, and then, before he steps into his sedan chair, should sum up his impressions in verbose admonitions to the assembled commune—then a smile flits over every face, people throw surreptitious glances at each other, and bend over their children so as not to be observed by the official. Why, they think to themselves, he's speaking of a dead man as if he were alive, this Emperor of his died long ago, the dynasty is blotted out, the good official is having his joke with us, but we will behave as if we did not notice it, so as not to offend him. But we shall obey in earnest no one but our present ruler, for not to do so would be a crime. And behind the departing sedan chair of the official there rises in might as ruler of the village some figure fortuitously exalted from an urn already crumbled to dust.

Similarly our people are but little affected by revolutions in the state or contemporary wars. I recall an incident in my youth. A revolt had broken out in a neighboring, but yet quite distant, province. What caused it I can no longer remember, nor is it of any importance now; occasions for revolt can be found there any day, the people are an excitable people. Well, one day a leaflet published by the rebels was brought to my father's house by a beggar who had crossed that province. It happened to be a feast day, our rooms were filled with guests, the priest sat in the center and studied the sheet. Suddenly everybody started to laugh, in the confusion the sheet was torn, the beggar, who however had already received abundant alms, was driven out of the room with blows, the guests dispersed to enjoy the beautiful day. Why? The dialect of this neighboring province differs in some essential respects from ours, and this difference occurs also in certain turns of the written word, which for us have an archaic character. Hardly had the priest read two pages before we had come to our decision. Ancient history told long ago, old sorrows long since healed. And though—so it seems to me in recollection—the gruesomeness of the living present was irrefutably conveyed by the beggar's words, we laughed and shook our heads and refused to listen any longer. So eager are our people to obliterate the present.

If from such appearances anyone should draw the conclusion that in reality we have no Emperor, he would not be far from the truth. Over and over again it must be repeated: There is perhaps no people more faithful to the Emperor than ours in the south, but the Emperor derives no advantage from our fidelity. True, the sacred dragon stands on the little column at the end of our village, and ever since the beginning of human memory it has breathed out its fiery breath in the direction of Peking in token of homage—but Peking itself is far stranger to the people in our village than the next world. Can there really be a village where the houses stand side by side, covering all the fields for a greater distance than one can see from our hills, and can there be dense crowds of people packed between these houses day and night? We find it more difficult to picture such a city than to believe that Peking and its Emperor are one, a cloud, say, peacefully voyaging beneath the sun in the course of the ages.

Now the result of holding such opinions is a life on the whole free and unconstrained. By no means immoral, however; hardly ever have I found in my travels such pure morals as in my native village. But yet a life that is subject to no contemporary law, and attends only to the exhortations and warnings which come to us from olden times.

I guard against generalizations, and do not assert that in all the ten thousand villages in my province it is so, far less in all the five hundred provinces of China. Yet perhaps I may venture to assert on the basis of the many writings on this subject which I have read, as well as from my own observation—the building of the wall in particular, with its abundance of human material, provided a man of sensibility with the opportunity of traversing the souls of almost all the provinces—on the basis of all this, then, perhaps I may venture to assert that the prevailing attitude to the Emperor shows persistently and universally something fundamentally in common with that of our village. Now I have no wish whatever to represent this attitude as a virtue; on the contrary. True, the essential responsibility for it lies with the government, which in the most ancient empire in the world has not yet succeeded in developing, or has neglected to develop, the institution of the empire to such precision that its workings extend directly and unceasingly to the farthest frontiers of the land. On the other hand, however, there is also involved a certain feebleness of faith and imaginative power on the part of the people, that prevents them from raising the empire out of its stagnation in Peking and clasping it in all its palpable living reality to their own breasts, which yet desire nothing better than but once to feel that touch and then to die.

This attitude then is certainly no virtue. All the more remarkable is it that this very weakness should seem to be one of the greatest unifying influences among our people; indeed, if one may dare to use the expression, the very ground on which we live. To set about establishing a fundamental defect here would mean undermining not only our consciences, but, what is far worse, our feet. And for that reason I shall not proceed any further at this stage with my inquiry into these questions.

A HUNGER ARTIST

DURING THESE LAST decades the interest in professional fasting has markedly diminished. It used to pay very well to stage such great performances under one's own management, but today that is quite impossible. We live in a different world now. At one time the whole town took a lively interest in the hunger artist; from day to day of his fast the excitement mounted; everybody wanted to see him at least once a day; there were people who bought season tickets for the last few days and sat from morning till night in front of his small barred cage; even in the nighttime there were visiting hours, when the whole effect was heightened by torch flares; on fine days the cage was set out in the open air, and then it was the children's special treat to see the hunger artist; for their elders he was often just a joke that happened to be in fashion, but the children stood open-mouthed, holding each other's hands for greater security, marveling at him as he sat there pallid in black tights, with his ribs sticking out so prominently, not even on a seat but down among straw on the ground, sometimes giving a courteous nod, answering questions with a constrained smile, or perhaps stretching an arm through the bars so that one might feel how thin it was, and then again withdrawing deep into himself, paying no attention to anyone or anything, not even to the all-important striking of the clock that was the only piece of furniture in his cage, but merely staring into vacancy with half-shut eyes, now and then taking a sip from a tiny glass of water to moisten his lips.

Besides casual onlookers there were also relays of permanent watchers selected by the public, usually butchers, strangely enough, and it was their task to watch the hunger artist day and night, three of them at a time, in case he should have some secret recourse to nourishment. This was nothing but a formality, instituted to reassure the masses, for the initiates knew well enough that during his fast the artist would never in any circumstances, not even under forcible compulsion, swallow the smallest morsel of food; the honor of his profession forbade it. Not every watcher, of course, was capable of understanding this, there were often groups of night watchers who were very lax in carrying out their duties and deliberately huddled together in a retired corner to play cards with great absorption, obviously intending to give the hunger artist the chance of a little refreshment, which they supposed he could draw from some private hoard. Nothing annoyed the artist more than such watchers; they made him miserable; they made his fast seem unendurable; sometimes he mastered his feebleness sufficiently to sing during their watch for as long as he could keep going, to show them how unjust their suspicions were. But that was of little use; they only wondered at his cleverness in being able to fill his mouth even while singing. Much more to his taste were the watchers who sat close up to the bars, who were not content with the dim night lighting of the hall but focused him in the full glare of the electric pocket torch given them by the impresario. The harsh light did not trouble him at all, in any case he could never sleep properly, and he could always drowse a little, whatever the light, at any hour, even when the hall

81

was thronged with noisy onlookers. He was quite happy at the prospect of spending a sleepless night with such watchers; he was ready to exchange jokes with them, to tell them stories out of his nomadic life, anything at all to keep them awake and demonstrate to them again that he had no eatables in his cage and that he was fasting as not one of them could fast. But his happiest moment was when the morning came and an enormous breakfast was brought them, at his expense, on which they flung themselves with the keen appetite of healthy men after a weary night of wakefulness. Of course there were people who argued that this breakfast was an unfair attempt to bribe the watchers, but that was going rather too far, and when they were invited to take on a night's vigil without a breakfast, merely for the sake of the cause, they made themselves scarce, although they stuck stubbornly to their suspicions.

Such suspicions, anyhow, were a necessary accompaniment to the profession of fasting. No one could possibly watch the hunger artist continuously, day and night, and so no one could produce first-hand evidence that the fast had really been rigorous and continuous; only the artist himself could know that, he was therefore bound to be the sole completely satisfied spectator of his own fast. Yet for other reasons he was never satisfied; it was not perhaps mere fasting that had brought him to such skeleton thinness that many people had regretfully to keep away from his exhibitions, because the sight of him was too much for them, perhaps it was dissatisfaction with himself that had worn him down. For he alone knew, what no other initiate knew, how easy it was to fast. It was the easiest thing in the world. He made no secret of this, yet people did not believe him, at the best they set him down as modest; most of them, however, thought he was out for publicity or else was some kind of cheat who found it easy to fast because he had discovered a way of making it easy, and then had the impudence to admit the fact, more or less. He had to put up with all that, and in the course of time had got used to it, but his inner dissatisfaction always rankled, and never yet, after any term of fasting—this must be granted to his credit—had he left the cage of his own free will. The longest period of fasting was fixed by his impresario at forty days, beyond that term he was not allowed to go, not even in great cities, and there was good reason for it, too. Experience had proved that for about forty days the interest of the public could be stimulated by a steadily increasing pressure of advertisement, but after that the town began to lose interest, sympathetic support began notably to fall off; there were of course local variations as between one town and another or one country and another, but as a general rule forty days marked the limit. So on the fortieth day the flower-bedecked cage was opened, enthusiastic spectators filled the hall, a military band played, two doctors entered the cage to measure the results of the fast, which were announced through a megaphone, and finally two young ladies appeared, blissful at having been selected for the honor, to help the hunger artist down the few steps leading to a small table on which was spread a carefully chosen invalid repast. And at this very moment the artist always turned stubborn. True, he would entrust his bony arms to the outstretched helping hands of the ladies bending over him, but stand up he would not. Why stop fasting at this particular moment, after forty days of it? He had held out for a long time, an illimitably long time; why stop now, when he was in his best fasting form, or rather, not yet quite in his best fasting form? Why should he be cheated of the fame he would get for fasting longer, for being not only the record hunger artist of all time, which presumably he was already, but for beating his own record by a performance beyond human imagination, since he felt that there were no limits to his capacity for fasting? His public pretended to admire him so much, why should it have so little patience with him; if he could endure fasting longer, why shouldn't the public endure it? Besides, he was tired, he was comfortable sitting in the straw, and now he was supposed to lift himself to his full height and go down to a meal the very thought of which gave him a nausea that only the presence of the ladies kept him from betraying, and

83

even that with an effort. And he looked up into the eyes of the ladies who were apparently so friendly and in reality so cruel, and shook his head, which felt too heavy on its strengthless neck. But then there happened yet again what always happened. The impresario came forward, without a word—for the band made speech impossible—lifted his arms in the air above the artist, as if inviting Heaven to look down upon its creature here in the straw, this suffering martyr, which indeed he was, although in quite another sense; grasped him round the emaciated waist, with exaggerated caution, so that the frail condition he was in might be appreciated; and committed him to the care of the blenching ladies, not without secretly giving him a shaking so that his legs and body tottered and swayed. The artist now submitted completely; his head lolled on his breast as if it had landed there by chance; his body was hollowed out; his legs in a spasm of self-preservation clung close to each other at the knees, yet scraped on the ground as if it were not really solid ground, as if they were only trying to find solid ground; and the whole weight of his body, a featherweight after all, relapsed onto one of the ladies, who, looking round for help and panting a little—this post of honor was not at all what she had expected it to be—first stretched her neck as far as she could to keep her face at least free from contact with the artist, then finding this impossible, and her more fortunate companion not coming to her aid but merely holding extended on her own trembling hand the little bunch of knucklebones that was the artist's, to the great delight of the spectators burst into tears and had to be replaced by an attendant who had long been stationed in readiness. Then came the food, a little of which the impresario managed to get between the artist's lips, while he sat in a kind of half-fainting trance, to the accompaniment of cheerful patter designed to distract the public's attention from the artist's condition; after that, a toast was drunk to the public, supposedly prompted by a whisper from the artist in the impresario's ear; the band confirmed it with a mighty flourish, the spectators melted away, and no one had any cause

84

to be dissatisfied with the proceedings, no one except the hunger artist himself, he only, as always.

So he lived for many years, with small regular intervals of recuperation, in visible glory, honored by the world, yet in spite of that troubled in spirit, and all the more troubled because no one would take his trouble seriously. What comfort could he possibly need? What more could he possibly wish for? And if some good-natured person, feeling sorry for him, tried to console him by pointing out that his melancholy was probably caused by fasting, it could happen, especially when he had been fasting for some time, that he reacted with an outburst of fury and to the general alarm began to shake the bars of his cage like a wild animal. Yet the impresario had a way of punishing these outbreaks which he rather enjoyed putting into operation. He would apologize publicly for the artist's behavior, which was only to be excused, he admitted, because of the irritability caused by fasting, a condition hardly to be understood by well-fed people; then by natural transition he went on to mention the artist's equally incomprehensible boast that he could fast for much longer than he was doing; he praised the high ambition, the good will, the great self-denial undoubtedly implicit in such a statement; and then quite simply countered it by bringing out photographs, which were also on sale to the public, showing the artist on the fortieth day of a fast lying in bed almost dead from exhaustion. This perversion of the truth, familiar to the artist though it was, always unnerved him afresh and proved too much for him. What was a consequence of the premature ending of his fast was here presented as the cause of it! To fight against this lack of understanding, against a whole world of non-understanding, was impossible. Time and again in good faith he stood by the bars listening to the impresario, but as soon as the photographs appeared he always let go and sank with a groan back on to his straw, and the reassured public could once more come close and gaze at him.

A few years later when the witnesses of such scenes called them to mind, they often failed to understand themselves at all. For meanwhile the aforementioned change in public interest had set in; it seemed to happen almost overnight; there may have been profound causes for it, but who was going to bother about that; at any rate the pampered hunger artist suddenly found himself deserted one fine day by the amusement seekers, who went streaming past him to other more favored attractions. For the last time the impresario hurried him over half Europe to discover whether the old interest might still survive here and there; all in vain; everywhere, as if by secret agreement, a positive revulsion from professional fasting was in evidence. Of course it could not really have sprung up so suddenly as all that, and many premonitory symptoms which had not been sufficiently remarked or suppressed during the rush and glitter of success now came retrospectively to mind, but it was now too late to take any countermeasures. Fasting would surely come into fashion again at some future date, yet that was no comfort for those living in the present. What, then, was the hunger artist to do? He had been applauded by thousands in his time and could hardly come down to showing himself in a street booth at village fairs, and as for adopting another profession, he was not only too old for that but too fanatically devoted to fasting. So he took leave of the impresario, his partner in an unparalleled career, and hired himself to a large circus; in order to spare his own feelings he avoided reading the conditions of his contract.

A large circus with its enormous traffic in replacing and recruiting men, animals and apparatus can always find a use for people at any time, even for a hunger artist, provided of course that he does not ask too much, and in this particular case anyhow it was not only the artist who was taken on but his famous and long-known name as well; indeed, considering the peculiar nature of his performance, which was not impaired by advancing age, it could not be objected that here was an artist past his prime, no longer at the height of his professional skill, seeking a refuge in some quiet corner of a circus; on the contrary, the hunger artist averred that he could fast as well as ever, which was entirely credible, he even alleged that if he were allowed to fast as he liked, and this was at once promised him without more ado, he could astound the world by establishing a record never yet achieved, a statement which certainly provoked a smile among the other professionals, since it left out of account the change in public opinion, which the hunger artist in his zeal conveniently forgot.

He had not, however, actually lost his sense of the real situation and took it as a matter of course that he and his cage should be stationed, not in the middle of the ring as a main attraction, but outside, near the animal cages, on a site that was after all easily accessible. Large and gaily painted placards made a frame for the cage and announced what was to be seen inside it. When the public came thronging out in the intervals to see the animals, they could hardly avoid passing the hunger artist's cage and stopping there for a moment, perhaps they might even have stayed longer had not those pressing behind them in the narrow gangway, who did not understand why they should be held up on their way towards the excitements of the menagerie, made it impossible for anyone to stand gazing quietly for any length of time. And that was the reason why the hunger artist, who had of course been looking forward to these visiting hours as the main achievement of his life, began instead to shrink from them. At first he could hardly wait for the intervals; it was exhilarating to watch the crowds come streaming his way, until only too soon—not even the most obstinate self-deception, clung to almost consciously, could hold out against the fact—the conviction was borne in upon him that these people, most of them, to judge from their actions, again and again, without exception, were all on their way to the menagerie. And the first sight of them from the distance remained the best. For when they reached his cage he was at once deafened by the storm of shouting and abuse that arose from the two contending factions, which renewed themselves continuously, of those who wanted to stop and stare at him—he soon began to dislike them more than the others—not out of real interest

87

but only out of obstinate self-assertiveness, and those who wanted to go straight on to the animals. When the first great rush was past, the stragglers came along, and these, whom nothing could have prevented from stopping to look at him as long as they had breath, raced past with long strides, hardly even glancing at him, in their haste to get to the menagerie in time. And all too rarely did it happen that he had a stroke of luck, when some father of a family fetched up before him with his children, pointed a finger at the hunger artist and explained at length what the phenomenon meant, telling stories of earlier years when he himself had watched similar but much more thrilling performances, and the children, still rather uncomprehending, since neither inside nor outside school had they been sufficiently prepared for this lesson—what did they care about fasting?—yet showed by the brightness of their intent eyes that new and better times might be coming. Perhaps, said the hunger artist to himself many a time, things would be a little better if his cage were set not quite so near the menagerie. That made it too easy for people to make their choice, to say nothing of what he suffered from the stench of the menagerie, the animals' restlessness by night, the carrying past of raw lumps of flesh for the beasts of prey, the roaring at feeding times, which depressed him continually. But he did not dare to lodge a complaint with the management; after all, he had the animals to thank for the troops of people who passed his cage, among whom there might always be one here and there to take an interest in him, and who could tell where they might seclude him if he called attention to his existence and thereby to the fact that, strictly speaking, he was only an impediment on the way to the menagerie.

A small impediment, to be sure, one that grew steadily less. People grew familiar with the strange idea that they could be expected, in times like these, to take an interest in a hunger artist, and with this familiarity the verdict went out against him. He might fast as much as he could, and he did so; but nothing could save him now, people passed him by. Just try to explain to anyone the art of fasting! Anyone who has no feeling for it cannot be made to understand it. The fine placards grew dirty and illegible, they were torn down; the little notice board telling the number of fast days achieved, which at first was changed carefully every day, had long stayed at the same figure, for after the first few weeks even this small task seemed pointless to the staff; and so the artist simply fasted on and on, as he had once dreamed of doing, and it was no trouble to him, just as he had always foretold, but no one counted the days; no one, not even the artist himself, knew what records he was already breaking, and his heart grew heavy. And when once in a time some leisurely passer-by stopped, made merry over the old figure on the board and spoke of swindling, that was in its way the stupidest lie ever invented by indifference and inborn malice, since it was not the hunger artist who was cheating, he was working honestly, but the world was cheating him of his reward.

Many more days went by, however, and that too came to an end. An overseer's eye fell on the cage one day and he asked the attendants why this perfectly good cage should be left standing there unused with dirty straw inside it; nobody knew, until one man, helped out by the notice board, remembered about the hunger artist. They poked into the straw with sticks and found him in it. "Are you still fasting?" asked the overseer, "when on earth do you mean to stop?" "Forgive me, everybody," whispered the hunger artist; only the overseer, who had his ear to the bars, understood him. "Of course," said the overseer, and tapped his forehead with a finger to let the attendants know what state the man was in, "we forgive you." "I always wanted you to admire my fasting," said the hunger artist. "We do admire it," said the overseer, affably. "But you shouldn't admire it," said the hunger artist. "Well then we don't admire it," said the overseer, "but why shouldn't we admire it?" "Because I have to fast, I can't help it," said the hunger artist. "What a fellow you are," said the overseer, "and why can't you help it?" "Because," said

89

the hunger artist, lifting his head a little and speaking, with his lips pursed, as if for a kiss, right into the overseer's ear, so that no syllable might be lost, "because I couldn't find the food I liked. If I had found it, believe me, I should have made no fuss and stuffed myself like you or anyone else." These were his last words, but in his dimming eyes remained the firm though no longer proud persuasion that he was still continuing to fast.

"Well, clear this out now!" said the overseer, and they buried the hunger artist, straw and all. Into the cage they put a young panther. Even the most insensitive felt it refreshing to see this wild creature leaping around the cage that had so long been dreary. The panther was all right. The food he liked was brought him without hesitation by the attendants; he seemed not even to miss his freedom; his noble body, furnished almost to the bursting point with all that it needed, seemed to carry freedom around with it too; somewhere in his jaws it seemed to lurk; and the joy of life streamed with such ardent passion from his throat that for the onlookers it was not easy to stand the shock of it. But they braced themselves, crowded round the cage, and did not want ever to move away.

THE BURROW

I HAVE COMPLETED the construction of my burrow and it seems to be successful. All that can be seen from outside is a big hole; that, however, really leads nowhere; if you take a few steps you strike against natural firm rock. I can make no boast of having contrived this ruse intentionally; it is simply the remains of one of my many abortive building attempts, but finally it seemed to me advisable to leave this one hole without filling it in. True, some ruses are so subtle that they defeat themselves, I know that better than anyone, and it is certainly a risk to draw attention by this hole to the fact that there may be something in the vicinity worth inquiring into. But you do not know me if you think I am afraid, or that I built my burrow simply out of fear. At a distance of some thousand paces from this hole lies, covered by a movable layer of moss, the real entrance to the burrow; it is secured as safely as anything in this world can be secured; yet someone could step on the moss or break through it, and then my burrow would lie open, and anybody who liked——please note, however, that quite uncommon abilities would also be required——could make his way in and destroy everything for good. I know that very well, and even now, at the zenith of my life, I can scarcely pass an hour in complete tranquillity; at that one point in the dark moss I am vulnerable, and in my dreams I often see a greedy muzzle sniffing around it persistently. It will be objected that I could quite well have filled in the entrance too, with a thin layer of hard earth on top and with loose soil further down, so that it would not cost me much trouble to dig my way out again whenever I liked. But that plan is impossible; prudence itself demands that I should have a way of leaving at a moment's notice if necessary, prudence itself demands, as alas! so often, to risk one's life. All this involves very laborious calculation, and the sheer pleasure of the mind in its own keenness is often the sole reason why one keeps it up. I must have a way of leaving at a moment's notice, for, despite all my vigilance, may I not be attacked from some quite unexpected quarter? I live in peace in the inmost chamber of my house, and meanwhile the enemy may be burrowing his way slowly and stealthily straight towards me. I do not say that he has a better scent than I; probably he knows as little about me as I of him. But there are insatiable robbers who burrow blindly through the ground, and to whom the very size of my house gives the hope of hitting by chance on some of its far-flung passages. I certainly have the advantage of being in my own house and knowing all the passages and how they run. A robber may very easily become my victim and a succulent one too. But I am growing old; I am not as strong as many others, and my enemies are countless; it could well happen that in flying from one enemy I might run into the jaws of another. Anything might happen! In any case I must have the confident knowledge that somewhere there is an exit easy to reach and quite free, where I have to do nothing whatever to get out, so that I might never—Heaven shield us!—suddenly feel the teeth of the pursuer in my flank while I am desperately burrowing away, even if it is at loose easy soil. And it is not only by external enemies that I am threatened. There are also enemies in the bowels of the earth. I have never seen them, but legend tells of them and I firmly believe in them. They are creatures of the inner earth; not even legend can describe them. Their very victims can scarcely have seen them; they come, you hear the scratching of their claws just under you in the ground, which is their element, and already you are lost. Here it is of no avail to console yourself with the thought that you are in your own house; far rather are you in theirs. Not even my exit could save me from them; indeed in all probability it would not save me in any case, but rather betray me; yet it is a hope, and I cannot live without it. Apart from this main exit I am also connected with the outer world by quite narrow, tolerably safe passages which provide me with good fresh air to breathe. They are the work of the field mice. I have made judicious use of them, transforming them into an organic part of my burrow. They also give me the possibility of scenting things from afar, and thus serve as a protection. All sorts of small fry, too, come running through them, and I devour these; so I can have a certain amount of subterranean hunting, sufficient for a modest way of life, without leaving my burrow at all; and that is naturally a great advantage.

But the most beautiful thing about my burrow is the

stillness. Of course, that is deceptive. At any moment it may be shattered and then all will be over. For the time being, however, the silence is still with me. For hours I can stroll through my passages and hear nothing except the rustling of some little creature, which I immediately reduce to silence between my jaws, or the pattering of soil, which draws my attention to the need for repair; otherwise all is still. The fragrance of the woods floats in; the place feels both warm and cool. Sometimes I lie down and roll about in the passage with pure joy. When autumn sets in, to possess a burrow like mine, and a roof over your head, is great good fortune for anyone getting on in years. Every hundred yards I have widened the passages into little round cells; there I can curl myself up in comfort and lie warm. There I sleep the sweet sleep of tranquillity, of satisfied desire, of achieved ambition; for I possess a house. I do not know whether it is a habit that still persists from former days, or whether the perils even of this house of mine are great enough to awaken me; but invariably every now and then I start up out of profound sleep and listen, listen into the stillness which reigns here unchanged day and night, smile contentedly and then sink with loosened limbs into still profounder sleep. Poor homeless wanderers in the roads and woods, creeping for warmth into a heap of leaves or a herd of their comrades, delivered to all the perils of heaven and earth! I lie here in a room secured on every side—there are more than fifty such rooms in my burrow—and pass as much of my time as I choose between dozing and unconscious sleep.

Not quite in the center of the burrow, carefully chosen to serve as a refuge in case of extreme danger from siege if not from immediate pursuit, lies the chief cell. While all the rest of the burrow is the outcome rather of intense intellectual than of physical labor, this Castle Keep was fashioned by the most arduous labor of my whole body. Several times, in the despair brought on by physical exhaustion, I was on the point of giving up the whole business, flung myself down panting and cursed the burrow, dragged myself outside and left the place lying open to all the world. I could afford to do that, for I had no longer any wish to return to it, until at last, after four hours or days, back I went repentantly, and when I saw that the burrow was unharmed I could almost have raised a hymn of thanksgiving, and in sincere gladness of heart started on the work anew. My labors on the Castle Keep were also made harder, and unnecessarily so (unnecessarily in that the burrow derived no real benefit from those labors) by the fact that just at the place where, according to my calculations, the Castle Keep should be, the soil was very loose and sandy and had literally to be hammered and pounded into a firm state to serve as a wall for the beautifully vaulted chamber. But for such tasks the only tool I possess is my forehead. So I had to run with my forehead thousands and thousands of times, for whole days and nights, against the ground, and I was glad when the blood came, for that was a proof that the walls were beginning to harden; and in that way, as everybody must admit, I richly paid for my Castle Keep.

In the Castle Keep I assemble my stores; everything over and above my daily wants that I capture inside the burrow, and everything I bring back with me from my hunting expeditions outside, I pile up here. The place is so spacious that food for half a year scarcely fills it. Consequently I can divide up my stores, walk about among them, play with them, enjoy their plenty and their various smells, and reckon up exactly how much they represent. That done, I can always arrange accordingly, and make my calculations and hunting plans for the future, taking into account the season of the year. There are times when I am so well provided for that in my indifference to food I never even touch the smaller fry that scuttle about the burrow, which, however, is probably imprudent of me. My constant preoccupation with defensive measures involves a frequent alteration or modification, though within narrow limits, of my views on how the building can best be organized for that end. Then it sometimes seems risky to make the Castle Keep the basis of defense; the ramifications of the burrow present me with manifold possibilities, and it seems more in accordance with prudence to divide up my stores somewhat, and put part of them in certain of the smaller rooms; thereupon I mark off every third room, let us say, as a reserve storeroom, or every fourth room as a main and every second as an auxiliary storeroom, and so forth. Or I ignore certain passages altogether and store no food in them, so as to throw any enemy off the scent, or I choose quite at random a very few rooms according to their distance from the main exit. Each of these new plans involves of course heavy work; I have to make my calculations and then carry my stores to their new places. True, I can do that at my leisure and without any hurry, and it is not at all unpleasant to carry such good food in your jaws, to lie down and rest whenever you like, and to nibble an occasional tasty tidbit. But it is not so pleasant when, as sometimes happens, you suddenly fancy, starting up from your sleep, that the present distribution of your stores is completely and totally wrong, might lead to great dangers, and must be set right at once, no matter how tired or sleepy you may be; then I rush, then I fly, then I have no time for calculation; and although I was about to execute a perfectly new, perfectly exact plan, I now seize whatever my teeth hit upon and drag it or carry it away, sighing, groaning, stumbling, and even the most haphazard change in the present situation, which seems so terribly dangerous, can satisfy me. Until little by little full wakefulness sobers me, and I can hardly understand my panic haste, breathe in deeply the tranquillity of my house, which I myself have disturbed, return to my resting place, fall asleep at once in a new-won exhaustion, and on awakening find hanging from my jaws, say, a rat, as indubitable proof of night labors which already seem almost unreal. Then again there are times when the storing of all my food in one place seems the best plan of all. Of what use to me could my stores in the smaller rooms be, how much could I store there in any case? And whatever I put there would block the passage, and be a greater hindrance than help to me if I were pursued and had to fly. Besides, it is stupid but true that one's self-conceit suffers if one cannot see all one's stores together, and so at one glance know how much one possesses. And in dividing up my food in those various ways might not a great deal get lost? I can't be always scouring through all my passages and cross-passages so as to make sure that everything is in order. The idea of dividing up my stores is of course a good one, but only if one had several rooms similar to my Castle Keep. Several such rooms! Indeed! And who is to build them? In any case, they could not be worked into the general plan of my burrow at this late stage. But I will admit that that is a fault in my burrow; it is always a fault to have only one piece of anything. And I confess too that during the whole time I was constructing the burrow a vague idea that I should have more such cells stirred in my mind, vaguely, yet clearly enough if I had only welcomed it; I did not yield to it, I felt too feeble for the enormous labor it would involve, more, I felt too feeble even to admit to myself the necessity for that labor, and comforted myself as best I could with the vague hope that a building which in any other case would clearly be inadequate, would in my own unique, exceptional, favored case suffice, presumably because providence was interested in the preservation of my forehead, that unique instrument. So I have only one Castle Keep, but my dark premonitions that one would not suffice, have faded. However that may be, I must content myself with the one big chamber, the smaller ones are simply no substitute for it, and so, when this conviction has grown on me, I begin once more to haul my stores back from them to the Castle Keep. For some time afterwards I find a certain comfort in having all the passages and rooms free, in seeing my stores growing in the Castle Keep and emitting their variegated and mingled smells, each of which delights me in its own fashion, and every one of which I can distinguish even at a distance, as far as the very remotest passages. Then I usually enjoy periods of particular tranquillity, in which I change my sleeping place by stages, always working in towards the center of the burrow, always steeping myself more profoundly in the mingled smells, until at last I can no longer restrain myself and one night rush into the Castle Keep, mightily fling myself upon my stores, and glut myself with the best that I can seize until I am completely gorged. Happy but dangerous hours; anyone who knew how to exploit them could destroy me with ease and without any risk. Here too the absence of a second or third large storeroom works to my detriment; for it is the single huge accumulated mass of food that seduces me. I try to guard myself in various ways against this danger; the distribution of my stores in the smaller rooms is really one of these expedients; but unfortunately, like other such expedients, it leads through renunciation to still greater greed, which, overruling my intelligence, makes me arbitrarily alter my plans of defense to suit its ends.

To regain my composure after such lapses I make a practice of reviewing the burrow, and after the necessary improvements have been carried out, frequently leave it, though only for a short spell. Even at such moments the hardship of being without it for a long time seems too punitive to me, yet I recognize clearly the need for occasional short excursions. It is always with a certain solemnity that I approach the exit again. During my spells of home life I avoid it, steer clear even of the outer windings of the corridor that leads to it; besides, it is no easy job to wander about out there, for I have contrived there a whole little maze of passages; it was there that I began my burrow, at a time when I had no hope of ever completing it according to my plans; I began, half in play, at that corner, and so my first joy in labor found riotous satisfaction there in a labyrinthine burrow which at the time seemed to me the crown of all burrows, but which I judge today, perhaps with more justice, to be too much of an idle *tour de force,* not really worthy of the rest of the burrow, and though perhaps theoretically brilliant—here is my main entrance, I said in those days, ironically addressing my invisible enemies and seeing them all already caught and stifled in the outer labyrinth—is in reality a flimsy piece of jugglery that would hardly withstand a serious attack or the struggles of an enemy fighting for his life. Should I reconstruct this part of my burrow? I keep on postponing the decision, and the labyrinth will probably remain as it is. Apart from the sheer hard work that I should have to face, the task would also be the most dangerous imaginable. When I began the burrow I could work away at it in comparative peace of mind, the risk wasn't much greater than any other risk; but to attempt that today would be to draw the whole world's attention, and gratuitously, to my burrow; today the whole thing is impossible. I am almost glad of that, for I still have a certain sentiment about this first achievement of mine. And if a serious attack were attempted, what pattern of entrance at all would be likely to save me? An entrance can deceive, can lead astray, can give the attacker no end of worry, and the present one too can do that at a pinch. But a really serious attack has to be met by an instantaneous mobilization of all the resources in the burrow and all the forces of my body and soul—that is self-evident. So this entrance can very well remain where it is. The burrow has so many unavoidable defects imposed by natural causes that it can surely stand this one defect for which I am responsible, and which I recognize as a defect, even if only after the event. In spite of that, however, I do not deny that this fault worries me from time to time, indeed always. If on my customary rounds I avoid this part of the burrow, the fundamental reason is that the sight of it is painful to me, because I don't want to be perpetually reminded of a defect in my house, even if that defect is only too disturbingly present in my mind. Let it continue to exist ineradicably at the entrance; I can at least refuse to look at it as long as that is possible. If I merely walk in the direction of the entrance, even though I may be separated from it by several passages and rooms, I find myself sensing an atmosphere of great danger, actually as if my hair were growing thin and in a moment might fly off and leave me bare and shivering, exposed to the howls of my enemies. Yes, the mere thought of the door itself, the end of the domestic protection, brings such feelings with it, yet it is the labyrinth leading up to it that torments me most of all. Sometimes I dream that I have reconstructed it, transformed it completely, quickly, in a night, with a giant's strength, nobody having noticed, and now it is impregnable; the nights in which such dreams come to me are the sweetest I know, tears of joy and deliverance still glisten on my beard when I awaken.

So I must thread the tormenting complications of this labyrinth physically as well as mentally whenever I go out, and I am both exasperated and touched when, as sometimes happens, I lose myself for a moment in my own maze, and the work of my hands seems to be still doing its best to prove its sufficiency to me, its maker, whose final judgment has long since been passed on it. But then I find myself beneath the mossy covering, which has been left untouched for so long—for I stay for long spells in my house—that it has grown fast to the soil around it, and now only a little push with my head is needed and I am in the upper world. For a long time I do not dare to make that little movement, and if it were not that I would have to traverse the labyrinth once more, I would certainly leave the matter for the time being and turn back again. Just think. Your house is protected and self-sufficient. You live in peace, warm, well-nourished, master, sole master of all your manifold passages and rooms, and all this you are prepared—not to give up, of course—but to risk it, so to speak; you nurse the confident hope, certainly, that you will regain it; yet is it not a dangerous, a far too dangerous stake that you are playing for? Can there be any reasonable grounds for such a step? No, for such acts as these there can be no reasonable grounds. But all the same, I then cautiously raise the trap door and slip outside, let it softly fall back again, and fly as fast as I can from the treacherous spot.

Yet I am not really free. True, I am no longer confined by narrow passages, but hunt through the open woods, and feel new powers awakening in my body for which there was no room, as it were, in the burrow, not even in the Castle Keep, though it had been ten times as big. The food too is better up here; though hunting is more difficult, success more rare, the results are more valuable from every point of view; I do not deny all this; I appreciate it and take advantage of it at least as fully as anyone else, and probably more fully, for I do not hunt like a vagrant out of mere idleness or desperation, but calmly and methodically. Also I am not permanently doomed to this free life, for I know that my term is measured, that I do not have to hunt here forever, and that, whenever I am weary of this life and wish to leave it, Someone, whose invitation I shall not be able to withstand, will, so to speak, summon me to him. And so I can pass my time here quite without care and in complete enjoyment, or rather I could, and yet I cannot. My burrow takes up too much of my thoughts. I fled from the entrance fast enough, but soon I am back at it again. I seek out a good hiding place and keep watch on the entrance of my house—this time from outside—for whole days and nights. Call it foolish if you like; it gives me infinite pleasure and reassures me. At such times it is as if I were not so much looking at my house as at myself sleeping, and had the joy of being in a profound slumber and simultaneously of keeping vigilant guard over myself. I am privileged, as it were, not only to dream about the specters of the night in all the helplessness and blind trust of sleep, but also at the same time to confront them in actuality with the calm judgment of the fully awake. And strangely enough I discover that my situation is not so bad as I had often thought, and will probably think again when I return to my house. In this connection—it may be in others too, but in this one especially—these excursions of mine are truly indispensable. Carefully as I have chosen an out-of-the-way place for my door, the traffic that passes it is nevertheless, if one takes a week's observation, very great; but so it is, no doubt, in all inhabited regions, and probably it is actually better to hazard the risks of dense traffic, whose very impetus carries it past, than to be delivered in complete solitude to the first persistently searching intruder. Here enemies are numerous and their allies and accomplices still more numerous, but they fight one another, and while thus employed rush past my burrow without noticing it. In all my time I have never seen anyone investigating the actual door of my house, which is fortunate both for me and for him, for I would certainly have launched myself at his throat, forgetting everything else in my anxiety for the burrow. True, creatures come, in whose vicinity I dare not remain, and from whom I have to fly as soon as I scent them in the distance; on their attitude to the burrow I really can't pronounce with certainty, but it is at least a reassurance that when I presently return I never find any of them there, and the entrance is undamaged. There have been happy periods in which I could almost assure myself that the enmity of the world towards me had ceased or been assuaged, or that the strength of the burrow had raised me above the destructive struggle of former times. The burrow has probably protected me in more ways than I thought or dared think while I was inside it. This fancy used to have such a hold over me that sometimes I have been seized by the childish desire never to return to the burrow again, but to settle down somewhere close to the entrance, to pass my life watching the entrance, and gloat perpetually upon the reflection—and in that find my happiness—how steadfast a protection my burrow would be if I were inside it. Well, one is soon roughly awakened from childish dreams. What does this protection which I am looking at here from the outside amount to after all? Dare I estimate the danger which I run inside the burrow from observations which I make when outside? Can my enemies, to begin with, have any proper awareness of me if I am not in my burrow? A certain awareness of me they certainly have, but not full awareness. And is not that full awareness the real definition of a state of danger? So the experiments I attempt here are only half-experiments or even less, calculated merely to reassure my fears and by giving me false reassurance to lay me open to great perils. No, I do not watch over my own sleep, as I imagined; rather it is I who sleep, while the destroyer watches. Perhaps he is one of those who pass the entrance without seeming to notice it, concerned merely to ascertain, just like myself, that the door is still untouched and waits for their attack, and only pass because they know that the master of the house is out, or because they are quite aware that he is guilelessly lying on the watch in the bushes close by. And I leave my post of observation and find I have had enough of this outside life; I feel that there is nothing more that I can learn here, either now or at any time. And I long to say a last goodbye to everything up here, to go down into my burrow never to return again, let things take their course, and not try to retard them with my profitless vigils. But spoilt by seeing for such a long time everything that happened around the entrance, I find great difficulty in summoning the resolution to carry out the actual descent, which might easily draw anyone's attention, and without knowing what is happening behind my back and behind the door after it is fastened. I take advantage of stormy nights to get over the necessary preliminaries, and quickly bundle in my spoil; that seems to have come off, but whether it has really come off will only be known when I myself have made the descent; it will be known, but not by me, or by me, but too late. So I give up the attempt and do not make the descent. I dig an experimental burrow, naturally at a good distance from the real entrance, a burrow just as long as myself, and seal it also with a covering of moss. I creep into my hole, close it after me, wait patiently, keep vigil for long or short spells, and at various hours of the day, then fling off the moss, issue from my hole, and summarize my observations. These are extremely heterogeneous, and both good and bad; but I have never been able to discover a universal principle or an infallible method of descent. In consequence of all this I have not yet summoned the resolution to make my actual descent, and am thrown into despair at the necessity of doing it soon. I almost screw myself to the point of deciding to emigrate to distant parts and take up my old comfortless life again, which had no security whatever, but was one indiscriminate succession of perils, yet in consequence prevented one from perceiving and fearing particular perils, as I am constantly reminded by comparing my secure burrow with ordinary life. Certainly such a decision would be an arrant piece of folly, produced simply by living too long in senseless freedom; the burrow is still mine, I have only to take a single step and I am safe. And I tear myself free from all my doubts and by broad daylight rush to the door, quite resolved to raise it now; but I cannot, I rush past it and fling myself into a thorn bush, deliberately, as a punishment, a punishment for some sin I do not know of. Then, at the last moment, I am forced to admit to myself that I was right after all, and that it was really impossible to go down into the burrow without exposing the thing I love best, for a little while at least, to all my enemies, on the ground, in the trees, in the air. And the danger is by no means a fanciful one, but very real. It need not be any particular enemy that is provoked to pursue me, it may very well be some chance innocent little creature, some disgusting little beast which follows me out of curiosity, and thus, without knowing it, becomes the leader of all the world against me; nor need it be even that, it may be—and that would be just as bad, indeed in some respects worse—it may be someone of my own kind, a connoisseur and prizer of burrows, a hermit, a lover of peace, but all the same a filthy scoundrel who wishes to be housed where he has not built. If he were actually to arrive now, if in his obscene lust he were to discover the entrance and set about working at it, lifting the moss, if he were actually to succeed, if he were actually to wriggle his way in in my stead, until only his hindquarters still showed; if all this were actually to happen, so that at last, casting all prudence to the winds, I might in my blind rage leap on him, maul him, tear the flesh from his bones, destroy him, drink his blood and fling his corpse among the rest of my spoil, but above all—that is the main thing—were at last back in my burrow once more, I would have it in my heart to greet the labryinth itself with rapture; but first I would draw the moss covering over me, and I would want to rest, it seems to me, for all the remainder of my life. But nobody comes and I am left to my own resources. Perpetually obsessed by the sheer difficulty of the attempt, I lose much of my timidity, I no longer attempt even to appear to avoid the entrance, but make a hobby of prowling around it; by now it is almost as if I were the enemy spying out a suitable opportunity for successfully breaking in. If I only had someone I could trust to keep watch at my post of observation; then of course I could descend in perfect peace of mind. I would make an agreement with this trusty confederate of mine that he would keep a careful note of the state of things during my descent and for quite a long time afterwards, and if he saw any sign of danger knock on the moss covering, and if he saw nothing do nothing. With that a clean sweep would be made of all my fears, no residue would be left, or at most my confidant. For would he not demand some counterservice from me; would he not at least want to see the burrow? That in itself, to let anyone freely into my burrow, would be exquisitely painful to me. I built it for myself, not for visitors, and I think I would refuse to admit him, not even though he alone made it possible for me to get into the burrow would I let him in. But I simply could not admit him, for either I must let him go in first by himself, which is simply unimaginable, or we must both descend at the same time, in which case the advantage I am supposed to derive from him, that of being kept watch over, would be lost. And what trust can I really put in him? Can I trust one whom I have had under my eyes just as fully when I can't see him, and the moss covering separates us? It is comparatively easy to trust anyone if you are supervising him or at least can supervise him; perhaps it is possible even to trust someone at a distance; but completely to trust someone outside the burrow when you are inside the burrow, that is, in a different world, that, it seems to me, is impossible. But such considerations are not in the least necessary; the mere reflection is enough that during or after my descent one of the countless accidents of existence might prevent my confidant from fulfilling his duty, and what incalculable results might not the smallest accident of that kind have for me? No, if one takes it by and large, I have no right to complain that I am alone and have nobody that I can trust. I certainly lose nothing by that and probably spare myself trouble. I can only trust myself and my burrow. I should have thought of that before and taken measures to meet the difficulty that worries me so much now. When I began the burrow it would at least have been partly possible. I should have so constructed the first passage that it had two entrances at a moderate distance from each other, so that after descending through the one entrance with that slowness which is unavoidable, I might rush at once through the passage to the second entrance, slightly raise the moss covering, which would be so arranged as to make that easy, and from there keep watch on the position for several days and nights. That would have been the only right way of doing it. True, the two entrances would double the risk, but that consideration need not delay me, for one of the entrances, serving merely as a post of observation, could be quite narrow. And with that I lose myself in a maze of technical speculations, I begin once more to dream my dream of a completely perfect burrow, and that somewhat calms me; with closed eyes I behold with delight perfect or almost perfect structural devices for enabling me to slip out and in unobserved. While I lie there thinking such things I admire these devices very greatly, but only as technical achievements, not as real advantages; for this freedom to slip out and in at will, what does it amount to? It is the mark of a restless nature, of inner uncertainty, disreputable desires, evil propensities that seem still worse when one thinks of the burrow, which is there at one's hand and can flood one with peace if one only remains quite open and receptive to it. For the present, however, I am outside it seeking some possibility of returning, and for

105

that the necessary technical devices would be very desirable. But perhaps not so very desirable after all. Is it not a very grave injustice to the burrow to regard it in moments of nervous panic as a mere hole into which one can creep and be safe? Certainly it is a hole among other things, and a safe one, or should be, and when I picture myself in the midst of danger, then I insist with clenched teeth and all my will that the burrow should be nothing but a hole set apart to save me, and that it should fulfill that clearly defined function with the greatest possible efficiency, and I am ready to absolve it from every other duty. Now the truth of the matter—and one has no eye for that in times of great peril, and only by a great effort even in times when danger is threatening—is that in reality the burrow does provide a considerable degree of security, but by no means enough, for is one ever free from anxieties inside it? These anxieties are different from ordinary ones, prouder, richer in content, often long repressed, but in their destructive effects they are perhaps much the same as the anxieties that existence in the outer world gives rise to. Had I constructed the burrow exclusively to assure my safety I would not have been disappointed, it is true; nevertheless the relation between the enormous labor involved and the actual security it would provide, at least insofar as I could feel it and profit by it, would not have been in my favor. It is extremely painful to have to admit such things to oneself, but one is forced to do it, confronted by that entrance over there which now literally locks and bars itself against me, the builder and possessor. Yet the burrow is not a mere hole for taking refuge in. When I stand in the Castle Keep surrounded by my piled-up stores, surveying the ten passages which begin there, raised and sunken passages, vertical and rounded passages, wide and narrow passages, as the general plan dictates, and all alike still and empty, ready by their various routes to conduct me to all the other rooms, which are also still and empty—then all thought of mere safety is far from my mind, then I know that here is my castle, which I have wrested from the refractory soil with tooth and claw, with pounding and hammering blows, my castle which can never belong to anyone else, and is so essentially mine that I can calmly accept in it even my enemy's mortal stroke at the final hour, for my blood will ebb away here in my own soil and not be lost. And what but that is the meaning of the blissful hours which I pass, now peacefully slumbering, now happily keeping watch, in these passages, these passages which suit me so well, where one can stretch oneself out in comfort, roll about in childish delight, lie and dream, or sink into blissful sleep. And the smaller rooms, each familiar to me, so familiar that in spite of their complete similarity I can clearly distinguish one from the other with my eyes shut by the mere feel of the wall: they enclose me more peacefully and warmly than a bird is enclosed in its nest. And all, all still and empty.

But if that is the case, why do I hang back? Why do I dread the thought of the intruding enemy more than the possibility of never seeing my burrow again? Well, the latter alternative is fortunately an impossibility; there is no need for me even to take thought to know what the burrow means to me; I and the burrow belong so indissolubly together that in spite of all my fears I could make myself quite comfortable out here, and not even need to overcome my repugnance and open the door; I could be quite content to wait here passively, for nothing can part us for long, and somehow or other I shall quite certainly find myself in my burrow again. But on the other hand how much time may pass before then, and how many things may happen in that time, up here no less than down there? And it lies with me solely to curtail that interval and to do what is necessary at once.

And then, too exhausted to be any longer capable of thought, my head hanging, my legs trembling with fatigue, half asleep, feeling my way rather than walking, I approach the entrance, slowly raise the moss covering, slowly descend, leaving the door open in my distraction for a needlessly long time, and presently remember my omission, and get out again to make it good—but what need was there to get out for that? All that was needed was to draw to the moss covering; right; so I creep in again and now at last draw to the moss covering. Only in this state, and in this state alone, can I achieve my descent. So at last I lie down beneath the moss on the top of my bloodstained spoil and can now enjoy my longed-for sleep. Nothing disturbs me, no one has tracked me down, above the moss everything seems to be quiet thus far at least, but even if all were not quiet I question whether I could stop to keep watch now; I have changed my place, I have left the upper world and am in my burrow, and I feel its effect at once. It is a new world, endowing me with new powers, and what I felt as fatigue up there is no longer that here. I have returned from a journey, dog-tired with my wanderings, but the sight of the old house, the thought of all the things that are waiting to be done, the necessity at least to cast a glance at all the rooms, but above all to make my way immediately to the Castle Keep; all this transforms my fatigue into ardent zeal; it is as though at the moment when I set foot in the burrow I had wakened from a long and profound sleep. My first task is a very laborious one and requires all my attention; I mean getting my spoil through the narrow and thin-walled passages of the labyrinth. I shove with all my might, and the work gets done too, but far too slowly for me; to hasten it I drag part of my flesh supply back again and push my way over it and through it; now I have only a portion of my spoil before me and it is easier to make progress; but my road is so blocked by all this flesh in these narrow passages, through which it is not always easy for me to make my way even when I am alone, that I could quite easily smother among my own stores; sometimes I can only rescue myself from their pressure by eating and drinking a clear space for myself. But the work of transport is successful, I finish it in quite a reasonable time, the labyrinth is behind me, I reach an ordinary passage and breathe freely, push my spoil through a communication passage into a main passage expressly designed for the purpose, a passage sloping down steeply to the Castle Keep. What is left to be done is not really work at all; my whole load rolls and flows down the passage almost of itself. The Castle Keep at last! At last I can dare to rest. Everything is unchanged, no great mishap seems to have occurred, the few little defects that I note at a first glance can soon be repaired; first, however, I must go my long round of all the passages, but that is no hardship, that is merely to commune again with friends, as I often did in the old days or—I am not so very old yet, but my memory of many things is already quite confused—as I often did, or as I have often heard that it was done. Now I begin with the second passage, purposefully slow, now that I have seen the Castle Keep I have endless time—inside the burrow I always have endless time—for everything I do there is good and important and satisfies me somehow. I begin with the second passage, but break off in the middle and turn into the third passage and let it take me back again to the Castle Keep, and now of course I have to begin at the second passage once more, and so I play with my task and lengthen it out and smile to myself and enjoy myself and become quite dazed with all the work in front of me, but never think of turning aside from it. It is for your sake, ye passages and rooms, and you, Castle Keep, above all, that I have come back, counting my own life as nothing in the balance, after stupidly trembling for it for so long, and postponing my return to you. What do I care for danger now that I am with you? You belong to me, I to you, we are united; what can harm us? What if my foes should be assembling even now up above there and their muzzles be preparing to break through the moss? And with its silence and emptiness the burrow answers me, confirming my words. But now a feeling of lassitude overcomes me and in some favorite room I curl myself up tentatively, I have not yet surveyed everything by a long way, though still resolved to examine everything to the very end; I have no intention of sleeping here,

I have merely yielded to the temptation of making myself comfortable and pretending I want to sleep, I merely wish to find out if this is as good a place for sleeping as it used to be. It is, but it is a better place for sleep than for waking, and I remain lying where I am in deep slumber.

I must have slept for a long time. I was only wakened when I had reached the last light sleep which dissolves of itself, and it must have been very light, for it was an almost inaudible whistling noise that wakened me. I recognized what it was immediately; the small fry, whom I had allowed far too much latitude, had burrowed a new channel somewhere during my absence, this channel must have chanced to intersect an older one, the air was caught there, and that produced the whistling noise. What an indefatigably busy lot these small fry are, and what a nuisance their diligence can be! First I shall have to listen at the walls of my passages and locate the place of disturbance by experimental excavations, and only then will I be able to get rid of the noise. However, this new channel may be quite welcome as a further means of ventilation, if it can be fitted into the plan of the burrow. But after this I shall keep a much sharper eye on the small fry than I used to; I shall spare none of them.

As I have a good deal of experience in investigations of this kind the work probably will not take me long and I can start upon it at once; there are other jobs awaiting me, it is true, but this is the most urgent. I must have silence in my passages. This noise, however, is a comparatively innocent one; I did not hear it at all when I first arrived, although it must certainly have been there; I must first feel quite at home before I could hear it; it is, so to speak, audible only to the ear of the householder. And it is not even constant, as such noises usually are; there are long pauses, obviously caused by stoppages of the current of air. I start on my investigations, but I can't find the right place to begin at, and though I cut a few trenches I do it at random; naturally that has no effect, and the hard work of digging and the still harder work of filling the trenches up again and beating the earth firm is so much labor lost. I don't seem to be getting any nearer to the place where the noise is, it goes on always on the same thin note, with regular pauses, now a sort of whistling, but again like a kind of piping. Now I could leave it to itself for the time being; it is very disturbing, certainly, but there can hardly be any doubt that its origin is what I took it to be at first; so it can scarcely become louder, on the contrary, such noises may quite well—though until now I have never had to wait so long for that to happen—may quite well vanish of themselves in the course of time through the continued labors of these little burrowers; and apart from that, often chance itself puts one on the track of the disturbance, where systematic investigation has failed for a long time. In such ways I comfort myself, and resolve simply to continue my tour of the passages, and visit the rooms, many of which I have not seen yet since my return, and enjoy myself contemplating the Castle Keep now and then between times; but my anxiety will not let me, and I must go on with my search. These little creatures take up much, far too much, time that could be better employed. In such cases as the present it is usually the technical problem that attracts me; for example, from the noise, which my ear can distinguish in all its finest shades, so that it has a perfectly clear outline to me, I deduce its cause, and now I am on fire to discover whether my conclusion is valid. And with good reason, for as long as that is not established I cannot feel safe, even if it were merely a matter of discovering where a grain of sand that had fallen from one of the walls had rolled to. And a noise such as this is by no means a trifling matter, regarded from that angle. But whether trifling or important, I can find nothing, no matter how hard I search, or it may be that I find too much. This had to happen just in my favorite room, I think to myself, and I walk a fair distance away from it, almost halfway along the passage leading to the next room; I do this more as a joke, pretending to myself that my favorite room is not alone

111

to blame, but that there are disturbances elsewhere as well, and with a smile on my face I begin to listen; but soon I stop smiling, for, right enough, the same whistling meets me here too. It is really nothing to worry about; sometimes I think that nobody but myself would hear it; it is true, I hear it now more and more distinctly, for my ear has grown keener through practice; though in reality it is exactly the same noise wherever I may hear it, as I have convinced myself by comparing my impressions. Nor is it growing louder; I recognize this when I listen in the middle of the passage instead of pressing my ear against the wall. Then it is only with an effort, indeed with great intentness, that I can more guess at than hear the merest trace of a noise now and then. But it is this very uniformity of the noise everywhere that disturbs me most, for it cannot be made to agree with my original assumption. Had I rightly divined the cause of the noise, then it must have issued with greatest force from some given place, which it would be my task to discover, and after that have grown fainter and fainter. But if my hypothesis does not meet the case, what can the explanation be? There still remains the possibility that there are two noises, that up to now I have been listening at a good distance from the two centers, and that while its noise increases, when I draw near to one of them, the total result remains approximately the same for the ear in consequence of the lessening volume of sound from the other center. Already I have almost fancied sometimes, when I have listened carefully, that I could distinguish, if very indistinctly, differences of tone which support this new assumption. In any case I must extend my sphere of investigation much farther than I have done. Accordingly I descend the passage to the Castle Keep and begin to listen there. Strange, the same noise there too. Now it is a noise produced by the burrowing of some species of small fry who have infamously exploited my absence; in any case they have no intention of doing me harm, they are simply busied with their own work, and so long as no obstacle comes in

112

their way they will keep on in the direction they have taken: I know all this, yet that they should have dared to approach the very Castle Keep itself is incomprehensible to me and fills me with agitation, and confuses the faculties which I need so urgently for the work before me. Here I have no wish to discover whether it is the unusual depth at which the Castle Keep lies, or its great extent and correspondingly powerful air suction, calculated to scare burrowing creatures away, or the mere fact that it is the Castle Keep, that by some channel or other has penetrated to their dull minds. In any case, I have never noticed any sign of burrowing in the walls of the Castle Keep until now. Crowds of little beasts have come here, it is true, attracted by the powerful smells; here I have had a constant hunting ground, but my quarry has always burrowed a way through in the upper passages, and come running down here, somewhat fearfully, but unable to withstand such a temptation. But now, it seems, they are burrowing in all the passages. If I had only carried out the best of the grand plans I thought out in my youth and early manhood, or rather, if I had only had the strength to carry them out, for there would have been no lack of will. One of these favorite plans of mine was to isolate the Castle Keep from its surroundings, that is to say, to restrict the thickness of its walls to about my own height, and leave a free space of about the same width all around the Castle Keep, except for a narrow foundation, which unfortunately would have to be left to bear up the whole. I had always pictured this free space, and not without reason, as the loveliest imaginable haunt. What a joy to lie pressed against the rounded outer wall, pull oneself up, let oneself slide down again, miss one's footing and find oneself on firm earth, and play all those games literally upon the Castle Keep and not inside it; to avoid the Castle Keep, to rest one's eyes from it whenever one wanted, to postpone the joy of seeing it until later and yet not have to do without it, but literally hold it safe be-between one's claws, a thing that is impossible if you

113

have only an ordinary open entrance to it; but above all to be able to stand guard over it, and in that way to be so completely compensated for renouncing the actual sight of it that, if one had to choose between staying all one's life in the Castle Keep or in the free space outside it, one would choose the latter, content to wander up and down there all one's days and keep guard over the Castle Keep. Then there would be no noises in the walls, no insolent burrowing up to the very Keep itself; then peace would be assured there and I would be its guardian; then I would not have to listen with loathing to the burrowing of the small fry, but with delight to something that I cannot hear now at all: the murmurous silence of the Castle Keep.

But that beautiful dream is past and I must set to work, almost glad that now my work has a direct connection with the Castle Keep, for that wings it. Certainly, as I can see more and more clearly, I need all my energies for this task, which at first seemed quite a trifling one. I listen now at the walls of the Castle Keep, and wherever I listen, high or low, at the roof or the floor, at the entrance or in the corners, everywhere, everywhere, I hear the same noise. And how much time, how much care must be wasted in listening to that noise, with its regular pauses. One can, if one wishes, find a tiny deceitful comfort in the fact that here in the Castle Keep, because of its vastness, one hears nothing at all, as distinguished from the passages, when one stands back from the walls. Simply as a rest and a means to regain my composure I often make this experiment, listen intently and am overjoyed when I hear nothing. But the question still remains, what can have happened? Confronted with this phenomenon my original explanation completely falls to the ground. But I must also reject other explanations which present themselves to me. One could assume, for instance, that the noise I hear is simply that of the small fry themselves at their work. But all my experience contradicts this; I cannot suddenly begin to hear now a thing that I have never heard before though it was always there. My sensitiveness to disturbances in the burrow has perhaps become greater with the years, yet my hearing has by no means grown keener. It is of the very nature of small fry not to be heard. Would I have tolerated them otherwise? Even at the risk of starvation I would have exterminated them. But perhaps—this idea now insinuates itself—I am concerned here with some animal unknown to me. That is possible. True, I have observed the life down here long and carefully enough, but the world is full of diversity and is never wanting in painful surprises. Yet it cannot be a single animal, it must be a whole swarm that has suddenly fallen upon my domain, a huge swarm of little creatures, which as they are audible, must certainly be bigger than the small fry, but yet cannot be very much bigger, for the sound of their labors is itself very faint. It may be, then, a swarm of unknown creatures on their wanderings, who happen to be passing by my way, who disturb me, but will presently cease to do so. So I could really wait for them to pass, and need not put myself to the trouble of work that will be needless in the end. Yet if these creatures are strangers, why is it that I never see any of them? I have already dug a host of trenches, hoping to catch one of them, but I can find not a single one. Then it occurs to me that they may be quite tiny creatures, far tinier than any I am acquainted with, and that it is only the noise they make that is greater. Accordingly I investigate the soil I have dug up, I cast the lumps into the air so that they break into quite small particles, but the noisemakers are not among them. Slowly I come to realize that by digging such small fortuitous trenches I achieve nothing; in doing that I merely disfigure the walls of my burrow, scratching hastily here and there without taking time to fill up the holes again; at many places already there are heaps of earth which block my way and my view. Still, that is only a secondary worry; for now I can neither wander about my house, nor review it, nor rest; often already I have fallen asleep at my work in some hole or other, with one paw clutching the soil above me, from which in a semi-stupor I have been trying to tear a lump. I intend now to alter my methods. I shall dig a wide and carefully constructed trench in the direction of the noise and not cease from digging until, independent of all theories, I find the real cause of the noise. Then I shall eradicate it, if that is within my power, and if it is not, at least I shall know the truth. That truth will bring me either peace or despair, but whether the one or the other, it will be beyond doubt or question. This decision strengthens me. All that I have done till now seems to me far too hasty; in the excitement of my return, while I had not yet shaken myself free from the cares of the upper world, and was not yet completely penetrated by the peace of the burrow, but rather hypersensitive at having had to renounce it for such a long time, I was thrown into complete confusion of mind by an unfamiliar noise. And what was it? A faint whistling, audible only at long intervals, a mere nothing to which I don't say that one could actually get used, for no one could get used to it, but which one could, without actually doing anything about it at once, observe for a while; that is, listen every few hours, let us say, and patiently register the results, instead of, as I had done, keeping one's ear fixed to the wall and at every hint of noise tearing out a lump of earth, not really hoping to find anything, but simply so as to do something to give expression to one's inward agitation. All that will be changed now, I hope. And then, with furious shut eyes, I have to admit to myself that I hope nothing of the kind, for I am still trembling with agitation just as I was hours ago, and if my reason did not restrain me I would probably like nothing better than to start stubbornly and defiantly digging, simply for the sake of digging, at some place or other, whether I heard anything there or not; almost like the small fry, who burrow either without any object at all or simply because they eat the soil. My new and reasonable plan both tempts me and leaves me cold. There is nothing in it to object to, I at least know of no objection; it is bound, so far as I can see, to achieve my aim. And yet at bottom I do not believe in it; I believe in it so little that I do not even fear the terrors which its success may well bring, I do not believe even in a dreadful denouement; indeed it seems to me that I have been thinking ever since the first appearance of the noise of such a methodical trench, and have not begun upon it until now simply because I put no trust in it. In spite of that I shall of course start on the trench; I have no other alternative; but I shall not start at once, I shall postpone the task for a little while. If reason is to be reinstated on the throne, it must be completely reinstated; I shall not rush blindly into my task. In any case I shall first repair the damage that I have done to the burrow with my wild digging; that will take a good long time, but it is necessary; if the new trench is really to reach its goal it will probably be long, and if it should lead to nothing at all it will be endless; in any case this task means a longish absence from the burrow, though an absence by no means so painful as an absence in the upper world, for I can interrupt my work whenever I like and pay a visit to my house; and even if I should not do that the air of Castle Keep will be wafted to me and surround me while I work; nevertheless it means leaving the burrow and surrendering myself to an uncertain fate, and consequently I want to leave the burrow in good order behind me; it shall not be said that I, who am fighting for its peace, have myself destroyed that peace without reinstating it at once. So I begin by shovelling the soil back into the holes from which it was taken, a kind of work I am familiar with, that I have done countless times almost without regarding it as work, and at which, particularly as regards the final pressing and smoothing down—and this is no empty boast, but the simple truth—I am unbeatable. But this time everything seems difficult, I am too distracted, every now and then, in the middle of my work, I press my ear to the wall and listen, and without taking any notice let the soil that I have just lifted trickle back into the passage again. The final embellishments, which demand a stricter attention, I can hardly achieve at all. Hideous protuberances, disturbing cracks remain, not to speak of the fact that the old buoyancy simply cannot be restored again to a wall patched up in such a way. I try to comfort myself with the reflection that my present work is only temporary. When I return after peace has been restored I shall repair everything properly; work will be mere play to me then. Oh yes, work is mere play in fairy tales, and this comfort of mine belongs to the realm of fairy tales too. It would be far better to do the work thoroughly now, at once, far more reasonable than perpetually to interrupt it and wander off through the passages to discover new sources of noise, which is easy enough, all that is needed being to stop at any point one likes and listen. And that is not the end of my useless discoveries. Sometimes I fancy that the noise has stopped, for it makes long pauses; sometimes such a faint whistling escapes one, one's own blood is pounding all too loudly in one's ears; then two pauses come one after another, and for a while one thinks that the whistling has stopped forever. I listen no longer, I jump up, all life is transfigured; it is as if the fountains from which flows the silence of the burrow were unsealed. I refrain from verifying my discovery at once, I want first to find someone to whom in all good faith I can confide it, so I rush to the Castle Keep, I remember, for I and everything in me has awakened to new life, that I have eaten nothing for a long time, I snatch something or other from among my store of food half buried under the debris and hurriedly begin to swallow it while I hurry back to the place where I made my incredible discovery, I only want to assure myself about it incidentally, perfunctorily, while I am eating; I listen, but the most perfunctory listening shows at once that I was shamefully deceived: away there in the distance the whistling still remains unshaken. And I spit out my food, and would like to trample it underfoot, and go back to my task, not caring which I take up; any place where it seems to be needed, and there are enough places like that, I mechanically start on something or other, just as if the overseer had appeared

118

and I must make a pretense of working for his benefit. But hardly have I begun to work in this fashion when it may happen that I make a new discovery. The noise seems to have become louder, not much louder, of course—here it is always a matter of the subtlest shades—but all the same sufficiently louder for the ear to recognize it clearly. And this growing-louder is like a coming-nearer; still more distinctly than you hear the increasing loudness of the noise, you can literally see the step that brings it closer to you. You leap back from the wall, you try to grasp at once all the possible consequences that this discovery will bring with it. You feel as if you had never really organized the burrow for defense against attack; you had intended to do so, but despite all your experience of life the danger of an attack, and consequently the need to organize the place for defense, seemed remote—or rather not remote (how could it possibly be!)—but infinitely less important than the need to put it in a state where one could live peacefully; and so that consideration was given priority in everything relating to the burrow. Many things in this direction might have been done without affecting the plan of the whole; most incomprehensibly they have been neglected. I have had a great deal of luck all those years, luck has spoilt me; I have had anxieties, but anxiety leads to nothing when you have luck to back you.

The thing to do, really to do now, would be to go carefully over the burrow and consider every possible means of defending it, work out a plan of defense and a corresponding plan of construction, and then start on the work at once with the vigor of youth. That is the work that would really be needed, for which, I may add, it is now far too late in the day; yet that is what would really be needed, and not the digging of a grand experimental trench, whose only real result would be to deliver me hand and foot to the search for danger, out of the foolish fear that it will not arrive quickly enough of itself. Suddenly I cannot comprehend my former plan. I can find no slightest trace of reason in what had seemed so reasonable; once more I lay aside my work and even my listening; I have no wish to discover any further signs that the noise is growing louder; I have had enough of discoveries; I let everything slide; I would be quite content if I could only still the conflict going on within me. Once more I let my passages lead me where they will, I come to more and more remote ones that I have not yet seen since my return, and that are quite unsullied by my scratching paws, and whose silence rises up to meet me and sinks into me. I do not surrender to it, I hurry on, I do not know what I want, probably simply to put off the hour. I stray so far that I find myself at the labyrinth; the idea of listening beneath the moss covering tempts me; such distant things, distant for the moment, chain my interest. I push my way up and listen. Deep stillness; how lovely it is here, outside there nobody troubles about my burrow, everybody has his own affairs, which have no connection with me; how have I managed to achieve this? Here under the moss covering is perhaps the only place in my burrow now where I can listen for hours and hear nothing. A complete reversal of things in the burrow; what was once the place of danger has become a place of tranquillity, while the Castle Keep has been plunged into the melee of the world and all its perils. Still worse, even here there is no peace in reality, here nothing has changed; silent or vociferous, danger lies in ambush as before above the moss, but I have grown insensitive to it, my mind is far too much taken up with the whistling in my walls. Is my mind really taken up with it? It grows louder, it comes nearer, but I wriggle my way through the labyrinth and make a couch for myself up here under the moss; it is almost as if I were already leaving the house to the whistler, content if I can only have a little peace up here. To the whistler? Have I come, then, to a new conclusion concerning the cause of the noise? But surely the noise is caused by the channels bored by the small fry? Is not that my considered opinion? It seems to me that I have not retreated from it thus far. And if the noise is not caused directly by these channels, it is indirectly. And even if it should have no connection with them whatever, one is not at liberty to make *a priori* assumptions, but must wait until one finds the cause, or it reveals itself. One could play with hypotheses, of course, even at this stage; for instance, it is possible that there has been a water burst at some distance away, and what seems a piping or whistling to me is in reality a gurgling. But apart from the fact that I have no experience in that sphere—the groundwater that I found at the start I drained away at once, and in this sandy soil it has never returned—apart from this fact the noise is undeniably a whistling and simply not to be translated into a gurgling. But what avail all exhortations to be calm; my imagination will not rest, and I have actually come to believe—it is useless to deny it to myself—that the whistling is made by some beast, and moreover not by a great many small ones, but by a single big one. Many signs contradict this. The noise can be heard everywhere and always at the same strength, and moreover uniformly, both by day and night. At first, therefore, one cannot but incline to the hypothesis of a great number of little animals; but as I must have found some of them during my digging and I have found nothing, it only remains for me to assume the existence of a great beast, especially as the things that seem to contradict the hypothesis are merely things which make the beast, not so much impossible, as merely dangerous beyond all one's powers of conception. For that reason alone have I resisted this hypothesis. I shall cease from this self-deception. For a long time already I have played with the idea that the beast can be heard at such a great distance because it works so furiously; it burrows as fast through the ground as another can walk on the open road; the ground still trembles at its burrowing when it has ceased; this reverberation and the noise of the boring itself unite into one sound at such a great distance, and I, as I hear only the last dying ebb of that sound, hear it always at the same uniform strength. It follows from this also that the beast is not making for me, seeing that the noise never changes; more likely it has a plan in view whose purpose I cannot decipher; I merely assume that the beast—and I make no claim whatever that it knows of my existence—is encircling me; it has probably made several circles around my burrow already since I began to observe it. The nature of the noise, the piping or whistling, gives me much food for thought. When I scratch and scrape in the soil in my own fashion the sound is quite different. I can explain the whistling only in this way: that the beast's chief means of burrowing is not its claws, which it probably employs merely as a secondary resource, but its snout or its muzzle, which, of course, apart from its enormous strength, must also be fairly sharp at the point. It probably bores its snout into the earth with one mighty push and tears out a great lump; while it is doing that I hear nothing; that is the pause; but then it draws in the air for a new push. This indrawal of its breath, which must be an earthshaking noise, not only because of the beast's strength, but of its haste, its furious lust for work as well, this noise I hear then as a faint whistling. But quite incomprehensible remains the beast's capacity to work without stopping; perhaps the short pauses provide also the opportunity of snatching a moment's rest; but apparently the beast has never yet allowed itself a really long rest, day and night it goes on burrowing, always with the same freshness and vigor, always thinking of its object, which must be achieved with the utmost expedition, and which it has the ability to achieve with ease. Now I could not have foreseen such an opponent. But apart altogether from the beast's peculiar characteristics, what is happening now is only something which I should really have feared all the time, something against which I should have been constantly prepared: the fact that someone would come. By what chance can everything have flowed on so quietly and happily for such a long time? Who can have diverted my enemies from their path, and forced them to make a wide detour around my property? Why have I been spared for so long, only to be delivered to such terrors now? Compared with this, what are all the petty dangers in brooding over which I have spent my life! Had I hoped, as owner of the burrow, to be in a stronger position than any enemy who might chance to appear? But simply by virtue of being owner of this great vulnerable edifice I am obviously defenseless against any serious attack. The joy of possessing it has spoilt me, the vulnerability of the burrow has made me vulnerable; any wound to it hurts me as if I myself were hit. It is precisely this that I should have foreseen; instead of thinking only of my own defense—and how perfunctorily and vainly I have done even that—I should have thought of the defense of the burrow. Above all, provision should have been made for cutting off sections of the burrow, and as many as possible of them, from the endangered sections when they are attacked; this should have been done by means of improvised landslides, calculated to operate at a moment's notice; moreover these should have been so thick, and have provided such an effectual barrier, that the attacker would not even guess that the real burrow only began at the other side. More, these landslides should have been so devised that they not only concealed the burrow, but also entombed the attacker. Not the slightest attempt have I made to carry out such a plan, nothing at all has been done in this direction, I have been as thoughtless as a child, I have passed my manhood's years in childish games, I have done nothing but play even with the thought of danger, I have shirked really taking thought for actual danger. And there has been no lack of warning.

Nothing, of course, approaching the present situation has happened before; nevertheless there was an incident not unlike it when the burrow was only beginning. The main difference between that time and this is simply that the burrow was only beginning then. . . . In those days I was literally nothing more than a humble apprentice, the labyrinth was only sketched out in rough outline, I had already dug a little room, but the proportions and the execution of the walls were sadly bungled; in short, everything was so tentative that it could only be regarded as an experiment, as something which, if one lost patience some day, one could leave behind without much regret. Then one day as I lay on a heap of earth resting from my labors —I have rested far too often from my labors all my life—suddenly I heard a noise in the distance. Being young at the time, I was less frightened than curious. I left my work to look after itself and set myself to listen; I listened and listened, and had no wish to fly up to my moss covering and stretch myself out there so that I might not have to hear. I did listen, at least. I could clearly recognize that the noise came from some kind of burrowing similar to my own; it was somewhat fainter, of course, but how much of that might be put down to the distance one could not tell. I was intensely interested, but otherwise calm and cool. Perhaps I am in somebody else's burrow, I thought to myself, and now the owner is boring his way towards me. If that assumption had proved to be correct I would have gone away, for I have never had any desire for conquest or bloodshed, and begun building somewhere else. But after all I was still young and still without a burrow, so I could remain quite cool. Besides, the further course of the noise brought no real cause for apprehension, except that it was not easy to explain. If whoever was boring there was really making for me, because he had heard me boring, then if he changed his direction, as now actually happened, it could not be told whether he did this because my pause for rest had deprived him of any definite point to make towards, or because—which was more plausible—he had himself changed his plans. But perhaps I had been deceived altogether, and he had never been actually making in my direction; at any rate the noise grew louder for a while as if he were drawing nearer, and being young at that time I probably would not have been displeased to see the burrower suddenly rising from the ground; but nothing of that kind happened, at a certain point the sound of boring began to weaken, it grew fainter and fainter, as if the burrower were gradually diverging from his first route, and suddenly it broke off altogether, as if he had decided now to take the diametrically opposite direction and were making straight away from me into the distance. For a long time I still went on listening for him in the silence, before I returned once more to my work. Now that warning was definite enough, but I soon forgot it, and it scarcely influenced my building plans.

Between that day and this lie my years of maturity, but is it not as if there were no interval at all between them? I still take long rests from my labors and listen at the wall, and the burrower has changed his intention anew, he has turned back, he is returning from his journey, thinking he has given me ample time in the interval to prepare for his reception. But on my side everything is worse prepared for than it was then; the great burrow stands defenseless, and I am no longer a young apprentice, but an old architect, and the powers I still have fail me when the decisive hour comes; yet old as I am it seems to me that I would gladly be still older, so old that I should never be able to rise again from my resting place under the moss. For to be honest I cannot endure the place, I rise up and rush, as if I had filled myself up there with new anxieties instead of peace, down into the house again. What was the state of things the last time I was here? Had the whistling grown fainter? No, it had grown louder. I listen at ten places chosen at random and clearly notice the deception; the whistling is just the same as ever, nothing has altered. Over there, there are no changes, there one is calm and not worried about time; but here every instant frets and gnaws at the listener. I go once more the long road to the Castle Keep, all my surroundings seem filled with agitation, seem to be looking at me, and then look away again so as not to disturb me, yet cannot refrain the very next moment from trying to read the saving solution from my expression. I shake my

125

head, I have not yet found any solution. Nor do I go to the Castle Keep in pursuance of any plan. I pass the spot where I had intended to begin the experimental trench, I look it over once more, it would have been an admirable place to begin at, the trench's course would have been in the direction where lay the majority of the tiny ventilation holes, which would have greatly lightened my labors; perhaps I should not have had to dig very far, should not even have had to dig to the source of the noise; perhaps if I had listened at the ventilation holes it would have been enough. But no consideration is potent enough to animate me to this labor of digging. This trench will bring me certainty, you say? I have reached the stage where I no longer wish to have certainty. In the Castle Keep I choose a lovely piece of flayed red flesh and creep with it into one of the heaps of earth; there I shall have silence at least, such silence, at any rate, as still can be said to exist here. I munch and nibble at the flesh, think of the strange beast going its own road in the distance, and then again that I should enjoy my store of food as fully as possible, while I still have the chance. This last is probably the sole plan I have left that I can carry out. For the rest I try to unriddle the beast's plans. Is it on its wanderings, or is it working on its own burrow? If it is on its wanderings then perhaps an understanding with it might be possible. If it should really break through to the burrow I shall give it some of my stores and it will go on its way again. It will go its way again, a fine story! Lying in my heap of earth I can naturally dream of all sorts of things, even of an understanding with the beast, though I know well enough that no such thing can happen, and that at the instant when we see each other, more, at the moment when we merely guess at each other's presence, we shall both blindly bare our claws and teeth, neither of us a second before or after the other, both of us filled with a new and different hunger, even if we should already be gorged to bursting. And with entire justice, for who, even if he were merely on his wanderings, would not change his itinerary and his plans for the future on catching sight of the burrow? But perhaps the beast is digging in its own burrow, in which case I cannot even dream of an understanding. Even if it should be such a peculiar beast that its burrow could tolerate a neighbor, my burrow could not tolerate a neighbor, at least not a clearly audible one. Now actually the beast seems to be a great distance away; if it would only withdraw a little farther the noise too would probably disappear; perhaps in that case everything would be peaceful again as in the old days; all this would then become a painful but salutary lesson, spurring me on to make the most diverse improvements on the burrow; if I have peace, and danger does not immediately threaten me, I am still quite fit for all sorts of hard work; perhaps, considering the enormous possibilities which its powers of work open before it, the beast has given up the idea of extending its burrow in my direction, and is compensating itself for that in some other one. That consummation also cannot, of course, be brought about by negotiation, but only by the beast itself, or by some compulsion exercised from my side. In both cases the decisive factor will be whether the beast knows about me, and if so what it knows. The more I reflect upon it the more improbable does it seem to me that the beast has even heard me; it is possible, though I can't imagine it, that it can have received news of me in some other way, but it has certainly never heard me. So long as I still knew nothing about it, it simply cannot have heard me, for at that time I kept very quiet, nothing could be more quiet than my return to the burrow; afterwards, when I dug the experimental trenches, perhaps it could have heard me, though my style of digging makes very little noise; but if it had heard me I must have noticed some sign of it, the beast must at least have stopped its work every now and then to listen. But all remained unchanged.

JOSEPHINE THE SINGER, OR THE MOUSE FOLK

OUR SINGER IS called Josephine. Anyone who has not heard her does not know the power of song. There is no one but is carried away by her singing, a tribute all the greater as we are not in general a music-loving race. Tranquil peace is the music we love best; our life is hard, we are no longer able, even on occasions when we have tried to shake off the cares of daily life, to rise to anything so high and remote from our usual routine as music. But we do not much lament that; we do not get even so far; a certain practical cunning, which admittedly we stand greatly in need of, we hold to be our greatest distinction, and with a smile born of such cunning we are wont to console ourselves for all shortcomings, even supposing—only it does not happen—that we were to yearn once in a way for the kind of bliss which music may provide. Josephine is the sole exception; she has a love for music and knows too how to transmit it; she is the only one; when she dies, music—who knows for how long—will vanish from our lives.

I have often thought about what this music of hers really means. For we are quite unmusical; how is it that we understand Josephine's singing or, since Josephine denies that, at least think we can understand it. The simplest answer would be that the beauty of her singing is so great that even the most insensitive cannot be deaf to it, but this answer is not satisfactory. If it were really so, her singing would have to give one an immediate and lasting feeling of being something out of the ordinary, a feeling that from her throat something is sounding which we have never heard before and which we are not even capable of hearing, something that Josephine alone and no one else can enable us to hear. But in my opinion that is just what does not happen, I do not feel this and have never observed that others feel anything of the kind. Among intimates we admit freely to one another that Josephine's singing, as singing, is nothing out of the ordinary.

Is it in fact singing at all? Although we are unmusical we have a tradition of singing; in the old days our people did sing; this is mentioned in legends and some songs have actually survived, which, it is true, no one can now sing. Thus we have an inkling of what singing is, and Josephine's art does not really correspond to it. So is it singing at all? Is it not perhaps just a piping? And piping is something we all know about, it is the real artistic accomplishment of our people, or rather no mere accomplishment but a characteristic expression of our life. We all pipe, but of course no one dreams of making out that our piping is an art, we pipe without thinking of it, indeed without noticing it, and there are even many among us who are quite unaware that piping is one of our characteristics. So if it were true that Josephine does not sing but only pipes and perhaps, as it seems to me at least, hardly rises above the level of our usual piping—yet, perhaps her strength is not even quite equal to our usual piping, whereas an ordinary farmhand can keep it up effortlessly all day long, besides doing his work—if that were all true, then indeed Josephine's alleged vocal skill might be disproved, but that would merely clear the ground for the real riddle which needs solving, the enormous influence she has.

After all, it is only a kind of piping that she produces. If you post yourself quite far away from her and listen, or, still better, put your judgment to the test, whenever she happens to be singing along with others, by trying to identify her voice, you will undoubtedly distinguish nothing but a quite ordinary piping tone, which at most differs a little from the others through being delicate or weak. Yet if you sit down before her, it is not merely a piping; to comprehend her art it is necessary not only to hear but to see her. Even if hers were only our usual workaday piping, there is first of all this peculiarity to consider, that here is someone making a ceremonial performance out of doing the usual thing. To crack a nut is truly no feat, so no one would ever dare to collect an audience in order to entertain it with nut-cracking. But if all the same one does do that and succeeds in entertaining the public, then it cannot be a matter of simple nut-cracking. Or it is a matter of nut-cracking, but it turns out that we have overlooked the art of cracking nuts because we were too skilled in it and that this newcomer to it first shows us its real nature, even finding it useful in making his effects to be rather less expert in nut-cracking than most of us.

Perhaps it is much the same with Josephine's singing; we admire in her what we do not at all admire in ourselves; in this respect, I may say, she is of one mind with us. I was once present when someone, as of course often happens, drew her attention to the folk piping everywhere going on, making only a modest reference to it, yet for Josephine that was more than enough. A smile so sarcastic and arrogant as she then assumed I have never seen; she, who in appearance is delicacy itself, conspicuously so even among our people who are prolific in such feminine types, seemed at that moment actually vulgar; she was at once aware of it herself, by the way, with her extreme sensibility, and controlled herself. At any rate she denies any connection between her art and ordinary piping. For those who are of the contrary opinion she has only contempt and probably unacknowledged hatred. This is not simple vanity, for the opposition, with which I too am half in sympathy, certainly admires her no less than the crowd does, but Josephine does not want mere admiration, she wants to be admired exactly in the way she prescribes, mere admiration leaves her cold. And when you take a seat before her, you understand her; opposition is possible only at a distance; when you sit before her, you know: this piping of hers is no piping.

Since piping is one of our thoughtless habits, one might think that people would pipe up in Josephine's audience too; her art makes us feel happy, and when we are happy we pipe; but her audience never pipes, it sits in mouselike stillness; as if we had become partakers in the peace we long for, from which our own piping at the very least holds us back, we make no sound. Is it her singing that enchants us or is it not rather the solemn stillness enclosing her frail little voice? Once it happened while Josephine was singing that some silly little thing in all innocence began to pipe up too. Now it was just the same as what we were hearing from Josephine; in front of us the piping sound that despite all rehearsal was still tentative and here in the audience the unself-conscious piping of a child; it would have been impossible to define the difference; but yet at once we hissed and whistled the interrupter down, although it would not really have been necessary, for in any case she would certainly have crawled away in fear and shame, whereas Josephine struck up her most triumphal notes and was quite beyond herself, spreading her arms wide and stretching her throat as high as it could reach.

That is what she is like always, every trifle, every casual incident, every nuisance, a creaking in the parquet, a grinding of teeth, a failure in the lighting incites her to heighten the effectiveness of her song; she believes anyhow that she is singing to deaf ears; there is no lack of enthusiasm and applause, but she has long learned not to expect real understanding, as she conceives it. So all disturbance is very welcome to her; whatever intervenes from outside to hinder the purity of her song, to be overcome with a slight effort, even with no effort at all, merely by confronting it, can help to awaken the masses, to teach them not perhaps understanding but awed respect.

And if small events do her such service, how much more do great ones. Our life is very uneasy, every day brings surprises, apprehensions, hopes and terrors, so that it would be impossible for a single individual to bear it all did he not always have by day and night the support of his fellows; but even so it often becomes very difficult; frequently as many as a thousand shoulders are trembling under a burden that was really meant only for one pair. Then Josephine holds that her time has come. So there she stands, the delicate creature, shaken by vibrations especially below the breastbone, so that one feels anxious for her, it is as if she has concentrated all her strength on her song, as if from everything in her that does not directly subserve her singing all strength has been withdrawn, almost all power of life, as if she were laid bare, abandoned, committed merely to the care of good angels, as if while she is so wholly withdrawn and living only in her song a cold breath blowing upon her might kill her. But just when she makes such an appearance, we who are supposed to be her opponents are in the habit of saying: "She can't even pipe; she has to put such a terrible strain on herself to force out not a song—we can't call it song—but some approximation to our usual customary piping." So it seems to us, but this impression although, as I said, inevitable is yet fleeting and transient. We too are soon sunk in the feeling of the mass, that, warmly pressed body to body, listens with indrawn breath.

And to gather around her this mass of our people who are almost always on the run and scurrying hither and thither for reasons that are often not very clear, Josephine mostly needs to do nothing else than take up her stand, head thrown back, mouth half open, eyes turned upwards, in the position that indicates her intention to sing. She can do this where she likes, it need not be a place visible a long way off, any secluded corner pitched on in a moment's caprice will serve as well. The news that she is going to sing flies round at once and soon whole processions are on the way there. Now, sometimes, all the same, obstacles intervene, Josephine likes best to sing just when things are most upset, many worries and dangers force us then to take devious ways, with the best will in the world we cannot assemble ourselves as quickly as Josephine wants, and on occasion she stands there in ceremonial state for quite a time without a sufficient audience—then indeed she turns furious, then she stamps her feet, swearing in most unmaidenly fashion; she actually bites. But even such behavior does no harm to her reputation; instead of curbing a little her excessive demands, people exert themselves to meet them; messengers are sent out to summon fresh hearers; she is kept in ignorance of the fact that this is being done; on the roads all around sentries can be seen posted who wave on newcomers and urge them to hurry; this goes on until at last a tolerably large audience is gathered.

What drives the people to make such exertions for Josephine's sake? This is no easier to answer than the first question about Josephine's singing, with which it is closely connected. One could eliminate that and combine them both in the second question, if it were possible to assert that because of her singing our people are unconditionally devoted to Josephine. But this is simply not the case; unconditional devotion is hardly known among us; ours are people who love slyness beyond everything, without any malice, to be sure, and childish whispering and chatter, innocent, superficial chatter, to be sure, but people of such a kind cannot go in for unconditional devotion, and that Josephine herself certainly feels, that is what she is fighting against with all the force of her feeble throat.

In making such generalized pronouncements, of course, one should not go too far, our people are all the same devoted to Josephine, only not unconditionally. For instance, they would not be capable of laughing at Josephine. It can be admitted: in Josephine there is much to make one laugh; and laughter for its own sake is never far away from us; in spite of all the misery of our lives quiet laughter is always, so to speak, at our elbows; but we do not laugh at Josephine. Many a time I have had the impression that our people interpret their relationship to Josephine in this way, that she, this frail creature, needing protection and in some way remarkable, in her own opinion remarkable for her gift of song, is entrusted to their care and they must look after her; the reason for this is not clear to anyone, only the fact

133

seems to be established. But what is entrusted to one's care one does not laugh at; to laugh would be a breach of duty; the utmost malice which the most malicious of us wreak on Josephine is to say now and then: "The sight of Josephine is enough to make one stop laughing."

So the people look after Josephine much as a father takes into his care a child whose little hand—one cannot tell whether in appeal or command—is stretched out to him. One might think that our people are not fitted to exercise such paternal duties, but in reality they discharge them, at least in this case, admirably; no single individual could do what in this respect the people as a whole are capable of doing. To be sure, the difference in strength between the people and the individual is so enormous that it is enough for the nursling to be drawn into the warmth of their nearness and he is sufficiently protected. To Josephine, certainly, one does not dare mention such ideas. "Your protection isn't worth an old song," she says then. Sure, sure, old song, we think. And besides, her protest is no real contradiction, it is rather a thoroughly childish way of doing, and childish gratitude, while a father's way of doing is to pay no attention to it.

Yet there is something else behind it which is not so easy to explain by this relationship between the people and Josephine. Josephine, that is to say, thinks just the opposite, she believes it is she who protects the people. When we are in a bad way politically or economically, her singing is supposed to save us, nothing less than that, and if it does not drive away the evil, at least gives us the strength to bear it. She does not put it in these words or in any other, she says very little anyhow, she is silent among the chatterers, but it flashes from her eyes, on her closed lips—few among us can keep their lips closed, but she can—it is plainly legible. Whenever we get bad news—and on many days bad news comes thick and fast at once, lies and half-truths included— she rises up at once, whereas usually she sits listlessly on the ground, she rises up and stretches her neck and tries to see over the heads of her flock like a shepherd before a thunderstorm. It is certainly a habit of children, in their wild, impulsive fashion, to make such claims, but Josephine's are not quite so unfounded as children's. True, she does not save us and she gives us no strength; it is easy to stage oneself as a savior of our people, inured as they are to suffering, not sparing themselves, swift in decision, well acquainted with death, timorous only to the eye in the atmosphere of reckless daring which they constantly breathe, and as prolific besides as they are bold—it is easy, I say, to stage oneself after the event as the savior of our people, who have always somehow managed to save themselves, although at the cost of sacrifices which make historians—generally speaking we ignore historical research entirely—quite horror-struck. And yet it is true that just in emergencies we hearken better than at other times to Josephine's voice. The menaces that loom over us make us quieter, more humble, more submissive to Josephine's domination; we like to come together, we like to huddle close to each other, especially on an occasion set apart from the troubles preoccupying us; it is as if we were drinking in all haste—yes, haste is necessary, Josephine too often forgets that—from a cup of peace in common before the battle. It is not so much a performance of songs as an assembly of the people, and an assembly where except for the small piping voice in front there is complete stillness; the hour is much too grave for us to waste it in chatter.

A relationship of this kind, of course, would never content Josephine. Despite all the nervous uneasiness that fills Josephine because her position has never been quite defined, there is still much that she does not see, blinded by her self-conceit, and she can be brought fairly easily to overlook much more, a swarm of flatterers is always busy about her to this end, thus really doing a public service—and yet to be only an incidental, unnoticed performer in a corner of an assembly of the people, for that, although in itself it would be no small thing, she would certainly not make us the sacrifice of her singing.

Nor does she need to, for her art does not go unnoticed. Although we are at bottom preoccupied with quite other things and it is by no means only for the sake of her singing that stillness prevails and many a listener does not even look up but buries his face in his neighbor's fur, so that Josephine up in front seems to be exerting herself to no purpose, there is yet something—it cannot be denied—that irresistibly makes its way into us from Josephine's piping. This piping, which rises up where everyone else is pledged to silence, comes almost like a message from the whole people to each individual; Josephine's thin piping amidst grave decisions is almost like our people's precarious existence amidst the tumult of a hostile world. Josephine exerts herself, a mere nothing in voice, a mere nothing in execution, she asserts herself and gets across to us; it does us good to think of that. A really trained singer, if ever such a one should be found among us, we could certainly not endure at such a time and we should unanimously turn away from the senselessness of any such performance. May Josephine be spared from perceiving that the mere fact of our listening to her is proof that she is no singer. An intuition of it she must have, else why does she so passionately deny that we do listen, only she keeps on singing and piping her intuition away.

But there are other things she could take comfort from: we do really listen to her in a sense, probably much as one listens to a trained singer; she gets effects which a trained singer would try in vain to achieve among us and which are only produced precisely because her means are so inadequate. For this, doubtless, our way of life is mainly responsible.

Among our people there is no age of youth, scarcely the briefest childhood. Regularly, it is true, demands are put forward that the children should be granted a special freedom, a special protection, that their right to be a little carefree, to have a little senseless giddiness, a little play, that this right should be respected and the exercise of it encouraged; such demands are put forward and nearly everyone approves them, there is nothing one could approve more, but there is also nothing, in the reality of our daily life, that is less likely to be granted, one approves these demands, one makes at-

136

tempts to meet them, but soon all the old ways are back again. Our life happens to be such that a child, as soon as it can run about a little and a little distinguish one thing from another, must look after itself just like an adult; the areas on which, for economic reasons, we have to live in dispersion are too wide, our enemies too numerous, the dangers lying everywhere in wait for us too incalculable—we cannot shelter our children from the struggle for existence; if we did so, it would bring them to an early grave. These depressing considerations are reinforced by another, which is not depressing: the fertility of our race. One generation—and each is numerous—treads on the heels of another, the children have no time to be children. Other races may foster their children carefully, schools may be erected for their little ones, out of these schools the children may come pouring daily, the future of the race, yet among them it is always the same children that come out day after day for a long time. We have no schools, but from our race come pouring at the briefest intervals the innumerable swarms of our children, merrily lisping or chirping so long as they cannot yet pipe, rolling or tumbling along by sheer impetus so long as they cannot yet run, clumsily carrying everything before them by mass weight so long as they cannot yet see, our children! And not the same children, as in those schools, no, always new children again and again, without end, without a break, hardly does a child appear than it is no more a child, while behind it new childish faces are already crowding so fast and so thick that they are indistinguishable, rosy with happiness. Truly, however delightful this may be and however much others may envy us for it, and rightly, we simply cannot give a real childhood to our children. And that has its consequences. A kind of unexpended, ineradicable childishness pervades our people; in direct opposition to what is best in us, our infallible practical common sense, we often behave with the utmost foolishness, with exactly the same foolishness as children, senselessly, wastefully, grandiosely, irresponsibly, and all that often for the sake of some trivial amusement. And although our enjoyment of it

137

cannot of course be so wholehearted as a child's enjoyment, something of this survives in it without a doubt. From this childishness of our people Josephine too has profited since the beginning.

Yet our people are not only childish, we are also in a sense prematurely old. Childhood and old age come upon us not as upon others. We have no youth, we are all at once grown-up, and then we stay grown-up too long, a certain weariness and hopelessness spreading from that leaves a broad trail through our people's nature, tough and strong in hope that it is in general. Our lack of musical gifts has surely some connection with this; we are too old for music, its excitement, its rapture do not suit our heaviness, wearily we wave it away; we content ourselves with piping, a little piping here and there, that is enough for us. Who knows, there may be talents for music among us; but if there were, the character of our people would suppress them before they could unfold. Josephine on the other hand can pipe as much as she will, or sing or whatever she likes to call it, that does not disturb us, that suits us, that we can well put up with; any music there may be in it is reduced to the least possible trace; a certain tradition of music is preserved, yet without making the slightest demand upon us.

But our people, being what they are, get still more than this from Josephine. At her concerts, especially in times of stress, it is only the very young who are interested in her singing as singing, they alone gaze in astonishment as she purses her lips, expels the air between her pretty front teeth, swoons in sheer wonderment at the sounds she herself is producing and after such a lying away swells her performance to new and more incredible heights, whereas the real mass of the people—this is plain to see—are quite withdrawn into themselves. Here in the brief intervals between their struggles our people dream, it is as if the limbs of each were loosened, as if the harried individual once in a while could relax and stretch himself at ease in the great, warm bed of the community. And into these dreams Josephine's piping drops note by note; she calls

138

it pearl-like, we call it staccato; but at any rate here it is in its right place, as nowhere else, finding the moment wait for it as music scarcely ever does. Something of our poor brief childhood is in it, something of lost happiness that can never be found again, but also something of active daily life, of its small gaieties, unaccountable and yet springing up and not to be obliterated. And indeed this is all expressed not in full round tones but softly, in whispers, confidentially, sometimes a little hoarsely. Of course it is a kind of piping. Why not? Piping is our people's daily speech, only many a one pipes his whole life long and does not know it, where here piping is set free from the fetters of daily life and it sets us free too for a little while. We certainly should not want to do without these performances.

But from that point it is a long, long way to Josephine's claim that she gives us new strength and so on and so forth. For ordinary people, at least, not for her train of flatterers. "What other explanation could there be?"—they say with quite shameless sauciness—"how else could you explain the great audiences, especially when danger is most imminent, which have even often enough hindered proper precautions being taken in time to avert danger." Now, this last statement is unfortunately true, but can hardly be counted as one of Josephine's titles to fame, especially considering that when such large gatherings have been unexpectedly flushed by the enemy and many of our people left lying for dead, Josephine, who was responsible for it all, and indeed perhaps attracted the enemy by her piping, has always occupied the safest place and was always the first to whisk away quietly and speedily under cover of her escort. Still, everyone really knows that, and yet people keep running to whatever place Josephine decides on next, at whatever time she rises up to sing. One could argue from this that Josephine stands almost beyond the law, that she can do what she pleases, at the risk of actually endangering the community, and will be forgiven for everything. If this were so, even Josephine's claims would be entirely comprehensible, yes, in this freedom to be allowed her, this extraordinary gift

139

granted to her and to no one else in direct contravention of the laws, one could see an admission of the fact that the people do not understand Josephine, just as she alleges, that they marvel helplessly at her art, feel themselves unworthy of it, try to assuage the pity she rouses in them by making really desperate sacrifices for her and, to the same extent that her art is beyond their comprehension, consider her personality and her wishes to lie beyond their jurisdiction. Well, that is simply not true at all, perhaps as individuals the people may surrender too easily to Josephine, but as a whole they surrender unconditionally to no one, and not to her either.

For a long time back, perhaps since the very beginning of her artistic career, Josephine has been fighting for exemption from all daily work on account of her singing; she should be relieved of all responsibility for earning her daily bread and being involved in the general struggle for existence, which—apparently—should be transferred on her behalf to the people as a whole. A facile enthusiast—and there have been such—might argue from the mere unusualness of this demand, from the spiritual attitude needed to frame such a demand, that it has an inner justification. But our people draw other conclusions and quietly refuse it. Nor do they trouble much about disproving the assumptions on which it is based. Josephine argues, for instance, that the strain of working is bad for her voice, that the strain of working is of course nothing to the strain of singing, but it prevents her from being able to rest sufficiently after singing and to recuperate for more singing, she has to exhaust her strength completely and yet, in these circumstances, can never rise to the peak of her abilities. The people listen to her arguments and pay no attention. Our people, so easily moved, sometimes cannot be moved at all. Their refusal is sometimes so decided that even Josephine is taken aback, she appears to submit, does her proper share of work, sings as best she can, but all only for a time, then with renewed strength—for this purpose her strength seems inexhaustible—she takes up the fight again.

Now it is clear that what Josephine really wants is not what she puts into words. She is honorable, she is not work-shy, shirking in any case is quite unknown among us; if her petition were granted she would certainly live the same life as before, her work would not at all get in the way of her singing nor would her singing grow any better—what she wants is public, unambiguous, permanent recognition of her art, going far beyond any precedent so far known. But while almost everything else seems within her reach, this eludes her persistently. Perhaps she should have taken a different line of attack from the beginning, perhaps she herself sees that her approach was wrong, but now she cannot draw back; retreat would be self-betrayal, now she must stand or fall by her petition.

If she really had enemies, as she avers, they could get much amusement from watching this struggle, without having to lift a finger. But she has no enemies, and even though she is often criticized here and there, no one finds this struggle of hers amusing. Just because of the fact that the people show themselves here in their cold, judicial aspect, which is otherwise rarely seen among us. And however one may approve it in this case, the very idea that such an aspect might be turned upon oneself some day prevents amusement from breaking in. The important thing, both in the people's refusal and in Josephine's position, is not the action itself, but the fact that the people are capable of presenting a stony, impenetrable front to one of their own, and that it is all the more impenetrable because in other respects they show an anxious paternal care, and more than paternal care, for this very member of the people.

Suppose that instead of the people one had an individual to deal with: one might imagine that this man had been giving in to Josephine all the time while nursing a wild desire to put an end to his submissiveness one fine day; that he had made superhuman sacrifices for Josephine in the firm belief that there was a natural limit to his capacity for sacrifice; yes, that he had sacrificed more than was needful merely to hasten the process, merely to spoil Josephine and encourage her to ask for more and more until she did indeed reach the limit with this last petition of hers; and that he then cut her off with a final refusal which was curt because long held in reserve. Now, this is certainly not how the matter stands, the people have no need of such guile, besides, their respect for Josephine is well tried and genuine, and Josephine's demands are after all so far-reaching that any simple child could have told her what the outcome would be; yet it may be that such considerations enter into Josephine's way of taking the matter and so add a certain bitterness to the pain of being refused.

But whatever her ideas on the subject, she does not let them deter her from pursuing the campaign. Recently she has even intensified her attack; hitherto she has used only words as her weapons but now she is beginning to have recourse to other means, which she thinks will prove more efficacious but which we think will run her into greater dangers.

Many believe that Josephine is becoming so insistent because she feels herself growing old and her voice falling off, and so she thinks it high time to wage the last battle for recognition. I do not believe it. Josephine would not be Josephine if that were true. For her there is no growing old and no falling off in her voice. If she makes demands it is not because of outward circumstances but because of an inner logic. She reaches for the highest garland not because it is momentarily hanging a little lower but because it is the highest; if she had any say in the matter she would have it still higher.

This contempt for external difficulties, to be sure, does not hinder her from using the most unworthy methods. Her rights seem beyond question to her; so what does it matter how she secures them; especially since in this world, as she sees it, honest methods are bound to fail. Perhaps that is why she has transferred the battle for her rights from the field of song to another which she cares little about. Her supporters have let it be known that, according to herself, she feels quite capable of singing in such a way that all levels of the populace, even to the remotest corners of the opposition, would find it a real delight, a real delight not by popular standards, for the people affirm that they have always delighted in her singing, but a delight by her own standards. However, she adds, since she cannot falsify the highest standards nor pander to the lowest, her singing will have to stay as it is. But when it comes to her campaign for exemption from work, we get a different story; it is of course also a campaign on behalf of her singing, yet she is not fighting directly with the priceless weapon of her song, so any instrument she uses is good enough. Thus, for instance, the rumor went round that Josephine meant to cut short her grace notes if her petition were not granted. I know nothing about grace notes, and have never noticed any in Josephine's singing. But Josephine is going to cut short her grace notes, not, for the present, to cut them out entirely, only to cut them short. Presumably she has carried out her threat, although I for one have observed no difference in her performance. The people as a whole listened in the usual way without making any pronouncement on the grace notes, nor did their response to her petition vary by a jot. It must be admitted that Josephine's way of thinking, like her figure, is often very charming. And so, for instance, after that performance, just as if her decision about the grace notes had been too severe or too sudden a move against the people, she announced that next time she would put in all the grace notes again. Yet after the next concert she changed her mind once more, there was to be definitely an end of these great arias with the grace notes, and until her petition was favorably regarded they would never recur. Well, the people let all these announcements, decisions and counterdecisions go in at one ear and out at the other, like a grown-up person deep in thought turning a deaf ear to a child's babble, fundamentally well disposed but not accessible.

Josephine, however, does not give in. The other day, for instance, she claimed that she had hurt her foot at work, so that it was difficult for her to stand up to sing; but since she could not sing except standing up, her songs would now have to be cut short. Although she limps and leans on her supporters, no one believes that she is really hurt. Granted that her frail body is extra sensitive, she is yet one of us and we are a race of workers; if we were to start limping every time we got a scratch, the whole people would never be done limping. Yet though she lets herself be led about like a cripple, though she shows herself in this pathetic condition oftener than usual, the people all the same listen to her singing thankfully and appreciatively as before, but do not bother much about the shortening of her songs.

Since she cannot very well go on limping forever, she thinks of something else, she pleads that she is tired, not in the mood for singing, feeling faint. And so we get a theatrical performance as well as a concert. We see Josephine's supporters in the background begging and imploring her to sing. She would be glad to oblige, but she cannot. They comfort and caress her with flatteries, they almost carry her to the selected spot where she is supposed to sing. At last, bursting inexplicably into tears, she gives way, but when she stands up to sing, obviously at the end of her resources, weary, her arms not widespread as usual but hanging lifelessly down, so that one gets the impression that they are perhaps a little too short—just as she is about to strike up, there, she cannot do it after all, an unwilling shake of the head tells us so and she breaks down before our eyes. To be sure, she pulls herself together again and sings, I fancy, much as usual; perhaps, if one has an ear for the finer shades of expression, one can hear that she is singing with unusual feeling, which is, however, all to the good. And in the end she is actually less tired than before, with a firm tread, if one can use such a term for her tripping gait, she moves off, refusing all help from her supporters and measuring with cold eyes the crowd which respectfully makes way for her.

That happened a day or two ago; but the latest is that she has disappeared, just at a time when she was supposed to sing. It is not only her supporters who are looking for her, many are devoting themselves to the search, but all in vain; Josephine has vanished, she will

144

not sing; she will not even be cajoled into singing, this time she has deserted us entirely.

Curious, how mistaken she is in her calculations, the clever creature, so mistaken that one might fancy she has made no calculations at all but is only being driven on by her destiny, which in our world cannot be anything but a sad one. Of her own accord she abandons her singing, of her own accord she destroys the power she has gained over people's hearts. How could she ever have gained that power, since she knows so little about these hearts of ours? She hides herself and does not sing, but our people, quietly, without visible disappointment, a self-confident mass in perfect equilibrium, so constituted, even though appearances are misleading, that they can only bestow gifts and not receive them, even from Josephine, our people continue on their way.

Josephine's road, however, must go downhill. The time will soon come when her last notes sound and die into silence. She is a small episode in the eternal history of our people, and the people will get over the loss of her. Not that it will be easy for us; how can our gatherings take place in utter silence? Still, were they not silent even when Josephine was present? Was her actual piping notably louder and more alive than the memory of it will be? Was it even in her lifetime more than a simple memory? Was it not rather because Josephine's singing was already past losing in this way that our people in their wisdom prized it so highly?

So perhaps we shall not miss so very much after all, while Josephine, redeemed from the earthly sorrows which to her thinking lay in wait for all chosen spirits, will happily lose herself in the numberless throng of the heroes of our people, and soon, since we are no historians, will rise to the heights of redemption and be forgotten like all her brothers.

A FRATRICIDE

THE EVIDENCE SHOWS that this is how the murder was committed:

Schmar, the murderer, took up his post about nine o'clock one night in clear moonlight by the corner where Wese, his victim, had to turn from the street where his office was into the street he lived in.

The night air was shivering cold. Yet Schmar was wearing only a thin blue suit; the jacket was unbuttoned, too. He felt no cold; besides, he was moving about all the time. His weapon, half a bayonet and half a kitchen knife, he kept firmly in his grasp, quite naked. He looked at the knife against the light of the moon; the blade glittered; not enough for Schmar; he struck it against the bricks of the pavement till the sparks flew; regretted that, perhaps; and to repair the damage drew it like a violin bow across his boot sole while he bent forward, standing on one leg, and listened both to the whetting of the knife on his boot and for any sound out of the fateful side street.

Why did Pallas, the private citizen who was watching it all from his window near by in the second story, permit it to happen? Unriddle the mysteries of human nature! With his collar turned up, his dressing gown girt round his portly body, he stood looking down, shaking his head.

And five houses further along, on the opposite side of the street, Mrs. Wese, with a fox-fur coat over her nightgown, peered out to look for her husband who was lingering unusually late tonight.

At last there rang out the sound of the doorbell before Wese's office, too loud for a doorbell, right over the town and up to heaven, and Wese, the industrious nightworker, issued from the building, still invisible in that street, only heralded by the sound of the bell; at once the pavement registered his quiet footsteps.

Pallas bent far forward; he dared not miss anything. Mrs. Wese, reassured by the bell, shut her window with a clatter. But Schmar knelt down; since he had no other parts of his body bare, he pressed only his face and his hands against the pavements; where everything else was freezing, Schmar was glowing hot.

At the very corner dividing the two streets Wese paused, only his walking stick came round into the other street to support him. A sudden whim. The night sky invited him, with its dark blue and its gold. Unknowing, he gazed up at it, unknowing he lifted his hat and stroked his hair; nothing up there drew together in a pattern to interpret the immediate future for him; everything stayed in its senseless, inscrutable place. In itself it was a highly reasonable action that Wese should walk on, but he walked on to Schmar's knife.

"Wese!" shrieked Schmar, standing on tiptoe, his arm outstretched, the knife sharply lowered, "Wese! You will never see Julia again!" And right into the throat and left into the throat and a third time deep into the belly stabbed Schmar's knife. Water rats, slit open, give out such a sound as came from Wese.

"Done," said Schmar, and pitched the knife, now superfluous blood-stained ballast, against the nearest house front. "The bliss of murder! The relief, the soaring ecstasy from the shedding of another's blood! Wese, old nightbird, friend, alehouse crony, you are oozing away into the dark earth below the street. Why aren't you simply a bladder of blood so that I could stamp on you and make you vanish into nothingness? Not all we want comes true, not all the dreams that blossomed have borne fruit, your solid remains lie here, already indifferent to every kick. What's the good of the dumb question you are asking?"

Pallas, choking on the poison in his body, stood at the double-leafed door of his house as it flew open. "Schmar! Schmar! I saw it all, I missed nothing." Pallas and Schmar scrutinized each other. The result of the scrutiny satisfied Pallas, Schmar came to no conclusion.

Mrs. Wese, with a crowd of people on either side, came rushing up, her face grown quite old with the shock. Her fur coat swung open, she collapsed on top of Wese, the nightgowned body belonged to Wese, the fur coat spreading over the couple like the smooth turf of a grave belonged to the crowd.

Schmar, fighting down with difficulty the last of his nausea, pressed his mouth against the shoulder of the policeman who, stepping lightly, led him away.

THE NEXT VILLAGE

MY GRANDFATHER USED to say: "Life is astoundingly short. To me, looking back over it, life seems so foreshortened that I scarcely understand, for instance, how a young man can decide to ride over to the next village without being afraid that—not to mention accidents—even the span of a normal happy life may fall far short of the time needed for such a journey."

THE BUCKET RIDER

COAL ALL SPENT; the bucket empty; the shovel useless; the stove breathing out cold; the room freezing; the leaves outside the window rigid, covered with rime; the sky a silver shield against any one who looks for help from it. I must have coal; I cannot freeze to death; behind me is the pitiless stove, before me the pitiless sky, so I must ride out between them and on my journey seek aid from the coaldealer. But he has already grown deaf to ordinary appeals; I must prove irrefutably to him that I have not a single grain of coal left, and that he means to me the very sun in the firmament. I must approach like a beggar, who, with the death rattle already in his throat, insists on dying on the doorstep, and to whom the grand people's cook accordingly decides to give the dregs of the coffeepot; just so must the coaldealer, filled with rage, but acknowledging the command, "Thou shalt not kill," fling a shovelful of coal into my bucket.

My mode of arrival must decide the matter; so I ride off on the bucket. Seated on the bucket, my hands on the handle, the simplest kind of bridle, I propel myself with difficulty down the stairs; but once down below my bucket ascends, superbly, superbly; camels humbly squatting on the ground do not rise with more dignity, shaking themselves under the sticks of their drivers. Through the hard frozen streets we go at a regular canter; often I am upraised as high as the first story of a house; never do I sink as low as the house doors. And at last I float at an extraordinary height above the vaulted cellar of the dealer, whom I see far below crouching over his table, where he is writing; he has opened the door to let out the excessive heat.

"Coaldealer!" I cry in a voice burned hollow by the frost and muffled in the cloud made by my breath, "please, coaldealer, give me a little coal. My bucket is so light that I can ride on it. Be kind. When I can I'll pay you."

The dealer puts his hand to his ear. "Do I hear rightly?" he throws the question over his shoulder to his wife. "Do I hear rightly? A customer."

"I hear nothing," says his wife, breathing in and out peacefully while she knits on, her back pleasantly warmed by the heat.

"Oh, yes, you must hear," I cry. "It's me; an old customer; faithful and true; only without means at the moment."

"Wife," says the dealer, "it's someone, it must be; my ears can't have deceived me so much as that; it must be an old, a very old customer, that can move me so deeply."

"What ails you, man?" says his wife, ceasing from her work for a moment and pressing her knitting to her bosom. "It's nobody, the street is empty, all our customers are provided for; we could close down the shop for several days and take a rest."

"But I'm sitting up here on the bucket," I cry, and unfeeling frozen tears dim my eyes, "please look up here, just once; you'll see me directly; I beg you, just a shovelful; and if you give me more it'll make me so happy that I won't know what to do. All the other customers are provided for. Oh, if I could only hear the coal clattering into the bucket!"

"I'm coming," says the coaldealer, and on his short legs he makes to climb the steps of the cellar, but his wife is already beside him, holds him back by the arm and says: "You stay here; seeing you persist in your fancies I'll go myself. Think of the bad fit of coughing you had during the night. But for a piece of business, even if it's one you've only fancied in your head,

150

you're prepared to forget your wife and child and sacrifice your lungs. I'll go."

"Then be sure to tell him all the kinds of coal we have in stock; I'll shout out the prices after you."

"Right," says his wife, climbing up to the street. Naturally she sees me at once. "Frau Coaldealer," I cry, "my humblest greetings; just one shovelful of coal; here in my bucket; I'll carry it home myself. One shovelful of the worst you have. I'll pay you in full for it, of course, but not just now, not just now." What a knell-like sound the words "not just now" have, and how bewilderingly they mingle with the evening chimes that fall from the church steeple near by!

"Well, what does he want?" shouts the dealer. "Nothing," his wife shouts back, "there's nothing here; I see nothing, I hear nothing; only six striking, and now we must shut up the shop. The cold is terrible; tomorrow we'll likely have lots to do again."

She sees nothing and hears nothing; but all the same she loosens her apron strings and waves her apron to waft me away. She succeeds, unluckily. My bucket has all the virtues of a good steed except powers of resistance, which it has not; it is too light; a woman's apron can make it fly through the air.

"You bad woman!" I shout back, while she, turning into the shop, half contemptuous, half reassured, flourishes her fist in the air. "You bad woman! I begged you for a shovelful of the worst coal and you would not give it me." And with that I ascend into the regions of the ice mountains and am lost for ever.

PROMETHEUS

THERE ARE FOUR legends concerning Prometheus:

According to the first he was clamped to a rock in the Caucasus for betraying the secrets of the gods to men, and the gods sent eagles to feed on his liver, which was perpetually renewed.

According to the second, Prometheus, goaded by the pain of the tearing beaks, pressed himself deeper and deeper into the rock until he became one with it.

According to the third his treachery was forgotten in the course of thousands of years, forgotten by the gods, the eagles, forgotten by himself.

According to the fourth everyone grew weary of the meaningless affair. The gods grew weary, the eagles grew weary, the wound closed wearily.

There remained the inexplicable mass of rock. The legend tried to explain the inexplicable. As it came out of a substratum of truth it had in turn to end in the inexplicable.

POSEIDON

POSEIDON SAT AT his desk, doing figures. The administration of all the waters gave him endless work. He could have had assistants, as many as he wanted—and he did have very many—but since he took his job very seriously, he would in the end go over all the figures and calculations himself, and thus his assistants were of little help to him. It cannot be said that he enjoyed his work; he did it only because it had been assigned to him; in fact, he had already filed many petitions for—as he put it—more cheerful work, but every time the offer of something different was made to him it would turn out that nothing suited him quite as well as his present position. And anyhow it was quite difficult to find something different for him. After all, it was impossible to assign him to a particular sea; aside from the fact that even then the work with figures would not become less but only pettier, the great Poseidon could in any case occupy only an executive position. And when a job away from the water was offered to him he would get sick at the very prospect, his divine breathing would become troubled and his brazen chest begin to tremble. Besides, his complaints were not really taken seriously; when one of the mighty is vexatious the appearance of an effort must be made to placate him, even when the case is most hopeless. In actuality a shift of posts was unthinkable for Poseidon—he had been appointed God of the Sea in the beginning, and that he had to remain.

What irritated him most—and it was this that was chiefly responsible for his dissatisfaction with his job—was to hear of the conceptions formed about him: how he was always riding about through the tides with his trident. When all the while he sat here in the depths of the world-ocean, doing figures uninterruptedly, with now and then a trip to Jupiter as the only break in the monotony—a trip, moreover, from which he usually returned in a rage. Thus he had hardly seen the sea—had seen it but fleetingly in the course of hurried ascents to Olympus, and he had never actually travelled around it. He was in the habit of saying that what he was waiting for was the fall of the world; then, probably, a quiet moment would yet be granted in which, just before the end and after having checked the last row of figures, he would be able to make a quick little tour.

Poseidon became bored with his sea. He let fall his trident. Silently he sat on the rocky coast and a gull, dazed by his presence, described wavering circles around his head.

THE PROBLEM OF
OUR LAWS

OUR LAWS ARE not generally known; they are kept secret by the small group of nobles who rule us. We are convinced that these ancient laws are scrupulously administered; nevertheless it is an extremely painful thing to be ruled by laws that one does not know. I am not thinking of possible discrepancies that may arise in the interpretation of the laws, or of the disadvantages involved when only a few and not the whole people are allowed to have a say in their interpretation. These disadvantages are perhaps of no great importance. For the laws are very ancient; their interpretation has been the work of centuries, and has itself doubtless acquired the status of law; and though there is still a possible freedom of interpretation left, it has now become very restricted. Moreover the nobles have obviously no cause to be influenced in their interpretation by personal interests inimical to us, for the laws were made to the advantage of the nobles from the very beginning, they themselves stand above the laws, and that seems to be why the laws were entrusted exclusively into their hands. Of course, there is wisdom in that—who doubts the wisdom of the ancient laws?—but also hardship for us; probably that is unavoidable.

The very existence of these laws, however, is at most a matter of presumption. There is a tradition that they exist and that they are a mystery confided to the nobility, but it is not and cannot be more than a mere tradition sanctioned by age, for the essence of a secret code is that it should remain a mystery. Some of us among the people have attentively scrutinized the doings of the nobility since the earliest times and possess records made by our forefathers—records which we have conscientiously continued—and claim to recognize amid the countless number of facts certain main tendencies which permit of this or that historical formulation; but when in accordance with these scrupulously tested and logically ordered conclusions we seek to adjust ourselves somewhat for the present or the future, everything becomes uncertain, and our work seems only an intellectual game, for perhaps these laws that we are trying to unravel do not exist at all. There is a small party who are actually of this opinion and who try to show that, if any law exists, it can only be this: The Law is whatever the nobles do. This party see everywhere only the arbitrary acts of the nobility, and reject the popular tradition, which according to them possesses only certain trifling and incidental advantages that do not offset its heavy drawbacks, for it gives the people a false, deceptive and over-confident security in confronting coming events. This cannot be gainsaid, but the overwhelming majority of our people account for it by the fact that the tradition is far from complete and must be more fully inquired into, that the material available, prodigious as it looks, is still too meager, and that several centuries will have to pass before it becomes really adequate. This view, so comfortless as far as the present is concerned, is lightened only by the belief that a time will eventually come when the tradition and our research into it will jointly reach their conclusion, and as it were gain a breathing space, when everything will have become clear, the law will belong to the people, and the nobility will vanish. This is not maintained in any spirit of hatred against the nobility; not at all, and by no one. We are more inclined to hate ourselves, because we have not yet shown ourselves worthy of being entrusted with the laws. And that is the real reason why the party who believe that there is no law have remained so few—although their doctrine is in certain ways so attractive, for it unequivocally recognizes the nobility and its right to go on existing.

Actually one can express the problem only in a sort of paradox: Any party which would repudiate, not only all belief in the laws, but the nobility as well, would have the whole people behind it; yet no such party can come into existence, for nobody would dare to repudiate the nobility. We live on this razor's edge. A writer once summed the matter up in this way: The sole visible and indubitable law that is imposed upon us is the nobility, and must we ourselves deprive ourselves of that one law?

A LITTLE FABLE

"ALAS," SAID THE mouse, "the whole world is growing smaller every day. At the beginning it was so big that I was afraid, I kept running and running, and I was glad when at last I saw walls far away to the right and left, but these long walls have narrowed so quickly that I am in the last chamber already, and there in the corner stands the trap that I must run into." "You only need to change your direction," said the cat, and ate it up.

GIVE IT UP!

IT WAS VERY early in the morning, the streets clean and deserted, I was on my way to the station. As I compared the tower clock with my watch I realized it was much later than I had thought and that I had to hurry; the shock of this discovery made me feel uncertain of the way, I wasn't very well acquainted with the town as yet; fortunately, there was a policeman at hand, I ran to him and breathlessly asked him the way. He smiled and said: "You asking me the way?" "Yes," I said, "since I can't find it myself." "Give it up! Give it up!" said he, and turned with a sudden jerk, like someone who wants to be alone with his laughter.

Translated by Tania and James Stern

ON PARABLES

MANY COMPLAIN THAT the words of the wise are always merely parables and of no use in daily life, which is the only life we have. When the sage says: "Go over," he does not mean that we should cross to some actual place, which we could do anyhow if the labor were worth it; he means some fabulous yonder, something unknown to us, something that he cannot designate more precisely either, and therefore cannot help us here in the very least. All these parables really set out to say merely that the incomprehensible is incomprehensible, and we know that already. But the cares we have to struggle with every day: that is a different matter.

Concerning this a man once said: Why such reluctance? If you only followed the parables you yourselves would become parables and with that rid of all your daily cares.

Another said: I bet that is also a parable.

The first said: You have won.

The second said: But unfortunately only in parable.

The first said: No, in reality: in parable you have lost.

Translated by Willa and Edwin Muir

158

AN IMPERIAL MESSAGE

THE EMPEROR, so it runs, has sent a message to you, the humble subject, the insignificant shadow cowering in the remotest distance before the imperial sun; the Emperor from his deathbed has sent a message to you alone. He has commanded the messenger to kneel down by the bed, and has whispered the message to him; so much store did he lay on it that he ordered the messenger to whisper it back into his ear again. Then by a nod of the head he has confirmed that it is right. Yes, before the assembled spectators of his death——all the obstructing walls have been broken down, and on the spacious and loftily-mounting open staircases stand in a ring the great princes of the Empire——before all these he has delivered his message. The messenger immediately sets out on his journey; a powerful, an indefatigable man; now pushing with his right arm, now with his left, he cleaves a way for himself through the throng; if he encounters resistance he points to his breast, where the symbol of the sun glitters; the way, too, is made easier for him than it would be for any other man. But the multitudes are so vast; their numbers have no end. If he could reach the open fields how fast he would fly, and soon doubtless you would hear the welcome hammering of his fists on your door. But instead how vainly does he wear out his strength; still he is only making his way through the chambers of the innermost palace; never will he get to the end of them; and if he succeeded in that nothing would be gained;

he must fight his way next down the stair; and if he
succeeded in that nothing would be gained; the courts
would still have to be crossed; and after the courts the
second outer palace; and once more stairs and courts;
and once more another palace; and so on for thousands
of years; and if at last he should burst through the outermost gate—but never, never can that happen—the
imperial capital would lie before him, the center of the
world, crammed to bursting with its own sediment. Nobody could fight his way through here, least of all one
with a message from a dead man.—But you sit at your
window when evening falls and dream it to yourself.

A COUNTRY DOCTOR

I WAS IN great perplexity; I had to start on an urgent
journey; a seriously ill patient was waiting for me in a
village ten miles off; a thick blizzard of snow filled all
the wide spaces between him and me; I had a gig, a light
gig with big wheels, exactly right for our country roads;
muffled in furs, my bag of instruments in my hand, I was
in the courtyard all ready for the journey; but there
was no horse to be had, no horse. My own horse had
died in the night, worn out by the fatigues of this icy
winter; my servant girl was now running around the
village trying to borrow a horse; but it was hopeless, I
knew it, and I stood there forlornly, with the snow gathering more and more thickly upon me, more and more
unable to move. In the gateway the girl appeared, alone,
and waved the lantern; of course, who would lend a
horse at this time for such a journey? I strode through

the courtyard once more; I could see no way out; in my
confused distress I kicked at the dilapidated door of
the yearlong uninhabited pigsty. It flew open and
flapped to and fro on its hinges. A steam and smell as
of horses came out from it. A dim stable lantern was
swinging inside from a rope. A man, crouching on his
hams in that low space, showed an open blue-eyed
face. "Shall I yoke up?" he asked, crawling out on all
fours. I did not know what to say and merely stooped
down to see what else was in the sty. The servant girl
was standing beside me. "You never know what you're
going to find in your own house," she said, and we both
laughed. "Hey there, Brother, hey there, Sister!" called
the groom, and two horses, enormous creatures with
powerful flanks, one after the other, their legs tucked
close to their bodies, each well-shaped head lowered like
a camel's, by sheer strength of buttocking squeezed out
through the door hole which they filled entirely. But at
once they were standing up, their legs long and their
bodies steaming thickly. "Give him a hand," I said, and
the willing girl hurried to help the groom with the har-
nessing. Yet hardly was she beside him when the groom
clipped hold of her and pushed his face against hers.
She screamed and fled back to me; on her cheek stood
out in red the marks of two rows of teeth. "You brute,"
I yelled in fury, "do you want a whipping?" but in the
same moment reflected that the man was a stranger;
that I did not know where he came from, and that of his
own free will he was helping me out when everyone else
had failed me. As if he knew my thoughts he took no
offense at my threat but, still busied with the horses,
only turned around once toward me. "Get in," he said
then, and indeed, everything was ready. A magnificent
pair of horses, I observed, such as I had never sat behind, and I climbed in happily. "But I'll drive, you don't
know the way," I said. "Of course," said he, "I'm
not coming with you anyway, I'm staying with Rose."
"No," shrieked Rose, fleeing into the house with a
justified presentiment that her fate was inescapable; I
heard the door chain rattle as she put it up; I heard
the key turn in the lock; I could see, moreover, how she

put out the lights in the entrance hall and in further flight all through the rooms to keep herself from being discovered. "You're coming with me," I said to the groom, "or I won't go, urgent as my journey is. I'm not thinking of paying for it by handing the girl over to you." "Gee up!" he said; clapped his hands; the gig whirled off like a log in a freshet; I could just hear the door of my house splitting and bursting as the groom charged at it and then I was deafened and blinded by a storming rush that steadily buffeted all my senses. But this only for a moment, since, as if my patient's farmyard had opened out just before my courtyard gate, I was already there; the horses had come quietly to a standstill; the blizzard had stopped; moonlight all around; my patient's parents hurried out of the house, his sister behind them; I was almost lifted out of the gig; from their confused ejaculations I gathered not a word; in the sickroom the air was almost unbreathable; the neglected stove was smoking; I wanted to push open a window; but first I had to look at my patient. Gaunt, without any fever, not cold, not warm, with vacant eyes, without a shirt, the youngster heaved himself up from under the feather bedding, threw his arms around my neck, and whispered in my ear: "Doctor, let me die." I glanced around the room; no one had heard it; the parents were leaning forward in silence waiting for my verdict; the sister had set a chair for my handbag; I opened the bag and hunted among my instruments; the boy kept clutching at me from his bed to remind me of his entreaty; I picked up a pair of tweezers, examined them in the candlelight, and laid them down again. "Yes," I thought blasphemously, "in cases like this the gods are helpful, send the missing horse, add to it a second because of the urgency, and to crown everything bestow even a groom——" And only now did I remember Rose again; what was I to do, how could I rescue her, how could I pull her away from under that groom at ten miles' distance, with a team of horses I couldn't control. These horses, now, they had somehow slipped the reins loose, pushed the windows open from outside, I did not know how; each of them had stuck a head in at a window and, quite unmoved by the startled cries of the family, stood eyeing the patient. "Better go back at once," I thought, as if the horses were summoning me to the return journey, yet I permitted the patient's sister, who fancied that I was dazed by the heat, to take my fur coat from me. A glass of rum was poured out for me, the old man clapped me on the shoulder, a familiarity justified by this offer of his treasure. I shook my head; in the narrow confines of the old man's thoughts I felt ill; that was my only reason for refusing the drink. The mother stood by the bedside and cajoled me toward it; I yielded, and, while one of the horses whinnied loudly to the ceiling, laid my head to the boy's breast, which shivered under my wet beard. I confirmed what I already knew; the boy was quite sound, something a little wrong with his circulation, saturated with coffee by his solicitous mother, but sound and best turned out of bed with one shove. I am no world reformer and so I let him lie. I was the district doctor and did my duty to the uttermost, to the point where it became almost too much. I was badly paid and yet generous and helpful to the poor. I had still to see that Rose was all right, and then the boy might have his way and I wanted to die too. What was I doing there in that endless winter! My horse was dead, and not a single person in the village would lend me another. I had to get my team out of the pigsty; if they hadn't chanced to be horses I should have had to travel with swine. That was how it was. And I nodded to the family. They knew nothing about it, and, had they known, would not have believed it. To write prescriptions is easy, but to come to an understanding with people is hard. Well, this should be the end of my visit, I had once more been called out needlessly, I was used to that, the whole district made my life a torment with my night bell, but that I should have to sacrifice Rose this time as well, the pretty girl who had lived in my house for years almost without my noticing her—that sacrifice was too much to ask, and I had somehow to get it reasoned out in my head with the help of what craft I could muster, in order not to let fly at this family, which with the best will in the world could not restore Rose to me. But as I shut my bag and put an arm out for my fur coat, the family meanwhile standing together, the father sniffing at the glass of rum in his hand, the mother, apparently disappointed in me—why, what do people expect?—biting her lips with tears in her eyes, the sister fluttering a blood-soaked towel, I was somehow ready to admit conditionally that the boy might be ill after all. I went toward him, he welcomed me smiling as if I were bringing him the most nourishing invalid broth—ah, now both horses were whinnying together; the noise, I suppose, was ordained by heaven to assist my examination of the patient—and this time I discovered that the boy was indeed ill. In his right side, near the hip, was an open wound as big as the palm of my hand. Rose-red, in many variations of shade, dark in the hollows, lighter at the edges, softly granulated, with irregular clots of blood, open as a surface mine to the daylight. That was how it looked from a distance. But on a closer inspection there was another complication. I could not help a low whistle of surprise. Worms, as thick and as long as my little finger, themselves rose-red and blood-spotted as well, were wriggling from their fastness in the interior of the wound toward the light, with small white heads and many little legs. Poor boy, you were past helping. I had discovered your great wound; this blossom in your side was destroying you. The family was pleased; they saw me busying myself; the sister told the mother, the mother the father, the father told several guests who were coming in, through the moonlight at the open door, walking on tiptoe, keeping their balance with outstretched arms. "Will you save me?" whispered the boy with a sob, quite blinded by the life within his wound. That is what people are like in my district. Always expecting the impossible from the doctor. They have lost their ancient beliefs; the parson sits at home and unravels his vestments, one after another; but the doctor is supposed to be omnipotent with his merciful surgeon's hand. Well, as it pleases them; I have not thrust my services on them; if they misuse me for sacred ends, I let that happen to me too; what better

164

do I want, old country doctor that I am, bereft of my servant girl! And so they came, the family and the village elders, and stripped my clothes off me; a school choir with the teacher at the head of it stood before the house and sang these words to an utterly simple tune:

> Strip his clothes off, then he'll heal us,
> If he doesn't, kill him dead!
> Only a doctor, only a doctor.

Then my clothes were off and I looked at the people quietly, my fingers in my beard and my head cocked to one side. I was altogether composed and equal to the situation and remained so, athough it was no help to me, since they now took me by the head and feet and carried me to the bed. They laid me down in it next to the wall, on the side of the wound. Then they all left the room; the door was shut; the singing stopped; clouds covered the moon; the bedding was warm around me; the horses' heads in the open windows wavered like shadows. "Do you know," said a voice in my ear, "I have very little confidence in you. Why, you were only blown in here, you didn't come on your own feet. Instead of helping me, you're cramping me on my death-bed. What I'd like best is to scratch your eyes out." "Right," I said, "it is a shame. And yet I am a doctor. What am I to do? Believe me, it is not too easy for me either." "Am I supposed to be content with this apology? Oh, I must be, I can't help it. I always have to put up with things. A fine wound is all I brought into the world; that was my sole endowment." "My young friend," said I, "your mistake is: you have not a wide enough view. I have been in all the sickrooms, far and wide, and I tell you, your wound is not so bad. Done in a tight corner with two strokes of the ax. Many a one proffers his side and can hardly hear the ax in the forest, far less that it is coming nearer to him." "Is that really so, or are you deluding me in my fever?" "It is really so, take the word of honor of an official doctor." And he took it and lay still. But now it was time for me to think of escaping. The horses were still standing faithfully in their places. My clothes, my fur coat, my bag were quickly collected; I didn't want to waste time dressing; if the horses raced home as they had come, I should only be springing, as it were, out of this bed into my own. Obediently a horse backed away from the window; I threw my bundle into the gig; the fur coat missed its mark and was caught on a hook only by the sleeve. Good enough. I swung myself onto the horse. With the reins loosely trailing, one horse barely fastened to the other, the gig swaying behind, my fur coat last of all in the snow. "Gee up!" I said, but there was no galloping; slowly, like old men, we crawled through the snowy wastes; a long time echoed behind us the new but faulty song of the children:

> O be joyful, all you patients,
> The doctor's laid in bed beside you!

Never shall I reach home at this rate; my flourishing practice is done for; my successor is robbing me, but in vain, for he cannot take my place; in my house the disgusting groom is raging; Rose is his victim; I do not want to think about it anymore. Naked, exposed to the frost of this most unhappy of ages, with an earthly vehicle, unearthly horses, old man that I am, I wander astray. My fur coat is hanging from the back of the gig, but I cannot reach it, and none of my limber pack of patients lifts a finger. Betrayed! Betrayed! A false alarm on the night bell once answered—it cannot be made good, not ever.

Translated by Willa and Edwin Muir

THE GREAT WALL AND
THE TOWER OF BABEL

FIRST, THEN, IT must be said that in those days things were achieved scarcely inferior to the construction of the Tower of Babel, although as regards divine approval, at least according to human reckoning, strongly at variance with that work. I say this because during the early days of building a scholar wrote a book in which he drew the comparison in the most exhaustive way. In it he tried to prove that the Tower of Babel failed to reach its goal, not because of the reasons universally advanced, or at least that among those recognised reasons the most important of all was not to be found. His proofs were drawn not merely from written documents and reports; he also claimed to have made enquiries on the spot, and to have discovered that the tower failed and was bound to fail because of the weakness of the foundation. In this respect at any rate our age was vastly superior to that ancient one. Almost every educated man of our time was a mason by profession and infallible in the matter of laying foundations. That, however, was not what our scholar was concerned to prove; for he maintained that the Great Wall alone would provide for the first time in the history of mankind a secure foundation for a new Tower of Babel. First the wall, therefore, and then the tower. His book was in everybody's hands at that time, but I admit that even today

I cannot quite make out how he conceived this tower. How could the wall, which did not form even a circle, but only a sort of quarter- or half-circle, provide the foundation for a tower? That could obviously be meant only in a spiritual sense. But in that case why build the actual wall, which after all was something concrete, the result of the lifelong labor of multitudes of people? And why were there in the book plans, somewhat nebulous plans, it must be admitted, of the tower, and proposals worked out in detail for mobilizing the people's energies for the stupendous new work?

There were many wild ideas in people's heads at that time—this scholar's book is only one example—perhaps simply because so many were trying to join forces as far as they could for the achievement of a single aim. Human nature, essentially changeable, unstable as the dust, can endure no restraint; if it binds itself it soon begins to tear madly at its bonds, until it rends everything asunder, the wall, the bonds and its very self.

PARADISE

THE EXPULSION FROM Paradise is in its main significance eternal: Consequently the expulsion from Paradise is final, and life in this world irrevocable, but the eternal nature of the occurrence (or, temporally expressed, the eternal recapitulation of the occurrence) makes it nevertheless possible that not only could we live continuously in Paradise, but that we are continuously there in actual fact, no matter whether we know it here or not.

Why do we lament over the fall of man? We were not driven out of Paradise because of it, but because of the Tree of Life, that we might not eat of it.

We are sinful not merely because we have eaten of the Tree of Knowledge, but also because we have not yet eaten of the Tree of Life. The state in which we find ourselves is sinful, quite independent of guilt.

We were fashioned to live in Paradise, and Paradise was destined to serve us. Our destiny has been altered; that this has also happened with the destiny of Paradise is not stated.

We were expelled from Paradise, but Paradise was not destroyed. In a sense our expulsion from Paradise was a stroke of luck, for had we not been expelled, Paradise would have had to be destroyed.

God said that Adam would have to die on the day he ate of the Tree of Knowledge. According to God, the instantaneous result of eating of the Tree of Knowledge would be death; according to the serpent (at least it can be understood so), it would be equality with God. Both were wrong in similar ways. Men did not die, but became mortal; they did not become like God, but received the indispensable capacity to become so. Both were right in similar ways. Man did not die, but the paradisiacal man did; men did not become God, but divine knowledge.

He is a free and secure citizen of the world, for he is fettered to a chain which is long enough to give him the freedom of all earthly space, and yet only so long that nothing can drag him past the frontiers of the world. But simultaneously he is a free and secure citizen of Heaven as well, for he is also fettered by a similarly designed heavenly chain. So that if he heads, say, for the earth, his heavenly collar throttles him, and if he heads for Heaven, his earthly one does the same. And yet all the possibilities are his, and he feels it; more, he actually refuses to account for the deadlock by an error in the original fettering.

Since the Fall we have been essentially equal in our capacity to recognize good and evil; nonetheless it is just here that we seek to show our individual superiority. But the real differences begin beyond that knowledge. The opposite illusion may be explained thus: nobody can remain content with the mere knowledge of good and evil in itself, but must endeavor as well to act in accordance with it. The strength to do so, however, is not likewise given him, consequently he must destroy himself trying to do so, at the risk of not achieving the necessary strength even then; yet there remains nothing for him but this final attempt. (That is moreover the meaning of the threat of death attached to eating of the Tree of Knowledge; perhaps too it was the original meaning of natural death.) Now, faced with this attempt, man is filled with fear; he prefers to annul his knowledge of good and evil (the term, "the fall of man," may be traced back to that fear); yet the accomplished cannot be annulled, but only confused. It was for this purpose that our rationalizations were created. The whole world is full of them, indeed the whole visible world is perhaps nothing more than the rationalization of a man who wants to find peace for a moment. An attempt to falsify the actuality of knowledge, to regard knowledge as a goal still to be reached.

THE TOWER OF BABEL

IF IT HAD been possible to build the Tower of Babel without ascending it, the work would have been permitted.

THE PIT OF BABEL

WHAT ARE YOU building?—I want to dig a subterranean passage. Some progress must be made. My station up there is much too high.

We are digging the pit of Babel.

171

ABRAHAM

ABRAHAM'S SPIRITUAL POVERTY and the inertia of this poverty are an asset, they make concentration easier for him, or, even more, they are concentration already—by this, however, he loses the advantage that lies in applying the powers of concentration.

Abraham falls victim to the following illusion: he cannot stand the uniformity of this world. Now the world is known, however, to be uncommonly various, which can be verified at any time by taking a handful of world and looking at it closely. Thus this complaint at the uniformity of the world is really a complaint at not having been mixed profoundly enough with the diversity of the world.

I could conceive of another Abraham for myself—he certainly would have never gotten to be a patriarch or even an old-clothes dealer—who was prepared to satisfy the demand for a sacrifice immediately, with the promptness of a waiter, but was unable to bring it off because he could not get away, being indispensable; the household needed him, there was perpetually something or other to put in order, the house was never ready; for without having his house ready, without having something to fall back on, he could not leave—this the Bible also realized, for it says: "He set his house in order." And, in fact, Abraham possessed everything in plenty to start with; if he had not had a house, where would he have raised his son, and in which rafter would he have stuck the sacrificial knife?

This Abraham—but it's all an old story not worth discussing any longer. Especially not the real Abraham; he had everything to start with, was brought up to it from childhood—I can't see the leap. If he already had everything, and yet was to be raised still higher, then something had to be taken away from him, at least in appearance: this would be logical and no leap. It was different for the other Abrahams, who stood in the houses they were building and suddenly had to go up on Mount Moriah; it is possible that they did not even have a son, yet already had to sacrifice him. These are impossibilities, and Sarah was right to laugh. Thus only the suspicion remains that it was by intention that these men did not ready their houses, and—to select a very great example—hid their faces in magic trilogies in order not to have to lift them and see the mountain standing in the distance.

But take another Abraham. One who wanted to perform the sacrifice altogether in the right way and had a correct sense in general of the whole affair, but could not believe that he was the one meant, he, an ugly old man, and the dirty youngster that was his child. True faith is not lacking to him, he has this faith; he would make the sacrifice in the right spirit if only he could believe he was the one meant. He is afraid that after starting out as Abraham with his son he would change on the way into Don Quixote. The world would have been enraged at Abraham could it have beheld him at the time, but this one is afraid that the world would laugh itself to death at the sight of him. However, it is not the ridiculousness as such that he is afraid of—though he is, of course, afraid of that too and, above all, of his joining in the laughter—but in the main he is afraid that this ridiculousness will make him even older and uglier, his son even dirtier, even more unworthy of being really called. An Abraham who should come unsummoned! It is as if, at the end of the year, when the best student was solemnly about to receive a prize, the worst student rose in the expectant stillness

173

and came forward from his dirty desk in the last row because he had made a mistake of hearing, and the whole class burst out laughing. And perhaps he had made no mistake at all, his name really was called, it having been the teacher's intention to make the rewarding of the best student at the same time a punishment for the worst one.

MOUNT SINAI

MANY PEOPLE PROWL round Mount Sinai. Their speech is blurred, either they are garrulous or they shout or they are taciturn. But none of them comes straight down a broad, newly made, smooth road that does its own part in making one's strides long and swifter.

BEFORE THE LAW

"BEFORE THE LAW stands a doorkeeper on guard. To this doorkeeper there comes a man from the country who begs for admittance to the Law. But the doorkeeper says that he cannot admit the man at the moment. The man, on reflection, asks if he will be allowed, then, to enter later. 'It is possible,' answers the doorkeeper, 'but not at this moment.' Since the door leading into the Law stands open as usual and the doorkeeper steps to one side, the man bends down to peer through the entrance. When the doorkeeper sees that, he laughs and says: 'If you are so strongly tempted, try to get in without my permission. But note that I am powerful. And I am only the lowest doorkeeper. From hall to hall keepers stand at every door, one more powerful than the other. Even the third of these has an aspect that even I cannot bear to look at.' These are difficulties which the man from the country has not expected to meet, the Law, he thinks, should be accessible to every man and at all times, but when he looks more closely at the doorkeeper in his furred robe, with his huge pointed nose and long, thin, Tartar beard, he decides that he had better wait until he gets permission to enter. The doorkeeper gives him a stool and lets him sit down at the side of the door. There he sits waiting for days and years. He makes many attempts to be allowed in and wearies the doorkeeper with his importunity. The doorkeeper often engages him in brief conversation, asking him about his home and about other matters, but the questions are put quite impersonally, as great men put questions, and always conclude with the statement that the man cannot be allowed to enter yet. The man, who has equipped himself with many things for his journey, parts with all he has, however valuable, in the hope of bribing the doorkeeper. The doorkeeper accepts it all, saying, however, as he takes each gift: 'I take this only to keep you from feeling that you have left something undone.' During all these long years the man watches the doorkeeper almost incessantly. He forgets about the other doorkeepers, and this one seems to him the only barrier between himself and the Law. In the first years he curses his evil fate aloud; later, as he grows old, he only mutters to himself. He grows childish, and since in his prolonged watch he has learned to know even the fleas in the doorkeeper's fur collar, he begs the very fleas to help him and to persuade the doorkeeper to change his mind. Finally his eyes grow dim and he does not know whether the world is really darkening around him or whether his eyes are only deceiving him. But in the darkness he can now perceive a radiance that streams immortally from the door of the Law. Now his life is drawing to a close. Before he dies, all that he has experienced during the whole time of his sojourn condenses in his mind into one question, which he has never yet put to the doorkeeper. He beckons the doorkeeper, since he can no longer raise his stiffening body. The doorkeeper has to bend far down to hear him, for the difference in size between them has increased very much to the man's disadvantage. 'What do you want to know now?' asks the doorkeeper, 'you are insatiable.' 'Everyone strives to attain the Law,' answers the man, 'how does it come about, then, that in all these years no one has come seeking admittance but me?' The doorkeeper perceives that the man is at the end of his strength and that his hearing is failing, so he bellows in his ear: 'No one but you could gain admittance through this door, since this door was intended only for you. I am now going to shut it.'"

"So the doorkeeper deluded the man," said K. immediately, strongly attracted by the story.

"Don't be too hasty," said the priest, "don't take over an opinion without testing it. I have told you the story in the very words of the scriptures. There's no mention of delusion in it."

"But it's clear enough," said K., "and your first interpretation of it was quite right. The doorkeeper gave the message of salvation to the man only when it could no longer help him."

"He was not asked the question any earlier," said the priest, "and you must consider, too, that he was only a doorkeeper, and as such he fulfilled his duty."

"What makes you think he fulfilled his duty?" asked K. "He didn't fulfill it. His duty might have been to keep all strangers away, but this man, for whom the door was intended, should have been let in."

"You have not enough respect for the written word and you are altering the story," said the priest. "The story contains two important statements made by the doorkeeper about admission to the Law, one at the beginning, the other at the end. The first statement is: that he cannot admit the man at the moment, and the other is: that this door was intended only for the man. But there is no contradiction. The first statement, on the contrary, even implies the second. One could almost say that in suggesting to the man the possibility of future admittance the doorkeeper is exceeding his duty. At that moment his apparent duty is only to refuse admittance, and indeed many commentators are surprised that the suggestion should be made at all, since the doorkeeper appears to be a precisian with a stern regard for duty. He does not once leave his post during these many years, and he does not shut the door until the very last minute; he is conscious of the importance of his office, for he says: 'I am powerful'; he is respectful to his superiors, for he says: 'I am only the lowest doorkeeper'; he is not garrulous, for during all these years he puts only what are called 'impersonal questions'; he is not to be bribed, for he says in accepting a gift: 'I take this only to keep you from feeling that you have left something undone'; where his duty is concerned he is to be moved neither by pity nor rage, for we are told that the man 'wearied the doorkeeper with his importunity'; and finally even his external appearance hints at a pedantic character, the large, pointed nose and the long, thin, black Tartar beard. Could one imagine a more faithful doorkeeper? Yet the doorkeeper has other elements in his character which are likely to advantage anyone seeking admittance and which make it comprehensible enough that he should somewhat exceed his duty in suggesting the possibility of future admittance. For it cannot be denied that he is a little simple-minded and consequently a little conceited. Take the statements he makes about his power and the power of the other doorkeepers and their dreadful aspect which even he cannot bear to see—I hold that these statements may be true enough, but that the way in which he brings them out shows that his perceptions are confused by simpleness of mind and conceit. The commentators note in

177

this connection: 'The right perception of any matter and a misunderstanding of the same matter do not wholly exclude each other.' One must at any rate assume that such simpleness and conceit, however sparingly indicated, are likely to weaken his defense of the door; they are breaches in the character of the doorkeeper. To this must be added the fact that the doorkeeper seems to be a friendly creature by nature, he is by no means always on his official dignity. In the very first moments he allows himself the jest of inviting the man to enter in spite of the strictly maintained veto against entry; then he does not, for instance, send the man away, but gives him, as we are told, a stool and lets him sit down beside the door. The patience with which he endures the man's appeals during so many years, the brief conversations, the acceptance of the gifts, the politeness with which he allows the man to curse loudly in his presence the fate for which he himself is responsible—all this lets us deduce certain motions of sympathy. Not every doorkeeper would have acted thus. And finally, in answer to a gesture of the man's he stoops low down to give him the chance of putting a last question. Nothing but mild impatience—the doorkeeper knows that this is the end of it all—is discernible in the words: 'You are insatiable.' Some push this mode of interpretation even further and hold that these words express a kind of friendly admiration, though not without a hint of condescension. At any rate the figure of the doorkeeper can be said to come out very differently from what you fancied."

"You have studied the story more exactly and for a longer time than I have," said K. They were both silent for a little while. Then K. said: "So you think the man was not deluded?"

"Don't misunderstand me," said the priest, "I am only showing you the various opinions concerning that point. You must not pay too much attention to them. The scriptures are unalterable and the comments often enough merely express the commentator's bewilderment. In this case there even exists an interpretation

178

which claims that the deluded person is really the door-keeper."

"That's a far-fetched interpretation," said K. "On what is it based?"

"It is based," answered the priest, "on the simple-mindedness of the doorkeeper. The argument is that he does not know the Law from inside, but he knows only the way that leads to it, where he patrols up and down. His ideas of the interior are assumed to be child-ish, and it is supposed that he himself is afraid of the other guardians whom he holds up as bogies before the man. Indeed, he fears them more than the man does, since the man is determined to enter after hearing about the dreadful guardians of the interior, while the door-keeper has no desire to enter, at least not so far as we are told. Others again say that he must have been in the interior already, since he is after all engaged in the ser-vice of the Law and can only have been appointed from inside. This is countered by arguing that he may have been appointed by a voice calling from the interior, and that anyhow he cannot have been far inside, since the aspect of the third doorkeeper is more than he can en-dure. Moreover, no indication is given that all these years he ever made any remarks showing a knowledge of the interior except for the one remark about the door-keepers. He may have been forbidden to do so, but there is no mention of that either. On these grounds the conclusion is reached that he knows nothing about the aspect and significance of the interior, so that he is in a state of delusion. But he is deceived also about his relation to the man from the country, for he is subject to the man and does not know it. He treats the man instead as his own subordinate, as can be recognized from many details that must still be fresh in your mind. But, according to this view of the story, it is just as clearly indicated that he is really subordinated to the man. In the first place, a bondman is always subject to a free man. Now the man from the country is really free, he can go where he likes, it is only the Law that is closed to him, and access to the Law is forbidden him only by one individual, the doorkeeper. When he sits down on the stool by the side of the door and stays there for the rest of his life, he does it of his own free will; in the story there is no mention of any compulsion. But the doorkeeper is bound to his post by his very office, he does not dare strike out into the country, nor apparently may he go into the interior of the Law, even should he wish to. Besides, although he is in the service of the Law, his service is confined to this one entrance; that is to say, he serves only this man for whom alone the entrance is intended. On that ground too he is subject to the man. One must assume that for many years, for as long as it takes a man to grow up to the prime of life, his service was in a sense empty formality, since he had to wait for a man to come, that is to say, someone in the prime of life, and so had to wait a long time before the purpose of his service could be fulfilled, and, moreover, had to wait on the man's pleasure, for the man came of his own free will. But the termination of his service also depends on the man's term of life, so that to the very end he is subject to the man. And it is emphasized throughout that the doorkeeper apparently realizes nothing of all this. That is not in itself remarkable, since according to this interpretation the doorkeeper is deceived in a much more important issue, affecting his very office. At the end, for example, he says regarding the entrance to the Law: 'I am now going to shut it,' but at the beginning of the story we are told that the door leading into the Law stands always open, and if it stands open always, that is to say, at all times, without reference to the life or death of the man, then the doorkeeper is incapable of closing it. There is some difference of opinions about the motive behind the doorkeeper's statement, whether he said he was going to close the door merely for the sake of giving an answer, or to emphasize his devotion to duty, or to bring the man into a state of grief and regret in his last moments. But there is no lack of agreement that the doorkeeper will not be able to shut the door. Many indeed profess to find that he is subordinate to the man even in wisdom, towards the end, at least, for the man sees the radiance that issues from the door of the Law while the doorkeeper in his official position must stand with his back to the door, nor does he say anything to show that he has perceived the change."

"That is well argued," said K., after repeating to himself in a low voice several passages from the priest's exposition. "It is well argued, and I am inclined to agree that the doorkeeper is deluded. But that has not made me abandon my former opinion, since both conclusions are to some extent compatible. Whether the doorkeeper is clear-sighted or deluded does not dispose of the matter. I said the man is deluded. If the doorkeeper is clear-sighted, one might have doubts about that, but if the doorkeeper himself is deluded, then his delusion must of necessity be communicated to the man. That makes the doorkeper not, indeed, a swindler, but a creature so simple-minded that he ought to be dismissed at once from his office. You mustn't forget that the doorkeeper's delusions do himself no harm but do infinite harm to the man."

"There are objections to that," said the priest. "Many aver that the story confers no right on anyone to pass judgment on the doorkeeper. Whatever he may seem to us, he is yet a servant of the Law; that is, he belongs to the Law and as such is set beyond human judgment. In that case one dare not believe that the doorkeeper is subordinate to the man. Bound as he is by his service, even at the door of the Law, he is incomparably freer than anyone at large in the world. The man is only seeking the Law, the doorkeeper is already attached to it. It is the Law that has placed him at his post; to doubt his integrity is to doubt the Law itself."

"I don't agree with that point of view," said K. shaking his head, "for if one accepts it, one must accept as true everything the doorkeeper says. But you yourself have sufficiently proved how impossible it is to do that."

"No," said the priest, "it is not necessary to accept everything as true, one must only accept it as necessary."

"A melancholy conclusion," said K. "It turns lying into a universal principle."

181

THE COMING OF
THE MESSIAH

THE MESSIAH WILL come as soon as the most unbridled individualism of faith becomes possible—when there is no one to destroy this possibility and no one to suffer its destruction; hence the graves will open themselves. This, perhaps, is Christian doctrine too, applying as much to the actual presentation of the example to be emulated, which is an individualistic example, as to the symbolic presentation of the resurrection of the Mediator in the single individual.

The Messiah will come only when he is no longer necessary; he will come only on the day after his arrival; he will come, not on the last day, but on the very last.

THE EMPEROR

A MAN DOUBTED that the emperor was descended
from the gods; he asserted that the emperor was our
rightful sovereign, he did not doubt the emperor's
divine mission (that was evident to him), it was only
the divine descent that he doubted. This, naturally, did
not cause much of a stir; when the surf flings a drop
of water on to the land, that does not interfere with
the eternal rolling of the sea, on the contrary, it is
caused by it.

THE CELL

---

"How DID I get here?" I exclaimed. It was a moderately large hall, lit by soft electric light, and I
was walking along close to the walls. Although there
were several doors, if one opened them one only
found oneself standing in front of a dark, smooth
rock-face, scarcely a handbreadth beyond the threshold

183

and extending vertically upwards and horizontally on both sides, seemingly without any end. Here was no way out. Only one door led into an adjoining room, the prospect there was more hopeful, but no less startling than that behind the other doors. One looked into a royal apartment, the prevailing colors were red and gold, there were several mirrors as high as the ceiling, and a large glass chandelier. But that was not all.

I do not have to go back again, the cell is burst open, I move, I feel my body.

THE TIGER

ONCE A TIGER was brought to the celebrated animal tamer Burson, for him to give his opinion as to the possibility of taming the animal. The small cage with the tiger in it was pushed into the training cage, which had the dimensions of a public hall; it was in a large hut-camp a long way outside the town. The attendants withdrew: Burson always wanted to be completely alone with an animal at his first encounter with it. The tiger lay quiet, having just been plentifully fed. It yawned a little, gazed wearily at its new surroundings, and immediately fell asleep.

COURIERS

THEY WERE OFFERED the choice between becoming kings or the couriers of kings. The way children would, they all wanted to be couriers. Therefore there are only couriers who hurry about the world, shouting to each other—since there are no kings—messages that have become meaningless. They would like to put an end to this miserable life of theirs but they dare not because of their oaths of service.

MY DESTINATION

I GAVE ORDERS for my horse to be brought round from the stable. The servant did not understand me. I myself went to the stable, saddled my horse and mounted. In the distance I heard a bugle call, I asked him what this meant. He knew nothing and had heard nothing. At the gate he stopped me, asking: "Where are you riding to, master?" "I don't know,"

I said, "only away from here, away from here. Always away from here, only by doing so can I reach my destination." "And so you know your destination?" he asked. "Yes," I answered, "didn't I say so? Away-From-Here, that is my destination." "You have no provisions with you," he said. "I need none," I said, "the journey is so long that I must die of hunger if I don't get anything on the way. No provisions can save me. For it is, fortunately, a truly immense journey."

LETTER TO HIS FATHER

DEAREST FATHER,

You asked me recently why I maintain that I am afraid of you. As usual, I was unable to think of any answer to your question, partly for the very reason that I am afraid of you, and partly because an explanation of the grounds for this fear would mean going into far more details than I could even approximately keep in mind while talking. And if I now try to give you an answer in writing, it will still be very incomplete, because, even in writing, this fear and its consequences hamper me in relation to you and because the magnitude of the subject goes far beyond the scope of my memory and power of reasoning.

To you the matter always seemed very simple, at least in so far as you talked about it in front of me, and indiscriminately in front of many other people. It looked to you more or less as follows: you have worked hard all your life, have sacrificed everything for your children, above all for me, consequently I have lived high and handsome, have been completely at liberty to learn whatever I wanted, and have had no cause for material worries, which means worries of any kind at all. You have not expected any gratitude for this, knowing what "children's gratitude" is like, but have expected at least some sort of obligingness, some sign of sympathy. Instead I have always hidden from you, in my room, among my books, with crazy friends, or with extravagant ideas. I have never talked to you frankly; I have never come to you when you were in the synagogue, never visited you at Franzensbad, nor indeed ever shown any family feeling; I have never taken any interest in the business or your other concerns; I left the factory on your hands and walked off; I encouraged Ottla in her obstinacy, and never lifted a finger for you (never even got you a theater ticket), while I do everything for my friends. If you sum up your judgment of me, the result you get is that, although you don't charge me with anything downright improper or wicked (with the exception perhaps of my latest marriage plan), you do charge me with coldness, estrangement, and ingratitude. And, what is more, you charge me with it in such a way as to make it seem my fault, as though I might have been able, with something like a touch on the steering wheel, to make everything quite different, while you aren't in the slightest to blame, unless it be for having been too good to me.

This, your usual way of representing it, I regard as accurate only in so far as I too believe you are entirely blameless in the matter of our estrangement. But I am equally entirely blameless. If I could get you to acknowledge this, then what would be possible is—not, I think, a new life, we are both much too old for that—but still, a kind of peace; no cessation, but still, a diminution of your unceasing reproaches.

Oddly enough you have some sort of notion of what I mean. For instance, a short time ago you said to me: "I have always been fond of you, even though outwardly I didn't act toward you as other fathers generally do, and this precisely because I can't pretend

187

as other people can." Now, Father, on the whole I have never doubted your goodness toward me, but this remark I consider wrong. You can't pretend, that is true, but merely for that reason to maintain that other fathers pretend is either mere opinionatedness, and as such beyond discussion, or on the other hand—and this in my view is what it really is—a veiled expression of the fact that something is wrong in our relationship and that you have played your part in causing it to be so, but without its being your fault. If you really mean that, then we are in agreement.

I'm not going to say, of course, that I have become what I am only as a result of your influence. That would be very much exaggerated (and I am indeed inclined to this exaggeration). It is indeed quite possible that even if I had grown up entirely free from your influence I still could not have become a person after your own heart. I should probably have still become a weakly, timid, hesitant, restless person, neither Robert Kafka nor Karl Hermann, but yet quite different from what I really am, and we might have got on with each other excellently. I should have been happy to have you as a friend, as a boss, an uncle, a grandfather, even (though rather more hesitantly) as a father-in-law. Only as a father you have been too strong for me, particularly since my brothers died when they were small and my sisters only came along much later, so that I alone had to bear the brunt of it—and for that I was much too weak.

Compare the two of us: I, to put it in a very much abbreviated form, a Löwy with a certain basis of Kafka, which, however, is not set in motion by the Kafka will to life, business, and conquest, but by a Löwyish spur that impels more secretly, more diffidently, and in another direction, and which often fails to work entirely. You, on the other hand, a true Kafka in strength, health, appetite, loudness of voice, eloquence, self-satisfaction, worldly dominance, endurance, presence of mind, knowledge of human nature, a certain way of doing things on a grand scale, of course also with all the defects and weaknesses that go with these advantages and into which your temperament and sometimes your hot temper drive you. You are perhaps not wholly a Kafka in your general outlook, in so far as I can compare you with Uncle Philipp, Ludwig, and Heinrich. That is odd, and here I don't see quite clear either. After all, they were all more cheerful, fresher, more informal, more easygoing, less severe than you. (In this, by the way, I have inherited a great deal from you and taken much too good care of my inheritance, without, admittedly, having the necessary counterweights in my own nature, as you have.) Yet you too, on the other hand, have in this respect gone through various phases. You were perhaps more cheerful before you were disappointed by your children, especially by me, and were depressed at home (when other people came in, you were quite different); perhaps you have become more cheerful again since then, now that your grandchildren and your son-in-law again give you something of that warmth which your children, except perhaps Valli, could not give you. In any case, we were so different and in our difference so dangerous to each other that if anyone had tried to calculate in advance how I, the slowly developing child, and you, the full-grown man, would stand to each other, he could have assumed that you would simply trample me underfoot so that nothing was left of me. Well, that did not happen. Nothing alive can be calculated. But perhaps something worse happened. And in saying this I would all the time beg of you not to forget that I never, and not even for a single moment, believe any guilt to be on your side. The effect you had on me was the effect you could not help having. But you should stop considering it some particular malice on my part that I succumbed to that effect.

I was a timid child. For all that, I am sure I was also obstinate, as children are. I am sure that Mother spoilt me too, but I cannot believe I was particularly difficult to manage; I cannot believe that a kindly word, a quiet taking by the hand, a friendly look, could not have got me to do anything that was wanted of me. Now you are, after all, at bottom a kindly and

189

softhearted person (what follows will not be in contradiction to this, I am speaking only of the impression you made on the child), but not every child has the endurance and fearlessness to go on searching until it comes to the kindliness that lies beneath the surface. You can only treat a child in the way you yourself are constituted, with vigor, noise, and hot temper, and in this case this seemed to you, into the bargain, extremely suitable, because you wanted to bring me up to be a strong brave boy.

Your educational methods in the very early years I can't, of course, directly describe today, but I can more or less imagine them by drawing retrospective conclusions from the later years and from your treatment of Felix. What must be considered as heightening the effect is that you were then younger and hence more energetic, wilder, more untrammeled, and still more reckless than you are today and that you were, besides, completely tied to the business, scarcely able to be with me even once a day, and therefore made all the more profound an impression on me, never really leveling out into the flatness of habit.

There is only one episode in the early years of which I have a direct memory. You may remember it, too. One night I kept on whimpering for water, not, I am certain, because I was thirsty, but probably partly to be annoying, partly to amuse myself. After several vigorous threats had failed to have any effect, you took me out of bed, carried me out onto the *pavlatche*, and left me there alone for a while in my nightshirt, outside the shut door. I am not going to say that this was wrong—perhaps there was really no other way of getting peace and quiet that night—but I mention it as typical of your methods of bringing up a child and their effect on me. I dare say I was quite obedient afterwards at that period, but it did me inner harm. What was for me a matter of course, that senseless asking for water, and the extraordinary terror of being carried outside were two things that I, my nature being what it was, could never properly connect with each other. Even years afterwards I suffered from the tormenting

190

fancy that the huge man, my father, the ultimate authority, would come almost for no reason at all and take me out of bed in the night and carry me out onto the *pavlatche*, and that meant I was a mere nothing for him.

That was only a small beginning, but this sense of nothingness that often dominates me (a feeling that is in another respect, admittedly, also a noble and fruitful one) comes largely from your influence. What I would have needed was a little encouragement, a little friendliness, a little keeping open of my road, instead of which you blocked it for me, though of course with the good intention of making me go another road. But I was not fit for that. You encouraged me, for instance, when I saluted and marched smartly, but I was no future soldier, or you encouraged me when I was able to eat heartily or even drink beer with my meals, or when I was able to repeat songs, singing what I had not understood, or prattle to you using your own favorite expressions, imitating you, but nothing of this had anything to do with my future. And it is characteristic that even today you really only encourage me in anything when you yourself are involved in it, when what is at stake is your own sense of self-importance, which I damage (for instance by my intended marriage) or which is damaged in me (for instance when Pepa is abusive to me). Then I receive encouragement, I am reminded of my worth, the matches I would be entitled to make are pointed out to me, and Pepa is condemned utterly. But apart from the fact that at my age I am now almost quite unsusceptible to encouragement, what help could it be to me anyway, if it only comes when it isn't primarily a matter of myself at all?

At that time, and at that time in every way, I would have needed encouragement. I was, after all, weighed down by your mere physical presence. I remember, for instance, how we often undressed in the same bathing hut. There was I, skinny, weakly, slight; you strong, tall, broad. Even inside the hut I felt a miserable specimen, and what's more, not only in your

191

eyes but in the eyes of the whole world, for you were for me the measure of all things. But then when we stepped out of the bathing hut before the people, you holding me by my hand, a little skeleton, unsteady, barefoot on the boards, frightened of the water, incapable of copying your swimming strokes, which you, with the best of intentions, but actually to my profound humiliation, always kept on showing me, then I was frantic with desperation and at such moments all my bad experiences in all spheres fitted magnificently together. I felt best when you sometimes undressed first and I was able to stay behind in the hut alone and put off the disgrace of showing myself in public until at last you came to see what I was doing and drove me out of the hut. I was grateful to you for not seeming to notice my anguish, and besides, I was proud of my father's body. By the way, this difference between us remains much the same to this very day.

In keeping, furthermore, was your intellectual domination. You had worked your way so far up by your own energies alone, and as a result you had unbounded confidence in your opinion. That was not yet so dazzling for me as a child as later for the boy growing up. From your armchair you ruled the world. Your opinion was correct, every other was mad, wild, *meshugge,* not normal. Your self-confidence indeed was so great that you had no need to be consistent at all and yet never ceased to be in the right. It did sometimes happen that you had no opinions whatsoever about a matter and as a result all opinions that were at all possible with respect to the matter were necessarily wrong, without exception. You were capable, for instance, of running down the Czechs, and then the Germans, and then the Jews, and what is more, not only selectively but in every respect, and finally nobody was left except yourself. For me you took on the enigmatic quality that all tyrants have whose rights are based on their person and not on reason. At least so it seemed to me.

Now, when I was the subject you were actually astonishingly often right; which in conversation was not surprising, for there was hardly ever any conversation between us, but also in reality. Yet this was nothing particularly incomprehensible, either; in all my thinking I was, after all, under the heavy pressure of your personality, even in that part of it—and particularly in that—which was not in accord with yours. All these thoughts, seemingly independent of you, were from the beginning burdened with your belittling judgments; it was almost impossible to endure this and still work out a thought with any measure of completeness and permanence. I am not here speaking of any sublime thoughts, but of every little childhood enterprise. It was only necessary to be happy about something or other, to be filled with the thought of it, to come home and speak of it, and the answer was an ironical sigh, a shaking of the head, a tapping on the table with a finger: "Is that all you're so worked up about?" or "Such worries I'd like to have!" or "The things some people have time to think about!" or "Where is that going to get you?" or "What a song and dance about nothing!" Of course, you couldn't be expected to be enthusiastic about every childish triviality, when you were in a state of fret and worry. But that was not the point. Rather, by virtue of your antagonistic nature, you could not help but always and inevitably cause the child such disappointments; and further, this antagonism, accumulating material, was constantly intensified; eventually the pattern expressed itself even if, for once, you were of the same opinion as I; finally, these disappointments of the child were not the ordinary disappointments of life but, since they involved you, the all-important personage, they struck to the very core. Courage, resolution, confidence, delight in this and that, could not last when you were against it or even if your opposition was merely to be assumed; and it was to be assumed in almost everything I did.

This applied to thoughts as well as to people. It was enough that I should take a little interest in a person—which in any case did not happen often, as a result of my nature—for you, without any consideration for my feelings or respect for my judgment, to move in with abuse, defamation, and denigration. Innocent, childlike people, such as, for instance, the Yiddish actor Löwy, had to pay for that. Without knowing him you compared him, in some dreadful way that I have now forgotten, to vermin and, as was so often the case with people I was fond of, you were automatically ready with the proverb of the dog and its fleas. Here I particularly recall the actor because at that time I made a note of your pronouncements about him, with the comment: "This is how my father speaks of my friend (whom he does not even know), simply because he is my friend. I shall always be able to bring this up against him whenever he reproaches me with the lack of a child's affection and gratitude." What was always incomprehensible to me was your total lack of feeling for the suffering and shame you could inflict on me with your words and judgments. It was as though you had no notion of your power. I too, I am sure, often hurt you with what I said, but then I always knew, and it pained me, but I could not control myself, could not keep the words back, I was sorry even while I was saying them. But you struck out with your words without much ado, you weren't sorry for anyone, either during or afterwards, one was utterly defenseless against you.

But your whole method of upbringing was like that. You have, I think, a gift for bringing up children; you could, I am sure, have been of help to a human being of your own kind with your methods; such a person would have seen the reasonableness of what you told him, would not have troubled about anything else, and would quietly have done things the way he was told. But for me as a child everything you called out at me was positively a heavenly commandment, I never forgot it, it remained for me the most important means of forming a judgment of the world, above all of forming a judgment of you yourself, and there you failed entirely. Since as a child I was with you chiefly during meals, your teaching was to a large extent the teaching of proper behavior at table. What was brought to the table had to be eaten, the quality of the food was not

194

to be discussed—but you yourself often found the food inedible, called it "this swill," said "that beast" (the cook) had ruined it. Because in accordance with your strong appetite and your particular predilection you ate everything fast, hot, and in big mouthfuls, the child had to hurry; there was a somber silence at table, interrupted by admonitions: "Eat first, talk afterwards," or "faster, faster, faster," or "there you are, you see, I finished ages ago." Bones mustn't be cracked with the teeth, but you could. Vinegar must not be sipped noisily, but you could. The main thing was that the bread should be cut straight. But it didn't matter that you did it with a knife dripping with gravy. Care had to be taken that no scraps fell on the floor. In the end it was under your chair that there were most scraps. At table one wasn't allowed to do anything but eat, but you cleaned and cut your fingernails, sharpened pencils, cleaned your ears with a toothpick. Please, Father, understand me correctly: in themselves these would have been utterly insignificant details, they only became depressing for me because you, so tremendously the authoritative man, did not keep the commandments you imposed on me. Hence the world was for me divided into three parts: one in which I, the slave, lived under laws that had been invented only for me and which I could, I did not know why, never completely comply with; then a second world, which was infinitely remote from mine, in which you lived, concerned with government, with the issuing of orders and with the annoyance about their not being obeyed; and finally a third world where everybody else lived happily and free from orders and from having to obey. I was continually in disgrace; either I obeyed your orders, and that was a disgrace, for they applied, after all, only to me; or I was defiant, and that was a disgrace too, for how could I presume to defy you; or I could not obey because I did not, for instance, have your strength, your appetite, your skill, although you expected it of me as a matter of course; this was the greatest disgrace of all. This was not the course of the child's reflections, but of his feelings.

My situation at that time becomes clearer, perhaps, if I compare it with that of Felix. You do, of course, treat him in a similar way, even indeed employing a particularly terrible method against him in his upbringing: whenever at meals he does anything that is in your opinion unclean, you are not content to say to him, as you used to say to me: "You are a pig," but add: "a thorough Hermann" or "just like your father." Now this may perhaps—one can't say more than "perhaps"—not really harm Felix in any essential way, because you are only a grandfather to him, an especially important one, of course, but still, not everything, as you were for me; and besides, Felix is of a quiet, even at this stage to a certain extent manly character, one who may perhaps be disconcerted by a great voice thundering at him, but not permanently conditioned by it. But above all he is, of course, only comparatively seldom with you, and besides, he is also under other influences; you are for him a rather endearing curiosity from which he can pick and choose whatever he likes. For me you were nothing in the least like a curiosity, I couldn't pick and choose, I had to take everything.

And this without being able to produce any arguments against any of it, for it is fundamentally impossible for you to talk calmly about a subject you don't approve of or even one that was not suggested by you; your imperious temperament does not permit it. In recent years you have been explaining this as due to your nervous heart condition. I don't know that you were ever essentially different. Rather, the nervous heart condition is a means by which you exert your domination more strongly, since the thought of it necessarily chokes off the least opposition from others. This is, of course, not a reproach, only a statement of fact. As in Ottla's case, when you say: "You simply can't talk to her at all, she flies straight in your face," but in reality she does not begin by flying out at all. You mistake the person for the thing. The thing under discussion is what flies in your face and you immediately made up your mind about it without listening to the person; whatever is brought forward afterwards merely serves to irritate you further, never to convince you. Then all one gets from you is: "Do whatever you like. So far as I'm concerned you have a free hand. You're of age, I've no advice to give you," and all this with that frightful, hoarse undertone of anger and utter condemnation that only makes me tremble less today than in my childhood because the child's exclusive sense of guilt has been partly replaced by insight into our helplessness, yours and mine.

The impossibility of getting on calmly together had one more result, actually a very natural one: I lost the capacity to talk. I dare say I would not have become a very eloquent person in any case, but I would, after all, have acquired the usual fluency of human language. But at a very early stage you forbade me to speak. Your threat, "Not a word of contradiction!" and the raised hand that accompanied it have been with me ever since. What I got from you—and you are, whenever it is a matter of your own affairs, an excellent talker—was a hesitant, stammering mode of speech, and even that was still too much for you, and finally I kept silent, at first perhaps out of defiance, and then because I could neither think nor speak in your presence. And because you were the person who really brought me up, this has had its repercussions throughout my life. It is altogether a remarkable mistake for you to believe I never fell in with your wishes. "Always agin you" was really not my basic principle where you were concerned, as you believe and as you reproach me. On the contrary: if I had obeyed you less, I am sure you would have been much better pleased with me. As it is, all your educational measures hit the mark exactly. There was no hold I tried to escape. As I now am, I am (apart, of course, from the fundamentals and the influence of life itself) the result of your upbringing and of my obedience. That this result is nevertheless distressing to you, indeed that you unconsciously refuse to acknowledge it as the result of your methods of upbringing, is due to the fact that your hand and the material I offered were so alien to each other.

You would say: "Not a word of contradiction!" thinking that that was a way of silencing the oppositional forces in me that were disagreeable to you, but the effect of it was too strong for me, I was too docile, I became completely dumb, cringed away from you, hid from you, and only dared to stir when I was so far away from you that your power could no longer reach me—at least not directly. But you were faced with all that, and it all seemed to you to be "agin," whereas it was only the inevitable consequence of your strength and my weakness.

Your extremely effective rhetorical methods in bringing me up, which never failed to work with me, were: abuse, threats, irony, spiteful laughter, and—oddly enough—self-pity.

I cannot recall your ever having abused me directly and in downright abusive terms. Nor was that necessary; you had so many other methods, and besides, in talk at home and particularly at business the words of abuse went flying around me in such swarms, as they were flung at other people's heads, that as a little boy I was sometimes almost stunned and had no reason not to apply them to myself too, for the people you were abusing were certainly no worse than I was and you were certainly not more displeased with them than with me. And here again was your enigmatic innocence and inviolability; you cursed and swore without the slightest scruple; yet you condemned cursing and swearing in other people and would not have it.

You reinforced abusiveness with threats, and this applied to me too. How terrible for me was, for instance, that "I'll tear you apart like a fish," although I knew, of course, that nothing worse was to follow (admittedly, as a little child I didn't know that), but it was almost exactly in accord with my notions of your power, and I saw you as being capable of doing this too. It was also terrible when you ran around the table, shouting, grabbing at one, obviously not really trying to grab, yet pretending to, and Mother (in the end) had to rescue one, as it seemed. Once again one had, so it seemed to the child, remained alive through your mercy and bore one's life henceforth as an undeserved gift from you. This is also the place to mention the threats about the consequences of disobedience. When I began to do something you did not like and you threatened me with the prospect of failure, my veneration for your opinion was so great that the failure became inevitable, even though perhaps it happened only at some later time. I lost confidence in my own actions. I was wavering, doubtful. The older I became, the more material there was for you to bring up against me as evidence of my worthlessness; gradually you began really to be right in a certain respect. Once again, I am careful not to assert that I became like this solely through you; you only intensified what was already there, but you intensified it greatly, simply because where I was concerned you were very powerful and you employed all your power to that end.

You put special trust in bringing up children by means of irony, and this was most in keeping with your superiority over me. An admonition from you generally took this form: "Can't you do it in such-and-such a way? That's too hard for you, I suppose. You haven't the time, of course?" and so on. And each such question would be accompanied by malicious laughter and a malicious face. One was, so to speak, already punished before one even knew that one had done something bad. Maddening were also those rebukes in which one was treated as a third person, in other words, considered not worthy even to be spoken to angrily; that is to say, when you would speak ostensibly to Mother but actually to me, who was sitting right there. For instance: "Of course, that's too much to expect of our worthy son," and the like. (This produced a corollary in that, for instance, I did not dare to ask you, and later from habit did not even really much think of asking, anything directly when Mother was there. It was much less dangerous for the child to put questions to Mother, sitting there beside you, and to ask Mother: "How is Father?"—so guarding oneself against surprises.) There were, of course, also cases when one was entirely in agreement with even the worst irony, namely, when it referred to someone else, such as Elli, with whom I was on bad terms for years. There was an orgy of malice and spiteful delight for me when such things were said of her, as they were at almost every meal: "She has to sit six feet away from the table, the great fat lump" and when you, morosely sitting on your chair without the slightest trace of pleasantness or good humor, a bitter enemy, would exaggeratedly imitate the way she sat, which you found utterly loathsome. How often such things happened, over and over again, and how little you really achieved as a result of them! I think the reason was that the expenditure of anger and malice seemed to be in no proper relation to the subject itself, one did not have the feeling that the anger was caused by this trifle of sitting some way back from the table, but that the whole bulk of it had already been there to begin with, then, only by chance, happened to settle on this matter as a pretext for breaking out. Since one was convinced that a pretext would be found anyway, one did not try very hard, and one's feelings became dulled by these continued threats. One had gradually become pretty sure of not getting a beating, anyway. One became a glum, inattentive, disobedient child, always intent on escape, mainly within one's own self. So you suffered, and so we suffered. From your own point of view you were quite right when, clenching your teeth and with that gurgling laughter that gave the child its first notions of hell, you used to say bitterly (as you did only just recently in connection with a letter from Constantinople): "A *nice* crowd that is!"

What seemed to be quite incompatible with this attitude toward your children was, and it happened very often, that you complained in public. I confess that as a child (though probably somewhat later) I was completely callous about this and could not understand how you could possibly expect to get any sympathy from anyone. You were such a giant in every respect. What could you care for our pity or even our help? Our help, indeed, you could not but despise, as you so often despised us ourselves. Hence, I did not take these complaints at their face value and looked for some hidden motive behind them. Only later did I come to understand that you really suffered a great deal because of your children; but at that time, when these complaints might under different circumstances still have met with a childish, candid sympathy, unhesitatingly ready to offer any help it could, to me they had to seem like overemphatic means of disciplining me and humiliating me, as such not in themselves very intense, but with the harmful side effect that the child became conditioned not to take very seriously the very things it should have taken seriously.

Fortunately, there were exceptions to all this, mostly when you suffered in silence, and affection and kindliness by their own strength overcame all obstacles, and moved me immediately. Rare as this was, it was wonderful. For instance, in earlier years, in hot summers, when you were tired after lunch, I saw you having a nap at the office, your elbow on the desk; or you joined us in the country, in the summer holidays, on Sundays, worn out from work; or the time Mother was gravely ill and you stood holding on to the bookcase, shaking with sobs; or when, during my last illness, you came tiptoeing to Ottla's room to see me, stopping in the doorway, craning your neck to see me, and out of consideration only waved to me with your hand. At such times one would lie back and weep for happiness, and one weeps again now, writing it down.

You have a particularly beautiful, very rare way of quietly, contentedly, approvingly smiling, a way of smiling that can make the person for whom it is meant entirely happy. I can't recall its ever having expressly been my lot in my childhood, but I dare say it may have happened, for why should you have refused it to me at a time when I still seemed blameless to you and was your great hope? Yet in the long run even such friendly impressions brought about nothing but an increased sense of guilt, making the world still more incomprehensible to me.

I would rather keep to the practical and permanent.

In order to assert myself even a little in relation to you, and partly too from a kind of vengefulness, I soon began to observe little ridiculous things about you, to collect them and to exaggerate them. For instance, how easily you let yourself be dazzled by people who were only seemingly above you, how you would keep on talking about them, as of some Imperial Councilor or some such (on the other hand, such things also pained me, to see you, my father, believing you had any need of such trifling confirmations of your own value, and boasting about them). Or I would observe your taste for indecent expressions, which you would produce in the loudest possible voice, laughing about them as though you had said something particularly good, while in point of fact it was only a banal little obscenity (at the same time this again was for me a humiliating manifestation of your vitality). There were, of course, plenty of such observations. I was happy about them; they gave me occasion for whispering and joking; you sometimes noticed it and were angry about it, took it for malice and lack of respect, but believe me, it was for me nothing other than a means—moreover, a useless one—of attempted self-preservation; they were jokes of the kind that are made about gods and kings, jokes that are not only compatible with the profoundest respect but are indeed part and parcel of it.

Incidentally, you too, in keeping with your similar position where I was concerned, tried a similar form of self-defense. You were in the habit of pointing out how exaggeratedly well off I was and how well I had in fact been treated. That is correct, but I don't believe it was of any real use to me under the prevailing circumstances.

It is true that Mother was illimitably good to me, but for me all that was in relation to you, that is to say, in no good relation. Mother unconsciously played the part of a beater during a hunt. Even if your method of upbringing might in some unlikely case have set me on my own feet by means of producing defiance, dislike, or even hate in me, Mother canceled that out again by kindness, by talking sensibly (in the maze and chaos of my childhood she was the very prototype of good sense and reasonableness), by pleading for me; and I was again driven back into your orbit, which I might perhaps otherwise have broken out of, to your advantage and to my own. Or it happened that no real reconciliation came about, that Mother merely shielded me from you in secret, secretly gave me something, or allowed me to do something, and then where you were concerned I was again the furtive creature, the cheat, the guilty one, who in his worthlessness could only pursue backstairs methods even to get the things he regarded as his right. Of course, I became used to taking such a course also in quest of things to which, even in my own view, I had no right. This again meant an increase in the sense of guilt.

It is also true that you hardly ever really gave me a whipping. But the shouting, the way your face got red, the hasty undoing of the braces and laying them ready over the back of the chair, all that was almost worse for me. It is as if someone is going to be hanged. If he really is hanged, then he is dead and it is all over. But if he has to go through all the preliminaries to being hanged and he learns of his reprieve only when the noose is dangling before his face, he may suffer from it all his life. Besides, from the many occasions on which I had, according to your clearly expressed opinion, deserved a whipping but was let off at the last moment by your grace, I again accumulated only a huge sense of guilt. On every side I was to blame, I was in your debt.

You have always reproached me (either alone or in front of others, since you have no feeling for the humiliation of the latter, and your children's affairs were always public) for living in peace and quiet, warmth and abundance, lacking nothing, thanks to your hard work. I think of remarks that must positively have worn grooves in my brain, such as: "When I was only seven I had to push a barrow from village to village." "We all had to sleep in one room." "We were glad when we got potatoes." "For years I had open sores on my legs because I did not have enough warm clothes." "I was only a little boy when I was sent to Pisek to work in a store." "I got nothing from home, not even when I was in the army, even then I was sending money home." "But for all that, for all that— Father was always Father to me. Ah, nobody knows what that means these days! What do these children know? Nobody's been through that! Does any child understand such things today?" Under other conditions such stories might have been very educational, they might have been a way of encouraging one and strengthening one to endure torments and deprivations similar to those one's father had undergone. But that wasn't what you wanted at all; the situation had, after all, become quite different as a result of all your efforts, and there was no opportunity to distinguish oneself as you had done. Such an opportunity would first of all have had to be created by violence and revolutions, it would have meant breaking away from home (assuming one had had the resolution and strength to do so and that Mother wouldn't have worked against it, for her part, with other means). But that was not what you wanted at all, that you termed ingratitude, extravagance, disobedience, treachery, madness. And so, while on the one hand you tempted me to it by means of example, story, and humiliation, on the other hand you forbade it with the utmost severity. Otherwise, for instance, you ought to have been delighted with Ottla's Zürau escapade—apart from the accompanying circumstances. She wanted to get back to the country from which you had come, she wanted work and hardship such as you had had, she did not want to batten on the results of your work, just as you yourself were independent of your father. Were those such dreadful intentions? Was that so remote from your example and your precept? Well, Ottla's intentions finally came to nothing in practice, were indeed perhaps carried out in a somewhat ridiculous way, with too much fuss, and she did not have enough consideration for her parents. But was that exclusively her fault and not also the fault of the circumstances and, above all, of the fact that you were so estranged from her? Was she any less estranged from you (as you later tried to convince yourself) in the business than afterwards at Zürau? And would you not quite certainly have had the power (assuming you could have brought yourself to do so) to turn that escapade into something very good by means of encouragement, advice, and supervision, perhaps even merely by means of toleration?

In connection with such experiences you used to say, in bitter jest, that we were too well off. But that joke is, in a sense, no joke at all. What you had to fight for we received from your hand, but the fight for external life, a fight that was instantly open to you and which we were, of course, not spared either, we had to fight for only late in life, in our maturity but with only childish strength. I do not say that our situation is therefore inevitably less favorable than yours was, on the contrary, it is probably no better and no worse (although this is said without reference to our different natures), only we have the disadvantage of not being able to boast of our wretchedness and not being able to humiliate anyone with it as you have done with your wretchedness. Nor do I deny that it might have been possible for me to really enjoy the fruits of your great and successful work; that I could have turned them to good account and, to your joy, continued to work with them; but here again, our estrangement stood in the way. I could enjoy what you gave, but only in humiliation, weariness, weakness, and with a sense of guilt. That was why I could be grateful to you for everything only as a beggar is, and could never show it by doing the right things.

The next external result of this whole method of upbringing was that I fled everything that even remotely reminded me of you. First, the business. In itself, especially in my childhood, so long as it was a shop, I ought to have liked it very much, it was so full of life, lit up in the evening, there was so much to see and hear; one was able to help now and then, to distinguish oneself, and, above all, to admire you for your magnificent commercial talents, for the way you sold things, managed people, made jokes, were untiring, in
205

case of doubt knew how to make the right decision immediately, and so forth; even the way you wrapped a parcel or opened a crate was a spectacle worth watching; all this was certainly not the worst school for a child. But since you gradually began to terrify me on all sides and the business and you became one for me, the business too made me feel uneasy. Things that had at first been a matter of course for me there now began to torment and shame me, particularly the way you treated the staff. I don't know, perhaps it was the same in most businesses (in the Assicurazioni Generali, for instance, in my time it was really similar, and the explanation I gave the director for my resignation was, though not strictly in accordance with the truth, still not entirely a lie: my not being able to bear the cursing and swearing, which incidentally had not actually been directed at me; it was something to which I had become too painfully sensitive from home), but in my childhood other businesses did not concern me. But you I heard and saw shouting, cursing, and raging in the shop, in a way that in my opinion at that time had no equal anywhere in the world. And not only cursing, but other sorts of tyrannizing. For instance, the way you pushed goods you did not want to have mixed up with others off the counter—only the thoughtlessness of your rage was some slight excuse—and how the clerk had to pick them up. Or your constant comment about a clerk who had TB: "The sooner he dies the better, the mangy dog." You called the employees "paid enemies," and that was what they were, but even before they became that, you seemed to me to be their "paying enemy." There, too, I learned the great lesson that you could be unjust; in my own case I would not have noticed it so soon, for here was too much accumulated sense of guilt, ready to admit that you were right; but there, in my childish view—which later, of course, became somewhat modified, although not too much so— were strangers, who were, after all, working for us and for that reason had to live in constant dread of you. Of course I exaggerated, because I simply assumed you had as terrible an effect on these people as on me. If it had been so, they could not have lived at all; since, however, they were grown-up people, most of them with excellent nerves, they shook off this abuse without any trouble and in the end it did you much more harm than it did them. But it made the business insufferable to me, reminding me far too much of my relations with you; quite apart from your proprietary interest and apart from your mania for domination even as a businessman, you were so greatly superior to all those who ever came to learn the business from you that nothing they ever did could satisfy you, and you must, as I assumed, in the same way be forever dissatisfied with me too. That was why I could not but side with the staff; incidentally also because, from sheer nervousness, I could not understand how anyone could be so abusive to a stranger, and hence from sheer nervousness tried somehow to reconcile the staff, which in my opinion must be in a terrible state of indignation, with you, with our family, if for no other reason than that of my own security. To this end it was not sufficient to behave in an ordinary decent way toward the staff, or even modestly; more than that, I had to be humble, not only be first to say "good morning" or "good evening," but if at all possible I had to prevent any return of the greeting. And even if I, insignificant creature that I was, down below, had licked their feet it would still have been no compensation for the way that you, the master, were lashing out at them up above. This relationship that I came to have toward my fellow man extended beyond the limits of the business and on into the future (something similar, but not so dangerous and deep-going as in my case, is for instance Ottla's taste for associating with poor people, sitting together with the maids, which annoys you so much, and the like). In the end I was almost afraid of the business and, in any case, it had long ceased to be any concern of mine even before I went to the Gymnasium and hence was taken even further away from it. Besides, it seemed to be entirely beyond my resources and capacities, since, as you said, it exhausted even yours. You then tried (today this seems to me both touching and shaming) to extract, nevertheless, some little sweetness for yourself from my dislike of the business, of your work—a dislike that was after all very distressing to you —by asserting that I had no business sense, that I had loftier ideas in my head, and the like. Mother was, of course, delighted with this explanation that you wrung from yourself, and I too, in my vanity and wretchedness, let myself be influenced by it. But if it had really been only or mainly "loftier ideas" that turned me against the business (which I now, but only now, have come really and honestly to hate), they would have had to express themselves differently, instead of letting me float quickly and timidly through my schooling and my law studies until I finally landed at a clerk's desk.

If I was to escape from you, I had to escape from the family as well, even from Mother. True, one could always get protection from her, but only in relation to you. She loved you too much and was too devoted and loyal to you to have been for long an independent spiritual force in the child's struggle. This was, incidentally, a correct instinct of the child, for with the passing of the years Mother became ever more closely allied to you; while, where she herself was concerned, she always kept her independence, within the narrowest limits, delicately and beautifully, and without ever essentially hurting you, still, with the passing of the years she did more and more completely, emotionally rather than intellectually, blindly adopt your judgments and your condemnations with regard to the children, particularly in the case—certainly a grave one—of Ottla. Of course, it must always be borne in mind how tormenting and utterly wearing Mother's position in the family was. She toiled in the business and in the house, and doubly suffered all the family illnesses, but the culmination of all this was what she suffered in her position between us and you. You were always affectionate and considerate toward her, but in this respect you spared her just as little as we spared her. We all hammered ruthlessly away at her, you from your side, we from ours. It was a diversion, nobody meant any harm, thinking of the battle that you were waging

208

with us and that we were waging with you, and it was Mother on whom we relieved our wild feelings. Nor was it at all a good contribution to the children's upbringing the way you—of course, without being in the slightest to blame for it yourself—tormented her on our account. It even seemed to justify our otherwise unjustifiable behavior toward her. How she suffered from us on your account, and from you on our account, even without counting those cases in which you were in the right because she was spoiling us, even though this "spoiling" may sometimes have been only a quiet, unconscious counterdemonstration against your system. Of course, Mother could not have borne all this if she had not drawn the strength to bear it from her love for us all and her happiness in that love.

My sisters were only partly on my side. The one who was happiest in her relation to you was Valli. Being closest to Mother, she fell in with your wishes in a similar way, without much effort and without suffering much harm. And because she reminded you of Mother, you did accept her in a more friendly spirit, although there was little Kafka material in her. But perhaps that was precisely what you wanted; where there was nothing of the Kafka's, even you could not demand anything of the sort, nor had you the feeling, as with the rest of us, that something was getting lost which had to be saved by force. Besides, it may be that you were never particularly fond of the Kafka element as it manifested itself in women. Valli's relationship to you would perhaps have become even friendlier if the rest of us had not disturbed it somewhat.

Elli is the only example of the almost complete success of a breaking away from your orbit. When she was a child she was the last person I should have expected it of. For she was such a clumsy, tired, timid, bad-tempered, guilt-ridden, overmeek, malicious, lazy, greedy, miserly child, I could hardly bring myself to look at her, certainly not to speak to her, so much did she remind me of myself, in so very much the same way was she under the same spell of our upbringing. Her miserliness was especially abhorrent to me, since

209

I had it to an, if possible, even greater extent. Miserliness is, after all, one of the most reliable signs of profound unhappiness; I was so unsure of everything that, in fact, I possessed only what I actually had in my hands or in my mouth or what was at least on the way there, and this was precisely what she, being in a similar situation, most enjoyed taking away from me. But all this changed when, at an early age—this is the most important thing—she left home, married, had children, and became cheerful, carefree, brave, generous, unselfish, and hopeful. It is almost incredible how you did not really notice this change at all, or at any rate did not give it its due, blinded as you were by the grudge you have always borne Elli and at bottom still bear her to this day; only this grudge matters much less now, since Elli no longer lives with us and, besides, your love for Felix and your affection for Karl have made it less important. Only Gerti sometimes has to suffer for it still.

I scarcely dare write of Ottla; I know that by doing so I jeopardize the whole effect I hope for from this letter. In ordinary circumstances, that is, so long as she is not in particular need or danger, all you feel is only hatred for her; you yourself have confessed to me that in your opinion she is always intentionally causing you suffering and annoyance, and while you are suffering on her account she is satisfied and pleased. In other words, a sort of fiend. What an immense estrangement, greater still than that between you and me, must have come about between you and her, for such an immense misunderstanding to be possible. She is so remote from you that you scarcely see her any more, instead, you put a specter in the place where you suppose her to be. I grant you that you have had a particularly difficult time with her. I don't, of course, quite see to the bottom of this very complicated case, but at any rate here was something like a kind of Löwy, equipped with the best Kafka weapons. Between us there was no real struggle; I was soon finished off; what remained was flight, embitterment, melancholy, and inner struggle. But you two were always in a fighting position, always fresh, always energetic. A sight as magnificent as it was desperate. At the very beginning you were, I am sure, very close to each other, because of the four of us Ottla is even today perhaps the purest representation of the marriage between you and Mother and of the forces it combined. I don't know what it was that deprived you both of the happiness of the harmony between father and child, but I can't help believing that the development in this case was similar to that in mine. On your side there was the tyranny of your own nature, on her side the Löwy defiance, touchiness, sense of justice, restlessness, and all that backed by the consciousness of the Kafka vigor. Doubtless I too influenced her, but scarcely of my own doing, simply through the fact of my existence. Besides, as the last to arrive, she found herself in a situation in which the balance of power was already established, and was able to form her own judgment from the large amount of material at her disposal. I can even imagine that she may, in her inmost being, have wavered for some time as to whether she should fling herself into your arms or into those of the adversaries; and it is obvious that at that time there was something you failed to do and that you rebuffed her, but if it had been possible, the two of you would have become a magnificently harmonious pair. That way I should have lost an ally, but the sight of you two would have richly compensated me; besides, the incredible happiness of finding complete contentment at least in one child would have changed you much to my advantage. All this, however, is today only a dream. Ottla has no contact with her father and has to seek her way alone, like me, and the degree of confidence, self-confidence, health, and ruthlessness by which she surpasses me makes her in your eyes more wicked and treacherous than I seem to you. I understand that. From your point of view she can't be different. Indeed, she herself is capable of regarding herself with your eyes, of feeling what you suffer and of being—not desperate (despair is my business) but very sad. You do see us together often enough, in apparent contradiction to this, whispering and laughing, and now and then you hear us mentioning you. The impression you get is that of impudent conspirators. Strange conspirators. You are, admittedly, a chief subject of our conversations, as of our thoughts ever since we can remember, but truly, not in order to plot against you do we sit together, but in order to discuss—with all our might and main, jokingly and seriously, in affection, defiance, anger, revulsion, submission, consciousness of guilt, with all the resources of our heads and hearts—this terrible trial that is pending between us and you, to examine it in all its details, from all sides, on all occasions, from far and near—a trial in which you keep on claiming to be the judge, whereas, at least in the main (here I leave a margin for all the mistakes I may naturally make) you are a party too, just as weak and deluded as we are.

An example of the effect of your methods of upbringing, one that is very instructive in the context of the whole situation, is the case of Irma. On the one hand, she was, after all, a stranger, already grown up when she entered your business, and had to deal with you mainly as her employer, so that she was only partially exposed to your influence, and this at an age when she had already developed powers of resistance; yet, on the other hand, she was also a blood relation, venerating you as her father's brother, and the power you had over her was far greater than that of a mere employer. And despite all this she, who, with her frail body, was so efficient, intelligent, hard-working, modest, trustworthy, unselfish and loyal, who loved you as her uncle and admired you as her employer, she who proved herself in previous and in subsequent positions, was not a very good clerk to you. Her relationship with you was, in fact, nearly that of one of your children—pushed, naturally, by us, too—and the power of your personality to bend others was, even in her case, so great that (admittedly only in relation to you and, it is to be hoped, without the deeper suffering of a child) she developed forgetfulness, carelessness, a sardonic sort of humor, and perhaps even a shade of defiance, in so far as she was capable of that at all. And I do not

212

even take into account that she was ailing, and not very happy in other respects either, and that she was burdened by a bleak home life. What was so illuminating to me in your relation to her, you yourself summed up in a remark that became classical for us, one that was almost blasphemous, but at the same time extraordinary evidence of the naïveté of your way of treating people: "The late lamented has left me quite a mess."

I might go on to describe further orbits of your influence and of the struggle against it, but there I would be entering uncertain ground and would have to construct things and apart from that, the farther you are away from your business and your family, the pleasanter you have always become, easier to get on with, better mannered, more considerate, and more sympathetic (I mean outwardly, too), in exactly the same way as for instance an autocrat, when he happens to be outside the frontiers of his own country, has no reason to go on being tyrannical and is able to associate good-humoredly even with the lowest of the low. In point of fact, in the group photographs taken at Franzensbad, for instance, you always looked as big and jolly, among those sulky little people, as a king on his travels. This was something, I grant you, from which your children might have benefited too, if they had been capable of recognizing this even as little children, which was impossible; and if I, for one, had not had to live constantly within the inmost, strictest, binding ring of your influence, as, in fact, I did.

Not only did I lose my family feeling, as you say; on the contrary, I did indeed have a feeling about the family, mostly in a negative sense, concerned with the breaking away from you (which, of course, could never be done completely). Relations with people outside the family, however, suffered possibly still more under your influence. You are entirely mistaken if you believe I do everything for other people out of affection and loyalty, and for you and the family nothing, out of coldness and betrayal. I repeat for the tenth time: even in other circumstances I should probably have become a shy and nervous person, but it is a long dark road from there to where I have really come. (Up to now I have intentionally passed over in silence relatively little in this letter, but now and later I shall have to keep silent about some things that are still too hard for me to confess—to you and to myself. I say this in order that, if the picture as a whole should be somewhat blurred here and there, you should not believe that this is due to lack of evidence; on the contrary, there is evidence that might well make the picture unbearably stark. It is not easy to find a middle way.) Here, it is enough to remind you of early days. I had lost my self-confidence where you were concerned, and in its place had developed a boundless sense of guilt. (In recollection of this boundlessness I once wrote of someone, accurately: "He is afraid the shame will outlive him, even.") I could not suddenly change when I was with other people; rather, I came to feel an even deeper sense of guilt with them, for, as I have already said, I had to make up to them for the wrongs you had done them in your business, wrongs in which I too had my share of responsibility. Besides, you always had some objection to make, frankly or covertly, about everyone I associated with, and for this too I had to atone. The mistrust that you tried to instill into me toward most people, at business and at home (name a single person who was of importance to me in my childhood whom you didn't at least once tear to shreds with your criticism), was, oddly enough, of no particular burden to you (you were strong enough to bear it; besides, it was perhaps really only a token of the autocrat). This mistrust (which was nowhere confirmed in the eyes of the little boy, since everywhere I saw only people excellent beyond any hope of emulation) turned in me to mistrust of myself and perpetual anxiety about everything else. There, then, I was in general certain of not being able to escape from you. That you were mistaken on this point was perhaps due to your actually never learning anything about my association with other people; and mistrustfully and jealously (I don't deny, do I, that you are fond of me?) you assumed that I had to compensate elsewhere for the lack of a family life, since it must be impossible that away from home I should live in the same way. Incidentally, in this respect, it was precisely in my childhood that I did find a certain comfort in my very mistrust of my own judgment. I would say to myself: "Oh, you're exaggerating, you tend too much to feel trivialities as great exceptions, the way young people always do." But this comfort I later lost almost entirely, when I gained a clearer perspective of the world.

I found as little escape from you in Judaism. Here some measure of escape would have been thinkable in principle, moreover, it would have been thinkable that we might both have found each other in Judaism or that we even might have begun from there in harmony. But what sort of Judaism was it that I got from you? In the course of the years, I have taken roughly three different attitudes to it.

As a child I reproached myself, in accord with you, for not going to the synagogue often enough, for not fasting, and so on. I thought that in this way I was doing a wrong not to myself but to you, and I was penetrated by a sense of guilt, which was, of course, always ready to hand.

Later, as a young man, I could not understand how, with the insignificant scrap of Judaism you yourself possessed, you could reproach me for not making an effort (for the sake of piety at least, as you put it) to cling to a similar, insignificant scrap. It was indeed, so far as I could see, a mere nothing, a joke—not even a joke. Four days a year you went to the synagogue, where you were, to say the least, closer to the indifferent than to those who took it seriously, patiently went through the prayers as a formality, sometimes amazed me by being able to show me in the prayer book the passage that was being said at the moment, and for the rest, so long as I was present in the synagogue (and this was the main thing) I was allowed to hang about wherever I liked. And so I yawned and dozed through the many hours (I don't think I was ever again so bored, except later at dancing lessons) and did my best to enjoy the few little bits of variety there were, as for instance when the Ark of the Covenant was opened, which always reminded me of the shooting galleries where a cupboard door would open in the same way whenever one hit a bull's eye; except that there something interesting always came out and here it was always just the same old dolls without heads. Incidentally, it was also very frightening for me there, not only, as goes without saying, because of all the people one came into close contact with, but also because you once mentioned in passing that I too might be called to the Torah. That was something I dreaded for years. But otherwise I was not fundamentally disturbed in my boredom, unless it was by the *bar mitzvah*, but that demanded no more than some ridiculous memorizing, in other words, it led to nothing but some ridiculous passing of an examination; and, so far as you were concerned, by little, not very significant incidents, as when you were called to the Torah and passed, in what to my way of feeling was a purely social event, or when you stayed on in the synagogue for the prayers for the dead, and I was sent away, which for a long time—obviously because of the being-sent-away and the lack of any deeper interest—aroused in me the more or less unconscious feeling that something indecent was about to take place.—That's how it was in the synagogue; at home it was, if possible, even poorer, being confined to the first Seder, which more and more developed into a farce, with fits of hysterical laughter, admittedly under the influence of the growing children. (Why did you have to give way to that influence? Because you had brought it about.) This was the religious material that was handed on to me, to which may be added at most the outstretched hand pointing to "the sons of the millionaire Fuchs," who attended the synagogue with their father on the high holy days. How one could do anything better with that material than get rid of it as fast as possible, I could not understand; precisely the getting rid of it seemed to me to be the devoutest action.

Still later, I did see it again differently and realized why it was possible for you to think that in this respect too I was malevolently betraying you. You really had brought some traces of Judaism with you from the ghetto-like village community; it was not much and it dwindled a little more in the city and during your military service; but still, the impressions and memories of your youth did just about suffice for some sort of Jewish life, especially since you did not need much help of that kind, but came of robust stock and could personally scarcely be shaken by religious scruples unless they were strongly mixed with social scruples. At bottom the faith that ruled your life consisted in your believing in the unconditional rightness of the opinions of a certain class of Jewish society, and hence actually, since these opinions were part and parcel of your own nature, in believing in yourself. Even in this there was still Judaism enough, but it was too little to be handed on to the child; it all dribbled away while you were passing it on. In part, it was youthful memories that could not be passed on to others; in part, it was your dreaded personality. It was also impossible to make a child, overacutely observant from sheer nervousness, understand that the few flimsy gestures you performed in the name of Judaism, and with an indifference in keeping with their flimsiness, could have any higher meaning. For you they had meaning as little souvenirs of earlier times, and that was why you wanted to pass them on to me, but since they no longer had any intrinsic value even for you, you could do this only through persuasion or threat; on the one hand, this could not be successful, and on the other, it had to make you very angry with me on account of my apparent obstinacy, since you did not recognize the weakness of your position in this.

The whole thing is, of course, no isolated phenomenon. It was much the same with a large section of this transitional generation of Jews, which had migrated from the still comparatively devout countryside to the cities. It happened automatically; only, it added to our relationship, which certainly did not lack in acrimony, one more, sufficiently painful source for it. Although you ought to believe, as I do, in your guiltlessness in this matter too, you ought to explain this guiltlessness by your nature and by the conditions of the times, not merely by external circumstances; that is, not by saying, for instance, that you had too much work and too many other worries to be able to bother with such things as well. In this manner you tend to twist your undoubted guiltlessness into an unjust reproach to others. That can be very easily refuted everywhere and here too. It was not a matter of any sort of instruction you ought to have given your children, but of an exemplary life. Had your Judaism been stronger, your example would have been more compelling too; this goes without saying and is, again, by no means a reproach, but only a refutation of your reproaches. You have recently been reading Franklin's memoirs of his youth. I really did purposely give you this book to read, though not, as you ironically commented, because of a little passage on vegetarianism, but because of the relationship between the author and his father, as it is there described, and of the relationship between the author and his son, as it is spontaneously revealed in these memoirs written for that son. I do not wish to dwell here on matters of detail.

I have received a certain retrospective confirmation of this view of your Judaism from your attitude in recent years, when it seemed to you that I was taking more interest in Jewish matters. As you have in advance an aversion to every one of my activities and especially to the nature of my interest, so you have had it here too. But in spite of this, one could have expected that in this case you would make a little exception. It was, after all, Judaism of your Judaism that was here stirring, and with it also the possibility to enter into a new relationship between us. I do not deny that, had you shown interest in them, these things might, for that very reason, have become suspect in my eyes. I do not even dream of asserting that I am in this respect any better than you are. But it never came to the test. Through my intervention Judaism became abhorrent to you, Jewish writings unreadable; they "nauseated" you.—This may have meant you insisted that only that

Judaism which you had shown me in my childhood was the right one, and beyond it there was nothing. Yet that you should insist on it was really hardly thinkable. But then the "nausea" (apart from the fact that it was directed primarily not against Judaism but against me personally) could only mean that unconsciously you did acknowledge the weakness of your Judaism and of my Jewish upbringing, did not wish to be reminded of it in any way, and reacted to any reminder with frank hatred. Incidentally, your negative high esteem of my new Judaism was much exaggerated; first of all, it bore your curse within it, and secondly, in its development the fundamental relationship to one's fellow men was decisive, in my case that is to say fatal.

You struck nearer home with your aversion to my writing and to everything that, unknown to you, was connected with it. Here I had, in fact, got some distance away from you by my own efforts, even if it was slightly reminiscent of the worm that, when a foot treads on its tail end, breaks loose with its front part and drags itself aside. To a certain extent I was in safety; there was a chance to breathe freely. The aversion you naturally and immediately took to my writing was, for once, welcome to me. My vanity, my ambition did suffer under your soon proverbial way of hailing the arrival of my books: "Put it on my bedside table!" (usually you were playing cards when a book came), but I was really quite glad of it, not only out of rebellious malice, not only out of delight at a new confirmation of my view of our relationship, but quite spontaneously, because to me that formula sounded something like: "Now you are free!" Of course it was a delusion; I was not, or, to put it most optimistically, was not yet, free. My writing was all about you; all I did there, after all, was to bemoan what I could not bemoan upon your breast. It was an intentionally long-drawn-out leave-taking from you, yet, although it was enforced by you, it did take its course in the direction determined by me. But how little all this amounted to! It is only worth talking about because it happened in my life, otherwise it would not even be noted; and also because in my childhood it ruled my life as a premonition, later as a hope, and still later often as despair, and it dictated—it may be said, yet again in your shape—my few small decisions.

For instance, the choice of a career. True, here you gave me complete freedom, in your magnanimous and, in this regard, even indulgent manner. Although here again you were conforming to the general method of treating sons in the Jewish middle class, which was the standard for you, or at least to the values of that class. Finally, one of your misunderstandings concerning my person played a part in this too. In fact, out of paternal pride, ignorance of my real life, and conclusions drawn from my feebleness, you have always regarded me as particularly diligent. As a child I was, in your view, always studying, and later always writing. This does not even remotely correspond to the facts. It would be more correct, and much less exaggerated, to say that I studied little and learnt nothing; that something did stick in my mind after those many years is, after all, not very remarkable, since I did have a moderately good memory and a not too inferior capacity for learning; but the sum total of knowledge and especially of a solid grounding of knowledge is extremely pitiable in comparison with the expenditure of time and money in the course of an outwardly untroubled, calm life, particularly also in comparison with almost all the people I know. It is pitiable, but to me understandable. Ever since I could think I have had such profound anxieties about asserting my spiritual existence that I was indifferent to everything else. Jewish schoolboys in our country often tend to be odd; among them one finds the most unlikely things; but something like my cold indifference, scarcely disguised, indestructible, childishly helpless, approaching the ridiculous, and brutishly complacent, the indifference of a self-sufficient but coldly imaginative child, I have never found anywhere else; to be sure, it was the sole defense against destruction of the nerves by fear and by a sense of guilt. All that occupied my mind was worry about myself, and this in various ways. There was, for instance, the worry about my health; it began imperceptibly enough, with now and then a little anxiety about digestion, hair falling out, a spinal curvature, and so on; intensifying in innumerable gradations, it finally ended with a real illness. But since there was nothing at all I was certain of, since I needed to be provided at every instant with a new confirmation of my existence, since nothing was in my very own, undoubted, sole possession, determined unequivocally only by me—in sober truth a disinherited son—naturally I became unsure even to the thing nearest to me, my own body. I shot up, tall and lanky, without knowing what to do with my lankiness, the burden was too heavy, the back became bent; I scarcely dared to move, certainly not to exercise, I remained weakly; I was amazed by everything I could still command as by a miracle, for instance, my good digestion; that sufficed to lose it, and now the way was open to every sort of hypochondria; until finally under the strain of the superhuman effort of wanting to marry (of this I shall speak later), blood came from the lung, something in which the apartment in the Schönbornpalais—which, however, I needed only because I believed I needed it for my writing, so that even this belongs here under the same heading—may have had a fair share. So all this did not come from excessive work, as you always imagine. There were years in which, in perfectly good health, I lazed away more time on the sofa than you in all your life, including all your illnesses. When I rushed away from you, frightfully busy, it was generally in order to lie down in my room. My total achievement in work done, both at the office (where laziness is, of course, not particularly striking, and besides, mine was kept in bounds by my timidity) and at home, is minute; if you had any real idea of it, you would be aghast. Probably I am constitutionally not lazy at all, but there was nothing for me to do. In the place where I lived I was spurned, condemned, fought to a standstill; and to escape to some other place was an enormous exertion, but that was not work, for it was something impossible, something that was, with small exceptions, unattainable for me.

This was the state in which I was given the freedom of choice of a career. But was I still capable of making any use of such freedom? Had I still any confidence in my own capacity to achieve a real career? My valuation of myself was much more dependent on you than on anything else, such as some external success. *That* was strengthening for a moment, nothing more, but on the other side your weight always dragged me down much more strongly. Never shall I pass the first grade in grammar school, I thought, but I succeeded, I even got a prize; but I shall certainly not pass the entrance exam for the Gymnasium, but I succeeded; but now I shall certainly fail in the first year at the Gymnasium; no, I did not fail, and I went on and on succeeding. This did not produce any confidence, however; on the contrary, I was always convinced—and I positively had the proof of it in your forbidding expression—that the more I achieved, the worse the final outcome would inevitably be. Often in my mind's eye I saw the terrible assembly of the teachers (the Gymnasium is only the most integral example, but it was the same all around me), as they would meet, when I had passed the first class, and then in the second class, when I had passed that, and then in the third, and so on, meeting in order to examine this unique, outrageous case, to discover how I, the most capable and, in any case, the most ignorant of all, had succeeded in creeping up so far as this class, which now, when everybody's attention had at last been focused on me, would of course instantly spew me out, to the jubilation of all the righteous liberated from this nightmare. To live with such fantasies is not easy for a child. In these circumstances, what could I care about my lessons? Who was able to strike a spark of real interest in me? Lessons, and not only lessons but everything around me, interested me as much, at that decisive age, as a defaulting bank clerk, still holding his job and trembling at the thought of discovery, is interested in the small current business of the bank, which he still has to

222

deal with as a clerk. That was how small and faraway everything was in comparison to the main thing. So it went on up to the qualifying exams which I really passed partly only through cheating, and then everything stagnated, for now I was free. If I had been concerned only with myself up to now, despite the discipline of the Gymnasium, how much more now that I was free. So there was actually no such thing for me as freedom to choose my career, for I knew: compared to the main thing everything would be exactly as much a matter of indifference to me as all the subjects taught at school, and so it was a matter of finding a profession that would let me indulge this indifference without injuring my vanity too much. Law was the obvious choice. Little contrary attempts on the part of vanity, of senseless hope, such as a fortnight's study of chemistry, or six months' German studies, only reinforced that fundamental conviction. So I studied law. This meant that in the few months before the exams, and in a way that told severely on my nerves, I was positively living, in an intellectual sense, on sawdust, which had, moreover, already been chewed for me in thousands of other people's mouths. But in a certain sense this was exactly to my taste, as in a certain sense the Gymnasium had been earlier, and later my job as a clerk, for it all suited my situation. At any rate, I did show astonishing foresight; even as a small child I had had fairly clear premonitions about my studies and my career. From this side I did not expect rescue; here I had given up long ago.

But I showed no foresight at all concerning the significance and possibility of a marriage for me; this up to now greatest terror of my life has come upon me almost completely unexpectedly. The child had developed so slowly, these things were outwardly all too remote; now and then the necessity of thinking of them did arise; but that here a permanent, decisive and indeed the most grimly bitter ordeal loomed was impossible to recognize. In reality, however, the marriage plans turned out to be the most grandiose and

223

hopeful attempts at escape, and, consequently, their failure was correspondingly grandiose.

I am afraid that, because in this sphere everything I try is a failure, I shall also fail to make these attempts to marry comprehensible to you. And yet the success of this whole letter depends on it, for in these attempts there was, on the one hand, concentrated everything I had at my disposal in the way of positive forces, and, on the other hand, there also accumulated, and with downright fury, all the negative forces that I have described as being the result in part of your method of upbringing, that is to say, the weakness, the lack of self-confidence, the sense of guilt, and they positively drew a cordon between myself and marriage. The explanation will be hard for me also because I have spent so many days and nights thinking and burrowing through the whole thing over and over again that now even I myself am bewildered by the mere sight of it. The only thing that makes the explanation easier for me is your—in my opinion—complete misunderstanding of the matter; slightly to correct so complete a misunderstanding does not seem excessively difficult.

First of all you rank the failure of the marriages with the rest of my failures; I should have nothing against this, provided you accepted my previous explanation of my failure as a whole. It does, in fact, form part of the same series, only you underrate the importance of the matter, underrating it to such an extent that whenever we talk of it we are actually talking about quite different things. I venture to say that nothing has happened to you in your whole life that had such importance for you as the attempts at marriage have had for me. By this I do not mean that you have not experienced anything in itself as important; on the contrary, your life was much richer and more care-laden and more concentrated than mine, but for that very reason nothing of this sort has happened to you. It is as if one person had to climb five low steps and another person only one step, but one that is, at least for him, as high as all the other five put together; the first person will not only manage the five, but hundreds and thousands more as well, he will have led a great and very strenuous life, but none of the steps he has climbed will have been of such importance to him as for the second person that one, first, high step, that step which it is impossible for him to climb even by exerting all his strength, that step which he cannot get up on and which he naturally cannot get past either.

Marrying, founding a family, accepting all the children that come, supporting them in this insecure world and perhaps even guiding them a little, is, I am convinced, the utmost a human being can succeed in doing at all. That so many seem to succeed in this is no evidence to the contrary; first of all, there are not many who do succeed, and secondly, these not-many usually don't "do" it, it merely "happens" to them; although this is not that Utmost, it is still very great and very honorable (particularly since "doing" and "happening" cannot be kept clearly distinct). And finally, it is not a matter of this Utmost at all, anyway, but only of some distant but decent approximation; it is, after all, not necessary to fly right into the middle of the sun, but it is necessary to crawl to a clean little spot on earth where the sun sometimes shines and one can warm oneself a little.

How was I prepared for this? As badly as possible. This is apparent from what has been said up to now. In so far as any direct preparation of the individual and any direct creation of the general basic conditions exist, you did not intervene much outwardly. And it could not be otherwise; what is decisive here are the general sexual customs of class, nation, and time. Yet you did intervene here too—not much, for such intervention must presuppose great mutual trust, and both of us had been lacking in this even long before the decisive time came—and not very happily, because our needs were quite different; what grips me need hardly touch you at all, and vice versa; what is innocence in you may be guilt in me, and vice versa; what has no consequences for you may be the last nail in my coffin.

I remember going for a walk one evening with you and Mother; it was on Josephsplatz near where the Länderbank is today; and I began talking about these interesting things, in a stupidly boastful, superior, proud, detached (that was spurious), cold (that was genuine), and stammering manner, as indeed I usually talked to you, reproaching the two of you with having left me uninstructed; with the fact that my schoolmates first had to take me in hand, that I had been close to great dangers (here I was brazenly lying, as was my way, in order to show myself brave, for as a consequence of my timidity I had, except for the usual sexual misdemeanors of city children, no very exact notion of these "great dangers"); but finally I hinted that now, fortunately, I knew everything, no longer needed any advice, and that everything was all right. I had begun talking about all this mainly because it gave me pleasure at least to talk about it, and also out of curiosity, and finally to avenge myself somehow on the two of you for something or other. In keeping with your nature you took it quite simply, only saying something to the effect that you could give me advice about how I could go in for these things without danger. Perhaps I did want to lure just such an answer out of you; it was in keeping with the pruriency of a child overfed with meat and all good things, physically inactive, everlastingly occupied with himself; but still, my outward sense of shame was so hurt by this—or I believed it ought to be so hurt—that against my will I could not go on talking to you about it and, with arrogant impudence, cut the conversation short.

It is not easy to judge the answer you gave me then; on the one hand, it had something staggeringly frank, sort of primeval, about it; on the other hand, as far as the lesson itself is concerned, it was uninhibited in a very modern way. I don't know how old I was at the time, certainly not much over sixteen. It was, nevertheless, a very remarkable answer for such a boy, and the distance between the two of us is also shown in the fact that it was actually the first direct instruction bearing on real life I ever received from you. Its real meaning, however, which sank into my mind even then, but which came partly to the surface of my consciousness only much later, was this: what you advised me to do was in your opinion and, even more, in my opinion at that time, the filthiest thing possible. That you wanted to see to it that I should not bring any of the physical filth home with me was unimportant, for you were only protecting yourself, your house. The important thing was rather that you yourself remained outside your own advice, a married man, a pure man, above such things; this was probably intensified for me at the time by the fact that even marriage seemed to me shameless; and hence it was impossible for me to apply to my parents the general information I had picked up about marriage. Thus you became still purer, rose still higher. The thought that you might have given yourself similar advice before your marriage was to me utterly unthinkable. So there was hardly any smudge of earthly filth on you at all. And it was you who pushed me down into this filth—just as though I were predestined to it—with a few frank words. And so, if the world consisted only of me and you (a notion I was much inclined to have), then this purity of the world came to an end with you and, by virtue of your advice, the filth began with me. In itself it was, of course, incomprehensible that you should thus condemn me; only old guilt, and profoundest contempt on your side, could explain it to me. And so again I was seized in my innermost being—and very hard indeed.

Here perhaps both our guiltlessness becomes most evident. A gives B a piece of advice that is frank, in keeping with his attitude to life, not very lovely but still, even today perfectly usual in the city, a piece of advice that might prevent damage to health. This piece of advice is for B morally not very invigorating —but why should he not be able to work his way out of it, and repair the damage in the course of the years? Besides, he does not even have to take the advice; and there is no reason why the advice itself should cause B's whole future world to come tumbling down. And yet something of this kind does happen, but only for the very reason that A is you and B is myself.

This guiltlessness on both sides I can judge especially well because a similar clash between us occurred some twenty years later, in quite different circumstances—horrible in itself but much less damaging—for what was there in me, the thirty-six-year-old, that could still be damaged? I am referring to a brief discussion on one of those few tumultuous days that followed the announcement of my latest marriage plans. You said to me something like this: "She probably put on a fancy blouse, something these Prague Jewesses are good at, and right away, of course, you decided to marry her. And that as fast as possible, in a week, tomorrow, today. I can't understand you: after all, you're a grown man, you live in the city, and you don't know what to do but marry the next best girl. Isn't there anything else you can do? If you're frightened, I'll go with you to see her." You put it in more detail and more plainly, but I can no longer recall the details, perhaps too things became a little vague before my eyes, I paid almost more attention to Mother who, though in complete agreement with you, took something from the table and left the room with it.

You have hardly ever humiliated me more deeply with words and shown me your contempt more clearly. When you spoke to me in a similar way twenty years earlier, one might, looking at it through your eyes, have seen in it some respect for the precocious city boy, who in your opinion could already be initiated into life without more ado. Today this consideration could only intensify the contempt, for the boy who was about to make his first start got stuck halfway and today does not seem richer oy any experience, only more pitiable by twenty years. My choice of a girl meant nothing at all to you. You had (unconsciously) always kept down my power of decision and now believed (unconsciously) that you knew what it was worth. Of my attempts at escape in other directions you knew nothing, thus you could not know anything, either, of the thought processes that had led me to this attempt to marry, and had to try to guess at them, and in keeping with your general opinion of me, you guessed at the most abominable, crude, and ridiculous. And you did not for a moment hesitate to tell me this in just such a manner. The shame you inflicted on me with this was nothing to you in comparison to the shame that I would, in your opinion, inflict on your name by this marriage.

Now, regarding my attempts at marriage there is much you can say in reply, and you have indeed done so: you could not have much respect for my decision since I had twice broken the engagement with F. and had twice renewed it, since I had needlessly dragged you and Mother to Berlin to celebrate the engagement, and the like. All this is true—but how did it come about?

The fundamental thought behind both attempts at marriage was quite sound: to set up house, to become independent. An idea that does appeal to you, only in reality it always turns out like the children's game in which one holds and even grips the other's hand, calling out: "Oh, go away, go away, why don't you go away?" Which in our case happens to be complicated by the fact that you have always honestly meant this "go away!" and have always unknowingly held me, or rather held me down, only by the strength of your personality.

Although both girls were chosen by chance, they were extraordinarily well chosen. Again a sign of your complete misunderstanding, that you can believe that I—timid, hesitant, suspicious—can decide to marry in a flash, out of delight over a blouse. Both marriages would rather have been common sense marriages, in so far as that means that day and night, the first time for years, the second time for months, all my power of thought was concentrated on the plan.

Neither of the girls disappointed me, only I disappointed both of them. My opinion of them is today exactly the same as when I wanted to marry them.

It is not true either that in my second marriage

attempt I disregarded the experience gained from the first attempt, that I was rash and careless. The cases were quite different; precisely the earlier experience held out a hope for the second case, which was altogether much more promising. I do not want to go into details here.

Why then did I not marry? There were certainly obstacles, as there always are, but then, life consists in taking such obstacles. The essential obstacle, however, which is, unfortunately, independent of the individual case, is that obviously I am mentally incapable of marrying. This manifests itself in the fact that from the moment I make up my mind to marry I can no longer sleep, my head burns day and night, life can no longer be called life, I stagger about in despair. It is not actually worries that bring this about; true, in keeping with my sluggishness and pedantry countless worries are involved in all this, but they are not decisive; they do, like worms, complete the work on the corpse, but the decisive blow has come from elsewhere. It is the general pressure of anxiety, of weakness, of self-contempt.

I will try to explain it in more detail. Here, in the attempt to marry, two seemingly antagonistic elements in my relations with you unite more intensely than anywhere else. Marriage certainly is the pledge of the most acute form of self-liberation and independence. I would have a family, in my opinion the highest one can achieve, and so too the highest you have achieved; I would be your equal; all old and ever new shame and tyranny would be mere history. It would be like a fairy tale, but precisely there does the questionable element lie. It is too much; so much cannot be achieved. It is as if a person were a prisoner, and he had not only the intention to escape, which would perhaps be attainable, but also, and indeed simultaneously, the intention to rebuild the prison as a pleasure dome for himself. But if he escapes, he cannot rebuild, and if he rebuilds, he cannot escape. If I, in the particular unhappy relationship in which I stand to you, want to become independent, I must do something that will have, if possible, no connection with you at all; though marrying is the greatest thing of all and provides the most honorable independence, it is also at the same time in the closest relation to you. To try to get out of all this has therefore a touch of madness about it, and every attempt is almost punished with it.

It is precisely this close relation that partly lures me toward marrying. I picture the equality which would then arise between us—and which you would be able to understand better than any other form of equality—as so beautiful because then I could be a free, grateful, guiltless, upright son, and you could be an untroubled, untyrannical, sympathetic, contented father. But to this end everything that ever happened would have to be undone, that is, we ourselves should have to be cancelled out.

But we being what we are, marrying is barred to me because it is your very own domain. Sometimes I imagine the map of the world spread out and you stretched diagonally across it. And I feel as if I could consider living in only those regions that either are not covered by you or are not within your reach. And in keeping with the conception I have of your magnitude, these are not many and not very comforting regions—and marriage is not among them.

This very comparison proves that I certainly do not mean to say that you drove me away from marriage by your example, as you had driven me away from your business. Quite the contrary, despite the remote similarity. In your marriage I had before me what was, in many ways, a model marriage, a model in constancy, mutual help, number of children; and even when the children grew up and increasingly disturbed the peace, the marriage as such remained undisturbed. Perhaps I formed my high idea of marriage on this model; the desire for marriage was powerless for other reasons. Those lay in your relation to your children, which is, after all, what this whole letter is about.

There is a view according to which fear of marriage sometimes has its source in a fear that one's children would some day pay one back for the sins one has committed against one's own parents. This, I believe, has no very great significance in my case, for my sense of guilt actually originates in you, and is filled with such conviction of its uniqueness—indeed, this feeling of uniqueness is an essential part of its tormenting nature—that any repetition is unthinkable. All the same, I must say that I should find such a mute, glum, dry, doomed son unbearable; I dare say that, if there were no other possibility, I should flee from him, emigrate, as you meant to do only because of my marriage. And this may also have had some influence on my incapacity to marry.

What is much more important in all this, however, is the anxiety about myself. This has to be understood as follows: I have already indicated that in my writing, and in everything connected with it, I have made some attempts at independence, attempts at escape, with the very smallest of success; they will scarcely lead any farther; much confirms this for me. Nevertheless it is my duty or, rather, the essence of my life, to watch over them, to let no danger that I can avert, indeed no possibility of such a danger, approach them. Marriage bears the possibility of such a danger, though also the possibility of the greatest help; for me, however, it is enough that there is the possibility of a danger. What should I do if it did turn out to be a danger! How could I continue living in matrimony in the perhaps undemonstrable, but nevertheless irrefutable impression of this danger? Faced with this I may waver, but the final outcome is certain: I must renounce. The simile of the bird in the hand and the two in the bush has only a very remote application here. In my hand I have nothing, in the bush is everything, and yet—so it is decided by the conditions of battle and the exigency of life—I must choose the nothing. I had to make a similar choice when I chose my profession.

The most important obstacle to marriage, however, is the no longer eradicable conviction that what is essential to the support of a family and especially to its guidance, is what I have recognized in you; and indeed everything rolled into one, good and bad, as it is organically combined in you—strength, and scorn of others, health, and a certain immoderation, eloquence and inadequacy, self-confidence and dissatisfaction with everyone else, a worldly wisdom and tyranny, knowledge of human nature and mistrust of most people; then also good qualities without any drawback, such as industry, endurance, presence of mind, and fearlessness. By comparison I had almost nothing or very little of all this; and was it on this basis that I wanted to risk marrying, when I could see for myself that even you had to fight hard in marriage and, where the children were concerned, had even failed? Of course, I did not put this question to myself in so many words and I did not answer it in so many words; otherwise everyday thinking would have taken over and shown me other men who are different from you (to name one, near at hand, who is very different from you: Uncle Richard) and yet have married and have at least not collapsed under the strain, which is in itself a great deal and would have been quite enough for me. But I did not ask this question, I lived it from childhood on. I tested myself not only when faced with marriage, but in the face of every trifle; in the face of every trifle you by your example and your method of upbringing convinced me, as I have tried to describe, of my incapacity; and what turned out to be true of every trifle and proved you right, had to be fearfully true of the greatest thing of all: of marriage. Up to the time of my marriage attempts I grew up more or less like a businessman who lives from day to day, with worries and forebodings, but without keeping proper accounts. He makes a few small profits—which he constantly pampers and exaggerates in his imagination because of their rarity—but otherwise he has daily losses. Everything is entered, but never balanced. Now comes the necessity of drawing a balance, that is, the attempt at marriage. And with the large sums that have to be taken into account here it is as though there had never been even the smallest profit, everything one single great liability. And now marry without going mad!

That is what my life with you has been like up to now, and these are the prospects inherent in it for the future.

If you look at the reasons I offer for the fear I have of you, you might answer: "You maintain I make things easy for myself by explaining my relation to you simply as being your fault, but I believe that despite your outward effort, you do not make things more difficult for yourself, but much more profitable. At first you too repudiate all guilt and responsibility; in this our methods are the same. But whereas I then attribute the sole guilt to you as frankly as I mean it, you want to be 'overly clever' and 'overly affectionate' at the same time and acquit me also of all guilt. Of course, in the latter you only seem to succeed (and more you do not even want), and what appears between the lines, in spite of all the 'turns of phrase' about character and nature and antagonism and helplessness, is that actually I have been the aggressor, while everything you were up to was self-defense. By now you would have achieved enough by your very insincerity, for you have proved three things: first, that you are not guilty; second, that I am the guilty one; and third, that out of sheer magnanimity you are ready not only to forgive me but (what is both more and less) also to prove and be willing to believe yourself that—contrary to the truth—I also am not guilty. That ought to be enough for you now, but it is still not enough. You have put it into your head to live entirely off me. I admit that we fight with each other, but there are two kinds of combat. The chivalrous combat, in which independent opponents pit their strength against each other, each on his own, each losing on his own, each winning on his own. And there is the combat of vermin, which not only sting but, on top of it, suck your blood in order to sustain their own life. That's what the real professional soldier is, and that's what you are. You are unfit for life; to make life comfortable for yourself, without worries and without self-reproaches, you prove that I have taken your fitness away from you and put it in my own pocket. Why should it bother you that you are unfit for life, since I have the responsibility for it, while you calmly stretch out and let yourself be hauled through life, physically and mentally, by me. For example: when you recently wanted to marry, you wanted—and this you do, after all, admit in this letter—at the same time not to marry, but in order not to have to exert yourself you wanted me to help you with this not-marrying, by forbidding this marriage because of the 'disgrace' this union would bring upon my name. I did not dream of it. First, in this as in everything else I never wanted to be 'an obstacle to your happiness,' and second, I never want to have to hear such a reproach from my child. But did the self-restraint with which I left the marriage up to you do me any good? Not in the least. My aversion to your marriage would not have prevented it; on the contrary, it would have been an added incentive for you to marry the girl, for it would have made the 'attempt at escape,' as you put it, complete. And my consent to your marriage did not prevent your reproaches, for you prove that I am in any case to blame for your not marrying. Basically, however, in this as in everything else you have only proved to me that all my reproaches were justified, and that one especially justified charge was still missing: namely, the charge of insincerity, obsequiousness, and parasitism. If I am not very much mistaken, you are preying on me even with this letter itself."

My answer to this is that, after all, this whole rejoinder—which can partly also be turned against you —does not come from you, but from me. Not even your mistrust of others is as great as my self-mistrust, which you have bred in me. I do not deny a certain justification for this rejoinder, which in itself contributes new material to the characterization of our relationship. Naturally things cannot in reality fit together the way the evidence does in my letter; life is more than a Chinese puzzle. But with the correction

235

made by this rejoinder—a correction I neither can nor will elaborate in detail—in my opinion something has been achieved which so closely approximates the truth that it might reassure us both a little and make our living and our dying easier.

Franz

REFLECTIONS ON SIN, PAIN, HOPE, AND THE TRUE WAY*

1

THE TRUE WAY goes over a rope which is not stretched at any great height but just above the ground. It seems more designed to make people stumble than to be walked upon.

3

There are two cardinal sins from which all the others spring: impatience and laziness. Because of impatience we were driven out of Paradise, because of laziness we cannot return. Perhaps, however, there is only one

* These aphorisms were carefully written out and numbered by Kafka himself on separate pieces of paper.

cardinal sin: impatience. Because of impatience we
were driven out, because of impatience we cannot return.

6

The decisive moment in human development is a continuous one. For this reason the revolutionary movements which declare everything before them to be null
and void are in the right, for nothing has yet happened.

10

A first sign of nascent knowledge is the desire for death.
This life seems unendurable, any other unattainable.
One is no longer ashamed of wishing to die; one prays
to be conducted from the old cell that one hates into a
new one that one has yet to hate. There is in this a
vestige of faith that during the change the Master may
chance to walk along the corridor, contemplate the
prisoner, and say: "You must not lock up this one
again. He is to come to me."

12

Like a road in autumn: Hardly is it swept clean before
it is covered again with dead leaves.

13

A cage went in search of a bird.

15

If it had been possible to build the Tower of Babel
without ascending it, the work would have been permitted.

24

What is laid upon us is to accomplish the negative; the positive is already given.

25

Once we have granted accommodation to the Evil One he no longer demands that we should believe him.

26

The afterthoughts with which you justify your accommodation of the Evil One are not yours but those of the Evil One.

The animal snatches the whip from its master and whips itself so as to become master, and does not know that all this is only a fantasy caused by a new knot in the master's whiplash.

29

The crows maintain that a single crow could destroy the heavens. Doubtless that is so, but it proves nothing against the heavens, for the heavens signify simply: the impossibility of crows.

36

One cannot pay the Evil One in installments—and yet one perpetually tries to do it.

*   *   *

It is conceivable that Alexander the Great, in spite of the martial successes of his early days, in spite of the excellent army that he had trained, in spite of the power he felt within him to change the world, might have remained standing on the bank of the Hellespont and never have crossed it, and not out of fear, not out of indecision, not out of infirmity of will, but because of the mere weight of his own body.

52

There is only a spiritual world; what we call the physical world is the evil in the spiritual one, and what we call evil is only a necessary moment in our endless development.

In a light that is fierce and strong one can see the world dissolve. To weak eyes it becomes solid, to weaker eyes it shows fists, before still weaker eyes it feels ashamed and smites down him who dares to look at it.

53

All is deception: one can try to live with the minimum of illusion, take things as they are, or try to live with the maximum of illusion. In the first case one betrays good by wanting to make its achievement too easy, and evil by imposing overwhelmingly unfavorable fighting conditions upon it. In the second case one betrays good by refusing to strive towards it even on the earthly plane. In the third case one betrays good by sundering oneself as far as possible from it, and evil by hoping that through its ubiquity it may be rendered innocuous. From this it seems that the second course is the one to be preferred, for in every case one betrays good, but in this case one does not betray evil, at least in appearance.

54

There are questions which we could never get over if we were not delivered from them by the operation of nature.

55

For all things outside the physical world language can be employed only as a sort of adumbration, but never with even approximate exactitude, since in accordance with the physical world it treats only of possession and its connotations.

66

Theoretically there exists a perfect possibility of happiness: to believe in the indestructible element in oneself and not strive after it.

73

Intercourse with human beings seduces one to self-contemplation.

75

Profane love can seem more sublime than sacred love; of itself it could not do this, but as, unknown to itself, it possesses an element of sacred love, it can.

83

A faith like a guillotine, as heavy, as light.

84

Death confronts us not unlike the historical battle scene that hangs on the wall of the classroom. It is our task to obscure or quite obliterate the picture by our deeds while we are still in this world.

98

We too must suffer all the suffering around us. What each of us possesses is not a body but a process of growth, and it conducts us through every pain, in this form or in that. Just as the child unfolds through all the stages of life to old age and death (and every stage seems unattainable to the previous one, whether in fear or longing) so we unfold (not less deeply bound to humanity than to ourselves) through all the sufferings of this world. In this process there is no place for justice, but no place either for dread of suffering or for the interpretation of suffering as a merit.

103

"But then he returned to his work as if nothing had happened." That is a saying which sounds familiar to us from an indefinite number of old tales, though in fact it perhaps occurs in none.

THE WISH TO BE
A RED INDIAN

IF ONE WERE only an Indian, instantly alert, and on a racing horse, leaning against the wind, kept on quivering jerkily over the quivering ground, until one shed one's spurs, for there needed no spurs, threw away the reins, for there needed no reins, and hardly saw that the land before one was smoothly shorn heath when horse's neck and head would be already gone.

THE TRUTH ABOUT
SANCHO PANZA

WITHOUT MAKING ANY boast of it Sancho Panza succeeded in the course of years, by feeding him a great number of romances of chivalry and adventure in the evening and night hours, in so diverting from himself his demon, whom he later called Don Quixote, that this demon thereupon set out, uninhibited, on the maddest exploits, which, however, for the lack of a preordained object, which should have been Sancho Panza himself, harmed nobody. A free man, Sancho Panza philosophically followed Don Quixote on his crusades, perhaps out of a sense of responsibility, and had of them a great and edifying entertainment to the end of his days.

THE NEWS OF THE
BUILDING OF THE WALL

A FRAGMENT

THE NEWS OF the building of the wall now penetrated into this world. This, too, arrived late, some thirty years after its announcement. It was on a summer's evening. Ten years old, I stood on the bank of the river with my father. As befits the significance of this much discussed moment, I remember the smallest circumstances. He held me by the hand—he liked to do that even when he was very old—and with his other hand he stroked his long and very thin pipe as if it were a flute. His large, sparse, stiff beard moved in the wind; enjoying his pipe, he looked upwards across the river. This made his pigtail, which was an object of reverence to children, sink lower, softly rustling against the gold-embroidered silk of his holiday gown. At that moment a bark came to a stop in front of us; the boatman beckoned to my father to descend the slope, while he himself climbed up to meet him. They met each other in the middle; the boatman whispered something into my father's ear. To get even closer to him, he embraced him. I did not understand what was said and saw only that my father did not seem to believe the news. The boatman tried to convince him that it was the truth, but Father still could not believe it; the boatman, with all the passion of a sailor, almost tore his clothes open on his breast in order to convince him that it was so. Father became quieter, and the boatman leaped back into the bark with a clatter and sailed away. Meditatively, my father turned back toward me, knocked out his pipe and stuck it in his belt, stroked my cheek, and pulled my head toward him. This was what I liked most, it made me very happy, and so we returned home. There the rice soup was already steaming on the table, several guests were already gathered, and the wine was just being poured into the cups. Without paying any attention to all this, my father began to report from the threshold what he had heard. Naturally, I have no exact recollection of his words, but because of the extraordinary nature of the circumstances involved, which was enough to impress even a child, their meaning sank into me so deeply that I still feel able to give a kind of verbatim version of them. And I do so now because these words were very characteristic of the popular interpretation. Thus, my father said more or less the following: A strange boatman—I know all those who usually sail past here, but this one was a stranger—has just told me that a great wall is going to be built to protect the Emperor. As you may know, the infidel nations, with demons among them too, often gather in front of the imperial palace and shoot their black arrows at the Emperor.

A REPORT TO
AN ACADEMY

HONORED MEMBERS OF the Academy!

You have done me the honor of inviting me to give your Academy an account of the life I formerly led as an ape.

I regret that I cannot comply with your request to the extent you desire. It is now nearly five years since I was an ape, a short space of time, perhaps, according to the calendar, but an infinitely long time to gallop through at full speed, as I have done, more or less accompanied by excellent mentors, good advice, applause, and orchestral music, and yet essentially alone, since all my escorters, to keep the image, kept well off the course. I could never have achieved what I have done had I been stubbornly set on clinging to my origins, to the remembrances of my youth. In fact, to give up being stubborn was the supreme commandment I laid upon myself; free ape as I was, I submitted myself to that yoke. In revenge, however, my memory of the past has closed the door against me more and more. I could have returned at first, had human beings allowed it, through an archway as wide as the span of heaven over the earth, but as I spurred myself on in my forced career, the opening narrowed and shrank behind me; I felt more comfortable in the world of men and fitted it better; the strong wind that blew after me out of my past began to slacken; today it is only a gentle puff of air that plays around my heels; and the opening in the distance, through which it comes and through which I once came myself, has grown so small that, even if my strength and my will power sufficed to get me back to it, I should have to scrape the very skin from my body to crawl through. To put it plainly, much as I like expressing myself in images, to put it plainly: your life as apes, gentlemen, insofar as something of that kind lies behind you, cannot be farther removed from you than mine is from me. Yet everyone on earth feels a tickling at the heels; the small chimpanzee and the great Achilles alike.

But to a lesser extent I can perhaps meet your demand, and indeed I do so with the greatest pleasure. The first thing I learned was to give a handshake; a handshake betokens frankness; well, today, now that I stand at the very peak of my career, I hope to add frankness in words to the frankness of that first handshake. What I have to tell the Academy will contribute nothing essentially new, and will fall far behind what you have asked of me and what with the best will in the world I cannot communicate—nonetheless, it should indicate the line an erstwhile ape has had to follow in entering and establishing himself in the world of men. Yet I could not risk putting into words even such insignificant information as I am going to give you if I were not quite sure of myself and if my position on all the great variety stages of the civilized world had not become quite unassailable.

I belong to the Gold Coast. For the story of my capture I must depend on the evidence of others. A hunting expedition sent out by the firm of Hagenbeck —by the way, I have drunk many a bottle of good red wine since then with the leader of that expedition— had taken up its position in the bushes by the shore when I came down for a drink at evening among a troop of apes. They shot at us; I was the only one that was hit; I was hit in two places.

Once in the cheek; a slight wound; but it left a large, naked, red scar which earned me the name of Red Peter, a horrible name, utterly inappropriate, which only some ape could have thought of, as if the only difference between me and the performing ape Peter, who died not so long ago and had some small local reputation, were the red mark on my cheek. This by the way.

The second shot hit me below the hip. It was a severe wound, it is the cause of my limping a little to this day. I read an article recently by one of the ten thousand windbags who vent themselves concerning me in the newspapers, saying: my ape nature is not yet quite under control; the proof being that when visitors come to see me, I have a predilection for taking down my trousers to show them where the shot went in. The hand which wrote that should have its fingers shot away one by one. As for me, I can take my trousers down before anyone if I like; you would find nothing but a well-groomed fur and the scar made—let me be particular in the choice of a word for this particular purpose, to avoid misunderstanding—the scar made by a wanton shot. Everything is open and aboveboard; there is nothing to conceal; when the plain truth is in question, great minds discard the niceties of refinement. But if the writer of the article were to take down his trousers before a visitor, that would be quite another story, and I will let it stand to his credit that he does not do it. In return, let him leave me alone with his delicacy!

After these two shots I came to myself—and this is where my own memories gradually begin—between decks in the Hagenbeck steamer, inside a cage. It was not a four-sided barred cage; it was only a three-sided cage nailed to a locker; the locker made the fourth side of it. The whole construction was too low for me to stand up in and too narrow to sit down in. So I had to squat with my knees bent and trembling all the time, and also, since probably for a time I wished to see no one, and to stay in the dark, my face was turned toward the locker while the bars of the cage cut into my flesh behind. Such a method of confining wild beasts is supposed to have its advantages during the first days of captivity, and out of my own experiences I cannot deny that from the human point of view this is really the case.

But that did not occur to me then. For the first time in my life I could see no way out; at least no direct way out; directly in front of me was the locker, board fitted close to board. True, there was a gap running right through the boards which I greeted with the blissful howl of ignorance when I first discovered it, but the hole was not even wide enough to stick one's tail through and not all the strength of an ape could enlarge it.

I am supposed to have made uncommonly little noise, as I was later informed, from which the conclusion was drawn that I would either soon die or if I managed to survive the first critical period would be very amenable to training. I did survive this period. Hopelessly sobbing, painfully hunting for fleas, apathetically licking a cocoanut, beating my skull against the locker, sticking out my tongue at anyone who came near me—that was how I filled in time at first in my new life. But over and above it all only the one feeling: no way out. Of course what I felt then as an ape I can represent now only in human terms, and therefore I misrepresent it, but although I cannot reach back to the truth of the old ape life, there is no doubt that it lies somewhere in the direction I have indicated.

Until then I had had so many ways out of everything, and now I had none. I was pinned down. Had I been nailed down, my right to free movement would not have been lessened. Why so? Scratch your flesh raw between your toes, but you won't find the answer. Press yourself against the bar behind you till it nearly cuts you in two, you won't find the answer. I had no way out but I had to devise one, for without it I could not live. All the time facing that locker—I should certainly have perished. Yet as far as Hagenbeck was concerned, the place for apes was in front of a locker—well then, I had to stop being an ape. A fine, clear train of thought, which I must have constructed somehow with my belly, since apes think with their bellies.

I fear that perhaps you do not quite understand what

I mean by "way out." I use the expression in its fullest and most popular sense. I deliberately do not use the word "freedom." I do not mean the spacious feeling of freedom on all sides. As an ape, perhaps, I knew that, and I have met men who yearn for it. But for my part I desired such freedom neither then nor now. In passing: may I say that all too often men are betrayed by the word freedom. And as freedom is counted among the most sublime feelings, so the corresponding disillusionment can be also sublime. In variety theaters I have often watched, before my turn came on, a couple of acrobats performing on trapezes high in the roof. They swung themselves, they rocked to and fro, they sprang into the air, they floated into each other's arms, one hung by the hair from the teeth of the other. "And that too is human freedom," I thought, "self-controlled movement." What a mockery of holy Mother Nature! Were the apes to see such a spectacle, no theater walls could stand the shock of their laughter.

No, freedom was not what I wanted. Only a way out; right or left, or in any direction; I made no other demand; even should the way out prove to be an illusion; the demand was a small one, the disappointment could be no bigger. To get out somewhere, to get out! Only not to stay motionless with raised arms, crushed against a wooden wall.

Today I can see it clearly; without the most profound inward calm I could never have found my way out. And indeed perhaps I owe all that I have become to the calm that settled within me after my first few days in the ship. And again for that calmness it was the ship's crew I had to thank.

They were good creatures, in spite of everything. I find it still pleasant to remember the sound of their heavy footfalls which used to echo through my half-dreaming head. They had a habit of doing everything as slowly as possible. If one of them wanted to rub his eyes, he lifted a hand as if it were a drooping weight. Their jests were coarse, but hearty. Their laughter had always a gruff bark in it that sounded dangerous but meant nothing. They always had something in their mouths to spit out and did not care where they spat it. They always grumbled that they got fleas from me; yet they were not seriously angry about it; they knew that my fur fostered fleas, and that fleas jump; it was a simple matter of fact to them. When they were off duty some of them often used to sit down in a semi-circle around me; they hardly spoke but only grunted to each other; smoked their pipes, stretched out on lockers; smacked their knees as soon as I made the slightest movement; and now and then one of them would take a stick and tickle me where I liked being tickled. If I were to be invited today to take a cruise on that ship I should certainly refuse the invitation, but just as certainly the memories I could recall between its decks would not all be hateful.

The calmness I acquired among these people kept me above all from trying to escape. As I look back now, it seems to me I must have had at least an inkling that I had to find a way out or die, but that my way out could not be reached through flight. I cannot tell now whether escape was possible, but I believe it must have been; for an ape it must always be possible. With my teeth as they are today I have to be careful even in simply cracking nuts, but at that time I could certainly have managed by degrees to bite through the lock of my cage. I did not do it. What good would it have done me? As soon as I had poked out my head I should have been caught again and put in a worse cage; or I might have slipped among the other animals without being noticed, among the pythons, say, who were opposite me, and so breathed out my life in their embrace; or supposing I had actually succeeded in sneaking out as far as the deck and leaping overboard, I should have rocked for a little on the deep sea and then been drowned. Desperate remedies. I did not think it out in this human way, but under the influence of my surroundings I acted as if I had thought it out.

I did not think things out; but I observed everything quietly. I watched these men go to and fro, always the same faces, the same movements, often it seemed to me there was only the same man. So this man or these men walked about unimpeded. A lofty goal faintly dawned before me. No one promised me that if I became like them the bars of my cage would be taken away. Such promises for apparently impossible contingencies are not given. But if one achieves the impossible, the promises appear later retrospectively precisely where one had looked in vain for them before. Now, these men in themselves had no great attraction for me. Had I been devoted to the aforementioned idea of freedom, I should certainly have preferred the deep sea to the way out that suggested itself in the heavy faces of these men. At any rate, I watched them for a long time before I even thought of such things, indeed, it was only the mass weight of my observations that impelled me in the right direction.

It was so easy to imitate these people. I learned to spit in the very first days. We used to spit in each other's faces; the only difference was that I licked my face clean afterwards and they did not. I could soon smoke a pipe like an old hand; and if I also pressed my thumb into the bowl of the pipe, a roar of appreciation went up between-decks; only it took me a very long time to understand the difference between a full pipe and an empty one.

My worst trouble came from the schnapps bottle. The smell of it revolted me; I forced myself to it as best I could; but it took weeks for me to master my repulsion. This inward conflict, strangely enough, was taken more seriously by the crew than anything else about me. I cannot distinguish the men from each other in my recollection, but there was one of them who came again and again, alone or with friends, by day, by night, at all kinds of hours; he would post himself before me with the bottle and give me instructions. He could not understand me, he wanted to solve the enigma of my being. He would slowly uncork the bottle and then look at me to see if I had followed him; I admit that I always watched him with wildly eager, too eager attention; such a student of humankind no human teacher ever found on earth. After the bottle was uncorked he lifted it to his mouth; I followed it with my

251

eyes right up to his jaws; he would nod, pleased with me, and set the bottle to his lips; I, enchanted with my gradual enlightenment, squealed and scratched myself comprehensively wherever scratching was called for; he rejoiced, tilted the bottle, and took a drink; I, impatient and desperate to emulate him, befouled myself in my cage, which again gave him great satisfaction; and then, holding the bottle at arm's length and bringing it up with a swing, he would empty it at one draught, leaning back at an exaggerated angle for my better instruction. I, exhausted by too much effort, could follow him no farther and hung limply to the bars, while he ended his theoretical exposition by rubbing his belly and grinning.

After theory came practice. Was I not already quite exhausted by theoretical instruction? Indeed I was, utterly exhausted. That was part of my destiny. And yet I would take hold of the proffered bottle as well as I was able; uncork it, trembling; this successful action would gradually inspire me with new energy; I would lift the bottle, already following my original model almost exactly; put it to my lips and—and then throw it down in disgust, utter disgust, although it was empty and filled only with the smell of the spirit, throw it down on the floor in disgust. To the sorrow of my teacher, to the greater sorrow of myself; neither of us being really comforted by the fact that I did not forget, even though I had thrown away the bottle, to rub my belly most admirably and to grin.

Far too often my lesson ended in that way. And to the credit of my teacher, he was not angry; sometimes indeed he would hold his burning pipe against my fur, until it began to smolder in some place I could not easily reach, but then he would himself extinguish it with his own kind, enormous hand; he was not angry with me, he perceived that we were both fighting on the same side against the nature of apes and that I had the more difficult task.

What a triumph it was then both for him and for me, when one evening before a large circle of spectators —perhaps there was a celebration of some kind, a gramophone was playing, an officer was circulating among the crew—when on this evening, just as no one was looking, I took hold of a schnapps bottle that had been carelessly left standing before my cage, uncorked it in the best style, while the company began to watch me with mounting attention, set it to my lips without hesitation, with no grimace, like a professional drinker, with rolling eyes and full throat, actually and truly drank it empty; then threw the bottle away, not this time in despair but as an artistic performer; forgot, indeed, to rub my belly; but instead of that, because I could not help it, because my senses were reeling, called a brief and unmistakable "Hallo!" breaking into human speech, and with this outburst broke into the human community, and felt its echo: "Listen, he's talking!" like a caress over the whole of my sweat-drenched body.

I repeat: there was no attraction for me in imitating human beings; I imitated them because I needed a way out, and for no other reason. And even that triumph of mine did not achieve much. I lost my human voice again at once; it did not come back for months; my aversion for the schnapps bottle returned again with even greater force. But the line I was to follow had in any case been decided, once for all.

When I was handed over to my first trainer in Hamburg I soon realized that there were two alternatives before me; the Zoological Gardens or the variety stage. I did not hesitate. I said to myself: do your utmost to get onto the variety stage; the Zoological Gardens means only a new cage; once there, you are done for.

And so I learned things, gentlemen. Ah, one learns when one has to; one learns when one needs a way out; one learns at all costs. One stands over oneself with a whip; one flays oneself at the slightest opposition. My ape nature fled out of me, head over heels and away, so that my first teacher was almost himself turned into an ape by it, had soon to give up teaching and was taken away to a mental hospital. Fortunately he was soon let out again.

But I used up many teachers, indeed, several teachers

at once. As I became more confident of my abilities, as the public took an interest in my progress and my future began to look bright, I engaged teachers for myself, established them in five communicating rooms, and took lessons from them all at once by dint of leaping from one room to the other.

That progress of mine! How the rays of knowledge penetrated from all sides into my awakening brain! I do not deny it: I found it exhilarating. But I must also confess: I did not overestimate it, not even then, much less now. With an effort which up till now has never been repeated I managed to reach the cultural level of an average European. In itself that might be nothing to speak of, but it is something insofar as it has helped me out of my cage and opened a special way out for me, the way of humanity. There is an excellent idiom: to fight one's way through the thick of things; that is what I have done, I have fought through the thick of things. There was nothing else for me to do, provided always that freedom was not to be my choice.

As I look back over my development and survey what I have achieved so far, I do not complain, but I am not complacent either. With my hands in my trouser pockets, my bottle of wine on the table, I half lie and half sit in my rocking chair and gaze out of the window; if a visitor arrives, I receive him with propriety. My manager sits in the anteroom; when I ring, he comes and listens to what I have to say. Nearly every evening I give a performance, and I have a success that could hardly be increased. When I come home late at night from banquets, from scientific receptions, from social gatherings, there sits waiting for me a half-trained little chimpanzee and I take comfort from her as apes do. By day I cannot bear to see her; for she has the insane look of the bewildered half-broken animal in her eye; no one else sees it, but I do, and I cannot bear it. On the whole, at any rate, I have achieved what I set out to achieve. But do not tell me that it was not worth the trouble. In any case, I am not appealing for any man's verdict, I am only imparting

254

knowledge, I am only making a report. To you also, honored Members of the Academy, I have only made a report.

Translated by Willa and Edwin Muir

SELECTIONS FROM
DIARIES, 1911-1923

February 19, 1911. The special nature of my inspiration in which I, the most fortunate and unfortunate of men, now go to sleep at 2 A.M. (perhaps, if I can only bear the thought of it, it will remain, for it is loftier than all before), is such that I can do everything, and not only what is directed to a definite piece of work. When I arbitrarily write a single sentence, for instance, "He looked out of the window," it already has perfection.

October 24, 1911. Yesterday it occurred to me that I did not always love my mother as she deserved and as I could, only because the German language prevented it. The Jewish mother is no "Mutter," to call her "Mutter" makes her a little comic (not to herself, because we are in Germany), we give a Jewish woman the name of a German mother, but forget the contradiction that sinks into the emotions so much the more heavily; "Mutter" is peculiarly German for a Jew, it unconsciously contains, together with the Christian splendor Christian coldness also, the Jewish woman who is called "Mutter" therefore becomes not only comic but strange. Mama would be a better name if only one didn't imagine "Mutter" behind it. I believe that it is only the memories of the ghetto that still preserve the Jewish family, for the word "Vater" too is far from meaning the Jewish father.

December 25, 1911. In Hebrew my name is Amschel, like my mother's maternal grandfather, whom my mother, who was six years old when he died, can remember as a very pious and learned man with a long, white beard. She remembers how she had to take hold of the toes of the corpse and ask forgiveness for any offense she may have committed against her grandfather. She also remembers her grandfather's many books which lined the walls. He bathed in the river every day, even in winter, when he chopped a hole in the ice for his bath. My mother's mother died of typhus at an early age. From the time of this death her grandmother became melancholy, refused to eat, spoke with no one; once, a year after the death of her daughter, she went for a walk and did not return, her body was found in the Elbe. An even more learned man than her grandfather was my mother's great-grandfather, Christians and Jews held him in equal honor; during a fire a miracle took place as a result of his piety, the flames jumped over and spared his house while the houses around it burned down. He had four sons, one was converted to Christianity and became a doctor. All but my mother's grandfather died young. He had one son, whom my mother knew as crazy Uncle Nathan, and one daughter, my mother's mother.

August 20, 1912. Miss F. B. When I arrived at Brod's on August 13th, she was sitting at the table. I was not at all curious about who she was, but rather took her for granted at once. Bony, empty face that wore its emptiness openly. Bare throat. A blouse thrown on. Looked very domestic in her dress although, as it later turned out, she by no means was. (I alienate myself from her a little by inspecting her so closely. What a state I'm in now, indeed, alienated in general from the whole of everything good, and don't even believe it yet. If the literary talk at Max's doesn't distract me too much, I'll try to write the story about Blenkelt today. It needn't be long, but I must hit it off right.) Almost broken nose. Blond, somewhat straight, unattractive hair, strong chin. As I was taking my seat I looked at her closely for the first time, by the time I was seated I already had an unshakable opinion.

September 23, 1912. This story, *The Judgment*, I wrote at one sitting during the night of the 22nd-23rd, from ten o'clock at night to six o'clock in the morning. I was hardly able to pull my legs out from under the desk, they had got so stiff from sitting. The fearful strain and joy, how the story developed before me, as if I were advancing over water. Several times during this night I heaved my own weight on my back. How everything can be said, how for everything, for the strangest fancies, there waits a great fire in which they perish and rise up again. How it turned blue outside the window. A wagon rolled by. Two men walked across the bridge. At two I looked at the clock for the last time. As the maid walked through the anteroom for the first time I wrote the last sentence. Turning out the light and the light of day. The slight pains around my heart. The weariness that disappeared in the middle of the night. The trembling entrance into my sisters' room. Reading aloud. Before that, stretching in the presence of the maid and saying, "I've been writing until now." The appearance of the undisturbed bed, as though it had just been brought in. The conviction verified that with my novel-writing I am in the shameful lowlands of writing. Only *in this way* can writing be done, only with such coherence, with such a complete opening out of the body and the soul. Morning in bed. The always clear eyes. Many emotions carried along in the writing, joy, for example, that I shall have something beautiful for Max's *Arkadia*, thoughts about Freud, of course; in one passage, of *Arnold Beer;* in another, of Wassermann; in one, of Werfel's giantess; of course, also of my "The Urban World."

September 24, 1912. My sister said: The house (in the story) is very like ours. I said: How? In that case, then, Father would have to be living in the toilet.

June 21, 1913. The tremendous world I have in my head. But how free myself and free it without being torn to pieces. And a thousand times rather be torn to pieces than retain it in me or bury it. That, indeed, is why I am here, that is quite clear to me.

July 21, 1913. Don't despair, not even over the fact that you don't despair. Just when everything seems over with, new forces come marching up, and precisely that means that you are alive. And if they don't, then everything is over with here, once and for all.

August 14, 1913. Conclusion for my case from *The Judgment*. I am indirectly in her debt for the story. But Georg goes to pieces because of his fiancée.

Coitus as punishment for the happiness of being together. Live as ascetically as possible, more ascetically than a bachelor, that is the only possible way for me to endure marriage. But she?

And despite all this, if we, I and F., had equal rights, if we had the same prospects and possibilities, I would not marry. But this blind alley into which I have slowly pushed her life makes it an unavoidable duty for me, although its consequences are by no means unpredictable. Some secret law of human relationship is at work here.

August 21, 1913. Today I got Kierkegaard's *Buch des Richters*. As I suspected, his case, despite essential differences, is very similar to mine, at least he is on the same side of the world. He bears me out like a friend. I drafted the following letter to her father, which, if I have the strength, I will send off tomorrow. [See Letters to Felice, p. 275.]

August 30, 1913. Where am I to find salvation? How many untruths I no longer even knew about will be brought to the surface. If they are going to pervade our marriage as they pervaded the goodbye, then I have certainly done the right thing. In me, by myself, without human relationship, there are no visible lies. The limited circle is pure.

January 8, 1914. What have I in common with Jews? I have hardly anything in common with myself and should stand very quietly in a corner, content that I can breathe.

May 27, 1914. A heavy downpour. Stand and face the rain, let its iron rays pierce you; drift with the water that wants to sweep you away but yet stand fast, and upright in this way abide the sudden and endless shining of the sun.

June 6, 1914. Back from Berlin. Was tied hand and foot like a criminal. Had they sat me down in a corner bound in real chains, placed policemen in front of me and let me look on simply like that, it could not have been worse. And that was my engagement; everybody made an effort to bring me to life, and when they couldn't, to put up with me as I was. F. least of all, of course, with complete justification, for she suffered the most. What was merely a passing occurrence to the others, to her was a threat.

July 23, 1914. The tribunal in the hotel. Trip in the cab. F.'s face. She patted her hair with her hand, wiped her nose, yawned. Suddenly she gathered herself together and said very studied, hostile things she had long been saving up. The trip back with Miss Bl. The room in the hotel; heat reflected from the wall across the street. Afternoon sun, in addition. Energetic waiter, almost an Eastern Jew in his manner. The courtyard noisy as a boiler factory. Bad smells. Bedbug. Crushing it a difficult decision. Chambermaid astonished:

There are no bedbugs anywhere, once only did a guest find one in the corridor.

At her parents'. Her mother's occasional tears. I recited my lesson. Her father understood the thing from every side. Made a special trip from Malmö to meet me, traveled all night; sat there in his shirt sleeves. They agreed that I was right, there was nothing, or not much, that could be said against me. Devilish in my innocence. Miss Bl.'s apparent guilt.

August 6, 1914. What will be my fate as a writer is very simple. My talent for portraying my dreamlike inner life has thrust all other matters into the background; my life has dwindled dreadfully, nor will it cease to dwindle. Nothing else will ever satisfy me. But the strength I can muster for that portrayal is not to be counted upon: perhaps it has already vanished forever, perhaps it will come back to me again, although the circumstances of my life don't favor its return. Thus I waver, continually fly to the summit of the mountain, but then fall back in a moment. Others waver too, but in lower regions, with greater strength; if they are in danger of falling, they are caught up by the kinsman who walks beside them for that very purpose. But I waver on the heights; it is not death, alas, but the eternal torments of dying.

September 30, 1915. Rossmann and K., the innocent and the guilty, both executed without distinction in the end, the guilty one with a gentler hand, more pushed aside than struck down.

July 5, 1916. The hardships of living together. Forced upon us by strangeness, pity, lust, cowardice, vanity, and only deep down, perhaps, a thin little stream worthy of the name of love, impossible to seek out, flashing once in the moment of a moment.

September 15, 1917. You have the chance, as far as it is at all possible, to make a new beginning. Don't throw it away. If you insist on digging deep into yourself,

you won't be able to avoid the muck that will well up.
But don't wallow in it. If the infection in your lungs
is only a symbol, as you say, a symbol of the infection
whose inflammation is called F. and whose depth is
its deep justification; if this is so then the medical
advice (light, air, sun, rest) is also a symbol. Lay hold
of this symbol.

September 25, 1917. I can still have passing satisfaction from works like *A Country Doctor*, provided I can
still write such things at all (very improbable). But
happiness only if I can raise the world into the pure,
the true, and the immutable.

October 8, 1917. Dickens' *Copperfield*. "The Stoker" a
sheer imitation of Dickens, the projected novel even
more so. The story of the trunk, the boy who delights
and charms everyone, the menial labor, his sweetheart
in the country house, the dirty houses, *et al.*, but above
all the method. It was my intention, as I now see, to
write a Dickens novel, but enhanced by the sharper
lights I should have taken from the times and the duller
ones I should have got from myself. Dickens' opulence
and great, careless prodigality, but in consequence
passages of awful insipidity in which he wearily works
over effects he has already achieved. Gives one a barbaric impression because the whole does not make
sense, a barbarism that I, it is true, thanks to my weakness and wiser for my epigonism, have been able to
avoid. There is a heartlessness behind his sentimentally
overflowing style. These rude characterizations which
are artificially stamped on everyone and without which
Dickens would not be able to get on with his story
even for a moment.

October 18, 1921. It is entirely conceivable that life's
splendor forever lies in wait about each one of us in all
its fulness, but veiled from view, deep down, invisible,
far off. It *is* there, though, not hostile, not reluctant,
not deaf. If you summon it by the right word, by

its right name, it will come. This is the essence of magic, which does not create but summons.

October 19, 1921. Anyone who cannot come to terms with his life while he is alive needs one hand to ward off a little his despair over his fate—he has little success in this—but with his other hand he can note down what he sees among the ruins, for he sees different (and more) things than do the others; after all, dead as he is in his own lifetime, he is the real survivor. This assumes that he does not need both hands, or more hands than he has, in his struggle against despair.

October 21, 1921. All is imaginary—family, office, friends, the street, all imaginary, far away or close at hand, the woman; the truth that lies closest, however, is only this, that you are beating your head against the wall of a windowless and doorless cell.

January 16, 1922. This past week I suffered something very like a breakdown; the only one to match it was on that night two years ago; apart from then I have never experienced its like. Everything seemed over with, even today there is no great improvement to be noticed. One can put two interpretations on the breakdown, both of which are probably correct.

First: breakdown, impossible to sleep, impossible to stay awake, impossible to endure life, or, more exactly, the course of life. The clocks are not in unison; the inner one runs crazily on at a devilish or demoniac or in any case inhuman pace, the outer one limps along at its usual speed. What else can happen but that the two worlds split apart, and they do split apart, or at least clash in a fearful manner. There are doubtless several reasons for the wild tempo of the inner process; the most obvious one is introspection, which will suffer no idea to sink tranquilly to rest but must pursue each one into consciousness, only itself to become an idea, in turn to be pursued by renewed introspection.

Second: This pursuit, originating in the midst of men, carries one in a direction away from them. The solitude that for the most part has been forced on me, in part voluntarily sought by me—but what was this if not compulsion too?—is now losing all its ambiguity and approaches its denouement. Where is it leading? The strongest likelihood is, that it may lead to madness; there is nothing more to say, the pursuit goes right through me and rends me asunder. Or I can—can I?—manage to keep my feet somewhat and be carried along in the wild pursuit. Where, then, shall I be brought? "Pursuit," indeed, is only a metaphor. I can also say, "assault on the last earthly frontier," an assault, moreover, launched from below, from mankind, and since this too is a metaphor, I can replace it by the metaphor of an assault from above, aimed at me from above.

All such writing is an assault on the frontiers; if Zionism had not intervened, it might easily have developed into a new secret doctrine, a Kabbalah. There are intimations of this. Though of course it would require genius of an unimaginable kind to strike root again in the old centuries, or create the old centuries anew and not spend itself withal, but only then begin to flower forth.

January 18, 1922. A moment of thought: Resign yourself, learn (learn, forty-year-old) to rest content in the moment (yes, once you could do it). Yes, in the moment, the terrible moment. It is not terrible, only your fear of the future makes it so. And also looking back on it in retrospect. What have you done with your gift of sex? It was a failure, in the end that is all that they will say. But it might easily have succeeded. A mere trifle, indeed so small as not to be perceived, decided between its failure and success. Why are you surprised? So it was with the greatest battles in the history of the world. Trifles decide trifles.

M. is right: fear means unhappiness but it does not follow from this that courage means happiness; not courage, which possibly aims at more than our strength can achieve (there were perhaps only two Jews in my class possessed of courage, and both shot themselves while still at school or shortly after); not courage, then,

263

but fearlessness with its calm, open eye and stoical resolution. Don't force yourself to do anything, yet don't feel unhappy that you force yourself, or that if you were to do anything, you would have to force yourself. And if you don't force yourself, don't hanker after the possibilities of being forced. Of course, it is never as clear as all that, or rather, it is; it is always as clear as all that; for instance: sex keeps gnawing at me, hounds me day and night, I should have to conquer fear and shame and probably sorrow too to satisfy it; yet on the other hand I am certain that I should at once take advantage, with no feeling of fear or sorrow or shame, of the first opportunity to present itself quickly, close at hand, and willingly; according to the above, then, I am left with the law that fear, etc. should not be conquered (but also that one should not continually dally with the idea of conquest), but rather take advantage of opportunities as they come (and not complain if none should come). It is true that there is a middle ground between "doing" and the "opportunity to do," namely this, to make, to tempt one's "opportunities" to one, a practice I have unfortunately followed not only in this but everything. As far as the "law" is concerned, there is hardly anything to be said against this, though this "tempting" of opportunities, especially when it makes use of ineffectual expedients, bears a considerable resemblance to "dallying with the idea of conquest," and there is no trace in it of calm, open-eyed fearlessness. Despite the fact that it satisfies the "letter" of the "law," there is something detestable in it which must be unconditionally shunned. To be sure, one would have to force oneself to shun it—and so I shall never have done with the matter.

January 19, 1922. What meaning have yesterday's conclusions today? They have the same meaning as yesterday, are true, except that the blood is oozing away in the chinks between the great stones of the law.

The infinite, deep, warm, saving happiness of sitting beside the cradle of one's child opposite its mother.

There is in it also something of this feeling: matters no longer rest with you, unless you wish it so. In contrast, this feeling of those who have no children: it perpetually rests with you, whether you will or no, every moment to the end, every nerve-racking moment, it perpetually rests with you, and without result. Sisyphus was a bachelor.

January 21, 1922. No one's task was as difficult, so far as I know. One might say that it is not a task at all, not even an impossible one, it is not even impossibility itself, it is nothing, it is not even as much of a child as the hope of a barren woman. But nevertheless it is the air I breathe, so long as I shall breathe at all.

Without forebears, without marriage, without heirs, with a fierce longing for forebears, marriage and heirs. They all of them stretch out their hands to me: forebears, marriage and heirs, but too far away for me.

January 24, 1922. Hesitation before birth. If there is a transmigration of souls then I am not yet on the bottom rung. My life is a hesitation before birth.

January 27, 1922. Despite my having legibly written my name to the hotel, despite their having correctly written to me twice already, they have Joseph K. down in the register. Shall I enlighten them, or shall I let them enlighten me?

January 28, 1922. A little dizzy, tired from the tobogganing; weapons still exist for me, however seldom I may employ them; it is so hard for me to lay hold of them because I am ignorant of the joys of their use, never learned how when I was a child. It is not only "Father's fault" that I never learned their use, but also my wanting to disturb the "peace," to upset the balance, and for this reason I could not allow a new person to be born elsewhere while I was bending every effort to bury him here. Of course, in this too there is a question of "fault," for why did I want to quit the world? Because "he" would not let me live in it, in his world. Though indeed I should not judge the matter so precisely, for I am now a citizen of this other world, whose relationship to the ordinary one is the relationship of the wilderness to cultivated land (I have been forty years wandering from Canaan); I look back at it like a foreigner, though in this other world as well— it is the paternal heritage I carry with me—I am the most insignificant and timid of all creatures and am able to keep alive thanks only to the special nature of its arrangements; in this world it is possible even for the humblest to be raised to the heights as if with lightning speed, though they can also be crushed forever as if by the weight of the seas. Should I not be thankful despite everything? Was it certain that I should find my way to this world? Could not "banishment" from one side, coming together with rejection from this, have crushed me at the border? Is not Father's power such that nothing (not I, certainly) could have resisted his decree? It is indeed a kind of Wandering in the Wilderness in reverse that I am undergoing: I think that I am continually skirting the wilderness and am full of childish hopes (particularly as regards women) that "perhaps I shall keep in Canaan after all"—when all the while I have been decades in the wilderness and these hopes are merely mirages born of despair, especially at those times when I am the wretchedest of creatures in the desert too, and Canaan is perforce my only Promised Land, for no third place exists for mankind.

January 29, 1922. Suffered some attacks on the road through the snow in the evening. There are conflicting thoughts always in my head, something like this: My situation in this world would seem to be a dreadful one, alone here in Spindelmühle, on a forsaken road, moreover, where one keeps slipping in the snow in the dark, a senseless road, moreover, without an earthly goal (to the bridge? Why there? Besides, I didn't even go that far); I too forsaken in this place (I cannot place a human, personal value on the help the doctor gives me, I haven't earned it; at bottom the fee is my only relationship to him), incapable of striking up a friendship with anyone, incapable of tolerating a friendship, at bottom full of endless astonishment when I see a group of people cheerfully assembled together (here in the hotel, indeed, there is little that is cheerful; I won't go so far as to say that I am the cause of this, in my character, perhaps, as "the man with the too-great shadow," though my shadow in this world *is* too great— with fresh astonishment I observe the capacity for resistance some people have, who, "in spite of everything," want to live under this shadow, directly under it; but there is much more than this to be said on the matter), or especially when I see parents with their children; forsaken, moreover, not only here but in general, even in Prague, my "home," and what is more, forsaken not by people (that would not be the worst thing, I could run after them as long as I was alive), but rather by myself vis-à-vis people, by my strength vis-à-vis people; I am fond of lovers but I cannot love, I am too far away, am banished, have—since I am human after all and my roots want nourishment—my proxies "down" (or up) there too, sorry, unsatisfactory comedians who can satisfy me (though indeed they don't satisfy me at all and it is for this reason that I am so forsaken) only because I get my principal nourishment from other roots in other climes, these roots too are sorry ones, but nevertheless better able to sustain life.

This brings me to the conflict in my thoughts. If things were only as they seem to be on the road in the snow, it would be dreadful; I should be lost, lost not in the sense of a dreadful future menacing me but in the sense of a present execution. But I live elsewhere; it is only that the attraction of the human world is so immense, in an instant it can make one forget everything. Yet the attraction of my world too is strong; those who love me love me because I am "forsaken"—not, I feel sure, on the principle of a Weissian vacuum, but because they sense that in happy moments I enjoy on another plane the freedom of movement completely lacking to me here.

If M., for example, should suddenly come here, it would be dreadful. Externally, indeed, my situation would at once seem comparatively brighter. I should be esteemed as one human being among others, I should have words spoken to me that were more than merely polite. I should sit at the actors' table (less erect, it is true, than now, when I am sitting here alone, though even now I am slumped down); outwardly, I should be almost a match in conviviality for Dr. H.— yet I should be plunged into a world in which I could not live. It only remains to solve the riddle of why I had fourteen days of happiness in Marienbad, and why, consequently, I might perhaps also be able to be happy here with M. (though of course only after a painful breaking down of barriers). But the difficulties would probably be much greater than in Marienbad, my opinions are more rigid, my experience larger. What used to be a dividing thread is now a wall, or a mountain range, or rather a grave.

June 12, 1923. More and more fearful as I write. It is understandable. Every word, twisted in the hands of the spirits—this twist of the hand is their characteristic gesture—becomes a spear turned against the speaker. Most especially a remark like this. And so ad infinitum. The only consolation would be: it happens whether you like or no. And what you like is of infinitesimally little help. More than consolation is: You too have weapons.

SELECTIONS FROM
LETTERS TO MILENA*

Dear Frau Milena,

(This mode of address is becoming tiresome, but it's one of those handles in the unsafe world to which the sick can hold on and it's not yet a proof of returning health when the handles become tiresome to them.) I have never lived among German people, German is my mother-tongue and therefore natural to me, but Czech feels to me far more intimate, which is why your letter dispels many an uncertainty, I see you clearer, the movements of your body, your hands, so quick, so determined, it's almost a meeting, although when I try to raise my eyes to your face, then in the flow of the letter—what a story!—fire breaks out and I see nothing but fire.

Of your husband I had made myself another picture. In the coffee-house circle he appeared to me as the most reliable, most understanding, the calmest person, almost exaggeratedly paternal, though also inscrutable, yet not to a point that would cancel what I've just said. I always had respect for him, for further insight I had neither opportunity nor ability, but friends, especially Max Brod, had a high opinion of him, and of this I was

* Franz Kafka first made Milena's acquaintance as the translator into Czech of his early short prose works.

always conscious when I thought of him. At one time I particularly liked his peculiarity of being called to the telephone in each coffee house several times during the evening. Presumably there must have been someone who, instead of sleeping, sat by the telephone dozing, his head on the back of his chair, and who started up from time to time to telephone him. A condition I understand so well that I mention it perhaps only for this reason.

Yours, Franz K.

As for Jewry. You ask me if I'm a Jew, perhaps this is only a joke, perhaps you're only asking me if I belong to those anxious Jews.

You may reproach the Jews for their specific anxiousness, although such a general reproach shows more theoretical than practical knowledge of human nature, more theoretical because first of all the reproach does not fit your husband at all according to your former description, nor secondly, in my experience, does it fit most Jews, and thirdly, it fits only isolated ones, but these most poignantly, for instance myself. The strangest thing is that in general the reproach does not fit. The insecure position of Jews, insecure within themselves, insecure among people, would make it above all comprehensible that they consider themselves to be allowed to own only what they hold in their hands or between their teeth, that furthermore only palpable possessions give them the right to live, and that they will never again acquire what they once have lost but that instead it calmly swims away from them forever. From the most improbable sides Jews are threatened with danger, or let us, to be more exact, leave the dangers aside and say they are threatened with threats.

Tomorrow I'll send the Father-letter to your apartment, please take good care of it, one day perhaps I might want to give it to my father. If possible let no one else read it. And in reading try to understand all the lawyer's tricks, it's a lawyer's letter. And in doing so never forget your big Nevertheless.

I somehow can no longer write of anything but what concerns us, us in the turmoil of the world, just us. Everything else is remote. Wrong! Wrong! But the lips are mumbling and my face lies in your lap.

The most beautiful of your letters (and that means a lot, for as a whole they are, almost in every line, the most beautiful thing that ever happened to me in my life) are those in which you agree with my "fear" and at the same time try to explain that I don't need to have it. For I too, even though I may sometimes look like a bribed defender of my "fear," probably agree with it deep down in myself, indeed it is part of me and perhaps the best part. And as it is my best, it is also perhaps this alone that you love. For what else worthy of love could be found in me? But this is worthy of love.

And when you once asked me how I could have called that Saturday "good" with that fear in my heart, it's not difficult to explain. Since I love you (*and I do love you, you stupid one, as the sea loves a pebble in its depths, this is just how my love engulfs you*—and may I in turn be the pebble with you, if Heaven permits), I love the whole world and this includes your left shoulder, no, it was first the right one, so I kiss it if I feel like it (and if you are nice enough to pull the blouse away from it) and this also includes your left shoulder and your face above me in the forest and my resting on your almost bare breast. And that's why you're right in saying that we were already one and I'm not afraid of it, rather it is my only happiness and my only pride and I don't confine it at all only to the forest.

But just between this day-world and that "half hour in bed" of which you once spoke contemptuously as "men's business," there lies for me an abyss which I cannot bridge, probably because I don't want to. That over there is a concern of the night, thoroughly and in every sense a concern of the night: this here is the world and I possess it and now I'm supposed to leap across

271

into the night in order to take possession of it once more. Can one take possession of anything twice? Does that not mean: to lose it? Here is the world which I possess, and I'm supposed to leap across for the sake of a sinister black-magic, of a hocus-pocus, a philosopher's stone, an alchemy, a wish-ring. Away with it, I'm terribly afraid of it.

To try and catch in one night by black magic, hastily, heavily breathing, helpless, obsessed, to try and obtain by black magic what every day offers to open eyes! ("Perhaps" children can't be begotten in any other way, "perhaps" children too are black magic. Let us leave this question for the moment.) This is the reason why I'm so grateful (to you and to everything) and it is therefore "samozřejmé" (natural) that by your side I'm most quiet and most unquiet, most inhibited and most free, and this also is why, after this realization, I have renounced all other life. Look into my eyes!

At last I've read the other letter, but actually only beginning with the passage: "Nechci abys na to odpovídal" —"I don't want you to answer that." I don't know what precedes this, but today, faced with your letters which confirm you irrefutably as I carry you locked within myself, I'm ready to sign it unread as true even if it should testify against me before the highest court. I'm dirty, Milena, infinitely dirty, which is why I make so much fuss about purity. No people sing with such pure voices as those who live in deepest hell; what we take for the song of angels is their song.

Nor is it perhaps really love when I say that for me you are the most beloved; love is to me that you are the knife which I turn within myself.

You say, Milena, that you don't understand it. Try to understand it by calling it illness. It's one of the many manifestations of illness which psychoanalysis believes it has uncovered. I don't call it illness and I consider the therapeutic part of psychoanalysis to be a hopeless error. All these so-called illnesses, sad as they may

272

appear, are matters of faith, efforts of souls in distress to find moorings in some maternal soil; thus psychoanalysis also considers the origin of religions to be nothing but what (in its opinion) causes the "illnesses" of the individual. Nowadays, of course, we generally lack a sense of religious community; the sects are countless and confined to single individuals—though perhaps it only appears so to the eye colored by the present.

Such moorings, however, which really take hold of solid ground, are after all not an isolated, interchangeable property of man, rather they are pre-existing in his nature and continue to form his nature (as well as his body) in this direction. And it's here they hope to cure?

It's a long time since I wrote to you, Frau Milena, and even today I'm writing only as the result of an incident. Actually, I don't have to apologize for my not writing, you know after all how I hate letters. All the misfortune of my life—I don't wish to complain, but to make a generally instructive remark—derives, one could say, from letters or from the possibility of writing letters. People have hardly ever deceived me, but letters always —and as a matter of fact not only those of other people, but my own. In my case this is a special misfortune of which I won't say more, but at the same time also a general one. The easy possibility of letter-writing must—seen merely theoretically—have brought into the world a terrible disintegration of souls. It is, in fact, an intercourse with ghosts, and not only with the ghost of the recipient but also with one's own ghost which develops between the lines of the letter one is writing and even more so in a series of letters where one letter corroborates the other and can refer to it as a witness. How on earth did anyone get the idea that people can communicate with one another by letter! Of a distant person one can think, and of a person who is near one can catch hold—all else goes beyond human strength. Writing letters, however, means to denude oneself before the ghosts, something for which they greedily wait.

Written kisses don't reach their destination, rather they are drunk on the way by the ghosts. It is on this ample nourishment that they multiply so enormously. Humanity senses this and fights against it and in order to eliminate as far as possible the ghostly element between people and to create a natural communication, the peace of souls, it has invented the railway, the motor car, the aeroplane. But it's no longer any good, these are evidently inventions being made at the moment of crashing. The opposing side is so much calmer and stronger; after the postal service it has invented the telegraph, the telephone, the radiograph. The ghosts won't starve, but we will perish.

SELECTIONS FROM
LETTERS TO FELICE

November 1, 1912

Dear Fräulein Felice,

You must not take offense at this form of address, at least not this time, for if I am to write about my mode of life, as you have asked me to do several times, I shall probably have some delicate things to say which I could hardly utter to a "Fräulein Bauer." Moreover this new form of address cannot be so very bad, or I should not have thought it out with so much and such lasting satisfaction.

My life consists, and basically always has consisted, of attempts at writing, mostly unsuccessful. But when I didn't write, I was at once flat on the floor, fit for the dustbin. My energies have always been pitifully weak; even though I didn't quite realize it, it soon became evident that I had to spare myself on all sides, renounce a little everywhere, in order to retain just enough strength for what seemed to me my main purpose. When I didn't do so (oh God, even on a holiday such as this, when I am acting as duty officer, there is no peace, just visitor after visitor, like a little hell let loose) but tried to reach beyond my strength, I was automatically forced back, wounded, humbled, forever weakened; yet this very fact which made me temporarily unhappy is precisely what gave me confidence in the long run, and I began to think that somewhere, however difficult to find, there must be a lucky star under which it would be possible to go on living. I once drew up a detailed list of the things I have sacrificed to writing, as well as the things that were taken from me for the sake of writing, or rather whose loss was only made bearable by this explanation.

Just as I am thin, and I am the thinnest person I know (and that's saying something, for I am no stranger to sanatoria), there is also nothing to me which, in relation to writing, one could call superfluous, superfluous in the sense of overflowing. If there is a higher power that wishes to use me, or does use me, then I am at its mercy, if no more than as a well-prepared instrument. If not, I am nothing, and will suddenly be abandoned in a dreadful void.

Now I have expanded my life to accommodate my thoughts about you, and there is hardly a quarter of an hour of my waking time when I haven't thought about you, and many quarter-hours when I do nothing else. But even this is related to my writing, my life is determined by nothing but the ups and downs of writing, and certainly during a barren period I should never have had the courage to turn to you. This is just as true as it is true that since that evening I have felt as though I had an opening in my chest through which there was an unrestrained drawing-in and drawing-out until one evening in bed, when, by calling to mind a story from the Bible, the necessity of this sensation, as well as the truth of the Bible story, were simultaneously confirmed.

Lately I have found to my amazement how intimately you have now become associated with my writing, although until recently I believed that the only time I did not think about you at all was while I was writing. In one short paragraph I had written, there were, among others, the following references to you and your letters: Someone was given a bar of chocolate. There was talk of small diversions someone had during working hours. Then there was a telephone call. And finally somebody urged someone to go to bed, and threatened to take him straight to his room if he did not obey, which was certainly prompted by the recollection of your mother's annoyance when you stayed so late at the office.—Such passages are especially dear to me; in them I take hold of you, without your feeling it, and therefore without your having to resist. And even if you were to read some of my writings, these little details would surely escape you. But believe me, probably nowhere in the world could you let yourself be caught with greater unconcern than here.

My mode of life is devised solely for writing, and if there are any changes, then only for the sake of perhaps fitting in better with my writing; for time is short, my strength is limited, the office is a horror, the apartment is noisy, and if a pleasant, straightforward life is not possible then one must try to wriggle through by subtle maneuvers. The satisfaction gained by maneuvering one's timetable successfully cannot be compared to the permanent misery of knowing that fatigue of any kind shows itself better and more clearly in writing than anything one is really trying to say. For the past six weeks, with some interruptions in the last few days, due to unbearable weakness, my timetable has been as follows: from 8 to 2 or 2:30 in the office, then lunch till 3 or 3:30, after that sleep in bed (usually only attempts: for a whole week I saw nothing but Montenegrins in my sleep, in extremely disagreeable clarity, which gave me headaches, I saw every detail of their complicated dress) till 7:30, then ten minutes of exercises, naked at the open window, then an hour's walk—alone, with Max, or with another friend, then dinner with my family (I have three sisters, one married, one engaged; the single one, without prejudicing my affection for the others, is easily my favorite); then at 10:30 (but often not till 11:30) I sit down to write, and I go on, depending on my strength, inclination, and luck, until 1, 2, or 3 o'clock, once even till 6 in the morning. Then again exercises, as above, but of course avoiding all exertions, a wash, and then, usually with a slight pain in my heart and twitching stomach muscles, to bed. Then every imaginable effort to get to sleep—i.e., to achieve the impossible, for one cannot sleep (Herr K. even demands dreamless sleep) and at the same time be thinking about one's work and trying to solve with certainty the one question that certainly is insoluble, namely, whether there will be a letter from you the next day, and at what time. Thus the night consists of two parts: one wakeful, the other sleepless, and if I were to tell you about it at length and you were prepared to listen, I should never finish. So it is hardly surprising if, at the office the next morning, I only just manage to start work with what little strength is left. In one of the corridors along which I always walk to reach my typist, there used to be a coffinlike trolley for the moving of files and documents, and each time I passed it I felt as though it had been made for me, and was waiting for me.

To be precise, I must not forget that I am not only a clerk, but also a manufacturer. For my brother-in-law owns an asbestos factory, and I (although only through money my father put into it) am a partner, and as such am on the board. This factory has already caused me enough pain and worry, but I don't want to talk about that now; in any case, I have neglected it for some time (i.e., I withhold my anyway useless collaboration) as much as I can, and more or less get by with it.

Once again I have told you so little, and have asked no questions, and once again I must close. But not a single answer and, even more certainly, not a single question shall be lost. There exists some kind of sorcery by which two people, without seeing each other, without talking to each other, can at least discover the greater part about each other's past literally in a flash, without having to tell each other all and everything; but this, after all, is almost an instrument of Black Magic (without seeming to be) which, although never without reward, one would certainly never resort to with impunity. Therefore I won't say it, unless you guess it first. It is terribly short, like all magic formulas.

Farewell, and let me reinforce this greeting by lingering over your hand.

Yours, Franz K.

[July] 10, 1913

If only I were with you. Felice, and had the capacity to make things clear to you, or rather the capacity just to see things clearly. It's all my fault. After all, we have never been as united as we are now; this Yes on both sides has tremendous power. But I am held back by what is almost a command from heaven; an apprehension that cannot be appeased; everything that used to be of the greatest importance to me—my health, my small income, my miserable disposition, all this for which there would be some justification—vanishes, is as nothing compared to this apprehension, and seems to be used only as a pretext. To be quite frank (as I have always been with you as far as my self-knowledge at the moment allows) and at long last to be recognized by you as the madman I am, it is my *dread of the union* even with the most beloved woman, above all with her. How can I explain to you what to me is so clear that I long to cover it, to stop it blinding me! And then of course it becomes less clear again when I read your sweet, trusting letter; then everything appears to be perfectly all right, and happiness seems to await us both.

Can you understand this, Felice, if only from a distance? I have a definite feeling that through marriage, *through the union, through the dissolution* of this nothingness that I am, I shall perish, and not alone but with my wife, and that the more I love her the swifter and more terrible it will be. Now you tell me what we should do, for I believe we are now so close to each other that neither of us, without the other's corroboration, could do anything on his own. Think carefully, too, about all that has been left unsaid! *Ask questions, I shall answer every one.* God, it really is about time to ease the pressure, and there surely isn't a girl who has been loved as I love you, and been tortured as I find it necessary to torture you.

Franz

To Felice's Father, Herr Carl Bauer

[August 28, 1913]

Dear Herr Bauer,

Now that I have extracted from you your two kind letters, I don't know whether you will have the patience and the desire to listen to what follows. But I do know that I have to say it. I would have to say it even if your letters had not inspired me with the confidence I now have in you.

What I told you in my first letter about my relationship with your daughter is true, and will remain so. But apart from one allusion which may have escaped your notice, something decisive was missing. Perhaps you thought there was no need to comment on it, because you believe that coming to grips with my character is entirely your daughter's affair and had already been achieved. This is not so. At times I used to think that it had, but again and again it turned out that it had not happened, and could not happen. I have deluded your daughter with my letters; as a rule I have not meant to deceive her (although sometimes I have, because I loved her, and love her, and have been terribly aware of our incompatibility), and perhaps by doing just this, I blinded her. I really don't know.

You know your own daughter: she is a gay, healthy, self-confident girl, who in order to live should be surrounded by gay, healthy, and lively people. You know me only from my visit (I was about to add that this should be enough), and I cannot repeat what I have told your daughter about myself in some 500 letters. But please consider this one important fact: my whole being is directed toward literature; I have followed this direction unswervingly until my 30th year, and the moment I abandon it I cease to live. Everything I am, and am not, is a result of this. I am taciturn, unsociable, morose, selfish, a hypochondriac, and actually in poor health. Fundamentally I deplore none of this: it is the earthly reflection of a higher necessity. (What I am really capable of is not the problem here, and has no connection with it.) I live within my family, among the kindest, most affectionate people—and am more

280

strange than a stranger. In recent years I have spoken hardly more than twenty words a day to my mother, and I exchange little more than a daily greeting with my father. To my married sisters and brothers-in-law I do not speak at all, although I have nothing against them. I lack all sense of family life.

And is your daughter, whose healthy nature has destined her for a happy married life, to live with this kind of man? Is she to tolerate a monastic existence with a person who, though he loves her as he can never love anyone else, spends most of his time in his room or wandering about by himself—simply because of his irrevocable vocation? Is she to tolerate a life utterly divorced from her parents, her family, and almost any other social contact—because I, who would lock my door against my best friend, cannot imagine any other kind of married life? Could she stand this? And what for? For my writing, which is highly problematic in her eyes and perhaps even in mine? And for this she is to live alone in a foreign town, in a marriage that may turn out to be a relationship of love and friendship rather than a real marriage?

I have said the minimum of what I intended to say. Above all: I want to make no excuses for myself. On our own, your daughter and I could find no solution: I love her too much, and she cannot see me as I am. And perhaps she wants the impossible only out of compassion, no matter how much she may deny it. Well, now we are three. You be the judge!

Very sincerely yours, Dr. F. Kafka

August 30, 1913

What is stopping me can hardly be said to be facts; it is fear, an insurmountable fear, fear of achieving happiness, a desire and a command to torment myself for some higher purpose. That you, dearest, should be forced to land under the wheels of this carriage, which is destined for me alone, is really terrible. I am consigned to darkness by my inner voice, yet in reality am drawn to you; this is irreconcilable; yet even if we were to try, the blows would fall alike on you and me.

I have calmed down, Felice; on Sunday I lay in the woods with a headache and kept turning my head in the grass with the pain; today it is better, but my self-control is no greater than it was before; when dealing with myself I am powerless. I can divide myself in my thoughts; I can stand at your side, calm and contented, and while doing so watch my utterly pointless self-torture; in my thoughts I can look down upon us both, and at the sight of the pain I inflict upon you, the kindest of girls, I can pray for some exquisite torture for myself; this I can do. The other day I wrote down the following wish: "When passing a house, to be pulled in through the ground-floor window by a rope tied around one's neck and to be hauled up, bloody and ragged, through all the ceilings, furniture, walls, and attics, without consideration, as if by a person who is paying no attention, until the empty noose, dropping the last shreds of me when breaking through the roof tiles, appears on the roof."

But in reality I can do nothing, am entirely shut in on myself, and hear your beloved voice only from afar. God knows from what source these perpetual, steadily revolving worries feed! I cannot get the better of them. I thought (and so did you) that I'd grow calmer once I had written to your father. The opposite has happened; intensified assault greatly intensifies the force of these worries and anxieties. This is the law by which all weaklings are governed, insisting on extreme atonement and extreme radical measures. The desire to renounce the greatest human happiness for the sake of writing keeps cutting every muscle in my body. I am unable to free myself. Everything is obscured by the apprehensions I feel at the idea of not renouncing.

Dearest, everything you say to me, I say almost all the time; the slightest detachment from you makes me smart; whatever happens between us is repeated with renewed intensity inside myself; faced with your letters, faced by your pictures, I succumb. And yet—of the four men I consider to be my true blood-relations (without comparing myself to them either in power or in range),

Grillparzer, Dostoevski, Kleist, and Flaubert, Dostoevski was the only one to get married, and perhaps Kleist, when compelled by outer and inner necessity to shoot himself on the Wannsee, was the only one to find the right solution. All this might be entirely irrelevant as far as we are concerned; after all, each one of us lives life anew—even if I were standing in the very center of the shadow they cast upon our own time. But this is a fundamental question of life and faith in general, and from this point of view interpreting the behavior of these four men makes more sense.

September [presumably October] 19, 1916

Dearest, for me to accept the things you say about Mother, parents, flowers, the New Year, and the company at table is not as simple as all that. You say that for you, too, to have to sit at table in my home with all my family won't "rank among your pleasantest experiences." Here you are merely expressing your opinion, and rightly so, regardless of whether I like it or not. Well, I don't like it. But I should certainly like it a great deal less had you said the opposite. Please tell me as plainly as possible what you think will make it unpleasant for you, and where the cause of this unpleasantness lies. We have often discussed this subject from my point of view, but in these matters it's hard to grasp even a little of the truth. One just has to keep on trying. Roughly—hence with rather more ruthlessness than the truth would warrant—I can describe my position as follows: Having as a rule depended on others, I have an infinite longing for independence, self-reliance, freedom in all directions; I would rather wear blinkers and go my own way to the bitter end, than have my vision distorted by being in the midst of frenzied family life. That's why every word I say to my parents, or they to me, so easily turns into a stumbling block under my feet. Any relationship not created by myself, even though it be opposed to parts of my own nature, is worthless; it hinders my movements, I hate it, or come near to hating it. The road is long, one's resources few, there is reason in plenty for this

283

hatred. Yet, I am my parents' progeny, am bound to them and to my sisters by blood; in my daily life, and because of the necessary obsession with my particular objectives, I am not conscious of this, yet fundamentally I respect it more than I know. Sometimes this too becomes the object of my hatred; at home the sight of the double bed, of sheets that have been slept in, of night-shirts carefully laid out, can bring me to the point of retching, can turn my stomach inside out; it is as though my birth had not been final, as though from this fusty life I keep being born again and again in this fusty room; as though I had to return there for confirmation, being—if not quite, at least in part—indissolubly connected with these distasteful things; something still clings to the feet as they try to break free, held fast as they are in the primeval slime. That is sometimes. At other times I know that after all they are my parents, are essential, strength-giving elements of my own self, belonging to me, not merely as obstacles but as human beings. At such times I want them as one wants perfection; since from way back and despite all my nastiness, rudeness, selfishness, and unkindness I have always trembled before them—and do so to this day, for in fact one never stops; and since they, Father on the one hand and Mother on the other, have —again quite naturally—almost broken my will, I want them to be worthy of their actions. (Now and again I think that Ottla would be the kind of mother I should like in the background: pure, truthful, honest, consistent—with humility and pride, receptiveness and reticence, devotion and self-reliance, timidity and courage, in unerring equilibrium. I mention Ottla because my mother after all is also part of her, though altogether unrecognizable.) So I want them to be worthy of their actions. In consequence, for me, they are a hundred times more unclean than they may be in reality, which doesn't really worry me; their foolishness is a hundred times greater, their absurdity a hundred times greater, their coarseness a hundred times greater. On the other hand their good qualities seem a hundred thousand times smaller than they are in reality. Thus they deceive me, and yet I cannot rebel against the laws of nature without going mad. So again there is hatred, and almost nothing but hatred. But you belong to me, I have made you mine; I do not believe that the battle for any woman in any fairy tale has been fought harder and more desperately than the battle for you within myself —from the beginning, over and over again, and perhaps forever. So you belong to me. Therefore my relationship with your relatives is not unlike my relationship with my own, albeit far less intense, of course, in regard to their good as well as their bad qualities. They too constitute a bond which hampers me (hampers me, even if we were never to exchange a word), and in the above-mentioned sense they are not worthy. In saying this I am being as frank with you as I am with myself. You mustn't hold it against me, nor see any arrogance in it; there is none, at least not where you would expect to find it. Suppose you were now in Prague, sitting at my parents' table, the area of conflict, which is what I fight against in my parents, would naturally have grown greater. They would assume that my bond with the family as a whole had grown greater (but it hasn't, and mustn't), and they would make me feel it: they would think of me as having joined their ranks, one outpost of which is the bedroom next door (but I have not joined); they would think that in you they had gained an ally against my opposition (they have not gained one), and in my eyes all that is ugly and contemptible about them is intensified, since I would expect them to rise to this greater occasion. Yet if this is so, why did I not like what you said? Because, literally, I stand facing my family perpetually brandishing knives, simultaneously to wound and to defend them. Leave me to act on your behalf in this matter, without acting on my behalf so far as your family is concerned. Isn't this too great a sacrifice for you to make, dearest? It is immense, and will only be made easier for you since, being what I am, should you fail to make it, I shall be forced to wrest it from you. But if you do make it, you will have done a lot for me.

The way you saw me this time is how I have seen myself for ages, only more clearly, which is why I can
explain what you saw:

As you know, there are two combatants at war
within me. During the past few days I have had fewer
doubts than ever that the better of the two belongs to
you. By word and silence, and a combination of both,
you have been kept informed about the progress of the
war for 5 years, and most of that time it has caused
you suffering. Were you to ask if I have always been
truthful, I could only say that with no one else have I
suppressed deliberate lies as strenuously, or—to be
more precise—more strenuously than I have with you.
Subterfuges there have been, lies very few, assuming
that it's possible to tell "very few" lies. I am a men-
dacious creature; for me it is the only way to maintain
an even keel, my boat is fragile. When I examine my
ultimate aim it shows that I do not actually strive to be
good, to answer to a supreme tribunal. Very much the
opposite. I strive to know the entire human and animal
community, to recognize their fundamental preferences,
desires, and moral ideals, to reduce them to simple
rules, and as quickly as possible to adopt these rules so
as to be pleasing to everyone, indeed (here comes the
inconsistency) to become so pleasing that in the end
I might openly act out my inherent baseness before the
eyes of the world without forfeiting its love—the only
sinner not to be roasted. In short, my only concern is
the human tribunal, and I would like to deceive even
this, and what's more without actual deception.

Apply this to our own case, which is not just an
arbitrary one, but altogether the one most truly representative of me. You are my human tribunal. Of the
two who are at war within me, or rather whose war I
consist of—excepting one small tormented remnant—
the one is good, the other evil. From time to time they
reverse their roles, which adds to the confusion of their
war, already so confused. Until very recently, however,
despite reverses, it was possible for me to imagine that
the most improbable would happen (the most probable

would be eternal war), which always seemed like the radiant goal, and I, grown pitiful and wretched over the years, would at last be allowed to have you.

Suddenly it appears that the loss of blood was too great. The blood shed by the good one (the one that now seems good to us) in order to win you, serves the evil one. Where the evil one on his own would probably or possibly not have found a decisive new weapon for his defense, the good one offers him just that. For secretly I don't believe this illness to be tuberculosis, at least not primarily tuberculosis, but rather a sign of my general bankruptcy. I had thought the war could last longer; but it can't. The blood issues not from the lung, but from a decisive stab delivered by one of the combatants.

From my tuberculosis this one now derives the kind of immense support a child gets from clinging to its mother's skirts. What more can the other one hope for? Has not the war been most splendidly concluded? It is tuberculosis, and that is the end. Weak and weary, almost invisible to you when in this state, what can the other one do but lean on your shoulder here in Zürau, and with you, the purest of the pure, stare in amazement, bewildered and hopeless, at the great man who— now that he feels sure of universal love, or of that of its female representative assigned to him—begins to display his atrocious baseness. It is a distortion of my striving, which in itself is already a distortion.

Please don't ask why I put up a barrier. Don't humiliate me in this way. One word like this from you and I would be at your feet again. But at once my actual, or rather, long before that, my alleged tuberculosis would stab me in the face, and I would have to give up. It is a weapon compared to which the countless others used earlier, ranging from "physical incapacity" up to my "work" and down to my "parsimony," look expedient and primitive.

And now I am going to tell you a secret which at the moment I don't even believe myself (although the distant darkness that falls about me at each attempt to work, or think, might possibly convince me), but which is bound to be true: I will never be well again. Simply because it is not the kind of tuberculosis that can be laid in a deckchair and nursed back to health, but a weapon that continues to be of supreme necessity as long as I remain alive. And both cannot remain alive.

Franz

SELECTIONS FROM
LETTERS TO FRIENDS

To Oskar Pollak

[January 27, 1904]

Dear Oskar,

You've written me a dear letter that should have been answered soon or not at all, and now two weeks have passed without my having written you; that would be unforgivable, but I had reasons. First of all, I wanted to write you only after careful reflection, because the answer to your letter seemed to me more important than any other previous letter to you (unfortunately I didn't get to it); and secondly I read Hebbel's diaries (some 1800 pages) all at once, whereas previously I had always just bitten out small pieces that struck me as insipid. All the same, I started to read consecutively. At first it was just a game, but eventually I came to feel like a caveman who rolls a block in front of the entrance to his cave, initially as a joke and out of boredom, but then, when the block makes the cave dark and shuts off the air, feels dully alarmed and with remarkable energy tries to push the rock away. But by then it has become ten times heavier and the man has to wrestle with it with all his might before light and air return. I simply could not take a pen in hand during these days. Because when you're surveying a life like that, which towers higher and higher without a gap, so high you can scarcely reach it with your field glasses, your conscience cannot settle down. But it's good when your conscience receives big wounds, because that makes it more sensitive to every twinge. I think we ought to read only the kind of books that wound and stab us. If the book we're reading doesn't wake us up with a blow on the head, what are we reading it for? So that it will make us happy, as you write? Good Lord, we would be happy precisely if we had no books, and the kind of books that make us happy are the kind we could write ourselves if we had to. But we need the books that affect us like a disaster, that grieve us deeply, like the death of someone we loved more than ourselves, like being banished into forests far from everyone, like a suicide. A book must be the axe for the frozen sea inside us. That is my belief.

To Max Brod

[Matliary, June, 1921]

Some time ago I read Kraus's *Literature.* I suppose you know it. My impression at the time, which of course has greatly faded by now, was that it was exceedingly acute, piercing straight to the heart. In this small world of German-Jewish writing he is really dominant, or rather the principle represented by him. He has so admirably subordinated himself to that principle that he has actually confounded himself with it and involved others in his confusion. I think I am distinguishing fairly well what in the book is only wit, although magnificent wit, what is whimpering, and finally what is truth, at least as much truth as there is in this hand with which I write, just as distinct and frighteningly physical. The wit principally consists of Yiddish-German—*mauscheln,* no one can *mauscheln* like Kraus, although in this German-Jewish world hardly anyone can do anything else. This *mauscheln*—taken in a wider sense, and that is the only way it should be taken—consists in a bumptious, tacit, or self-pitying appropriation of someone else's property, something not earned, but stolen by means of a relatively casual gesture. Yet it remains someone else's property, even though there is no evidence of a single solecism. That does not matter, for in this realm, the whispering voice of conscience confesses the whole crime in a penitent hour. This is not to say anything against *mauscheln*—in itself it is fine. It is an organic compound of bookish German and pantomime. (How expressive this is: "So he's got talent? Who says?" Or this, jerking the arm out of its socket and tossing up the chin: "*You* think so?" Or this, scraping the knees together: "He writes? Who about?") What we have here is the product of a sensitive feeling for language which has recognized that in German only the dialects are really alive, and except for them, only the most individual High German, while all the rest, the linguistic middle ground, is nothing but embers which can only be brought to a semblance of life when excessively lively Jewish hands rummage through them. That is a fact, funny or terrible as you like.

But why should the Jews be so irresistibly drawn to this language? German literature existed before the emancipation of the Jews and attained great glory. After all, that literature was, as far as I can see, in no way less varied than today—in fact, today there may be less variety. And there is a relationship between all this and Jewishness, or more precisely between young Jews and their Jewishness, with the frightful inner predicament of these generations. This is something Kraus especially recognized, or more precisely, this was something that came to light by being contrasted with him. He is in some way like the grandfather in the operetta, differing only to the extent that instead of simply saying *Oy*, he composes long tedious poems. (With a certain justification, by the way, the same justification with which Schopenhauer lived a tolerably cheerful life even though he recognized that man was continually plunging straight to hell.)

Psychoanalysis lays stress on the father-complex and many find the concept intellectually fruitful. In this case I prefer another version, where the issue revolves not around the innocent father but around the father's Jewishness. Most young Jews who began to write German wanted to leave Jewishness behind them, and their fathers approved of this, but vaguely (this vague-

291

ness was what was outrageous to them). But with their posterior legs they were still glued to their father's Jewishness and with their waving anterior legs they found no new ground. The ensuing despair became their inspiration.

An inspiration as honorable as any other, but on closer examination certain sad peculiarities. First of all, the product of their despair could not be German literature, though outwardly it seemed to be so. They existed among three impossibilities, which I just happen to call linguistic impossibilities. It is simplest to call them that. But they might also be called something entirely different. These are: The impossibility of not writing, the impossibility of writing German, the impossibility of writing differently. One might also add a fourth impossibility, the impossibility of writing (since the despair could not be assuaged by writing, was hostile to both life and writing; writing is only an expedient, as for someone who is writing his will shortly before he hangs himself—an expedient that may well last a whole life). Thus what resulted was a literature impossible in all respects, a gypsy literature which had stolen the German child out of its cradle and in great haste put it through some kind of training, for someone has to dance on the tightrope. (But it wasn't even a German child, it was nothing; people merely said that somebody was dancing) [BREAKS OFF]

To Max Brod

[Planá; postmark: July 5, 1922]
Last night as I lay sleepless and let everything continually veer back and forth between my aching temples, what I had almost forgotten during the last relatively quiet time became clear to me: namely, on what frail ground or rather altogether nonexistent ground I live, over a darkness from which the dark power emerges when it wills and, heedless of my stammering, destroys my life. Writing sustains me, but is it not more accurate to say that it sustains this kind of life? By this I don't mean, of course, that my life is better when I don't write. Rather it is much worse then and wholly unbear-

able and has to end in madness. But that, granted, only follows from the postulate that I am a writer, which is actually true even when I am not writing, and a non-writing writer is a monster inviting madness. But what about being a writer itself? Writing is a sweet and wonderful reward, but for what? In the night it became clear to me, as clear as a child's lesson book, that it is the reward for serving the devil. This descent to the dark powers, this unshackling of spirits bound by nature, these dubious embraces and whatever else may take place in the nether parts which the higher parts no longer know, when one writes one's stories in the sunshine. Perhaps there are other forms of writing, but I know only this kind; at night, when fear keeps me from sleeping, I know only this kind. And the diabolic element in it seems very clear to me. It is vanity and sensuality which continually buzz about one's own or even another's form—and feast on him. The movement multiplies itself—it is a regular solar system of vanity. Sometimes a naïve person will wish, "I would like to be dead and see how everyone mourns me." Such a writer is continually staging such a scene: He dies (or rather he does not live) and continually mourns himself. From this springs a terrible fear of death, which need not reveal itself as fear of death but may also appear as fear of change, as fear of Georgental. The reasons for this fear of death may be divided into two main categories. First he has a terrible fear of dying because he has not yet lived. By this I do not mean that wife and child, fields and cattle are essential to living. What is essential to life is only to forgo complacency, to move into the house instead of admiring it and hanging garlands around it. In reply to this, one might say that this is a matter of fate and is not given into anyone's hand. But then why this sense of repining, this repining that never ceases? To make oneself finer and more savory? That is a part of it. But why do such nights leave one always with the refrain: I could live and I do not live. The second reason—perhaps it is all really one, the two do not want to stay apart for me now—is the belief: "What I have

293

playacted is really going to happen. I have not bought myself off by my writing. I died my whole life long and now I will really die. My life was sweeter than other peoples' and my death will be more terrible by the same degree. Of course the writer in me will die right away, since such a figure has no base, no substance, is less than dust. He is only barely possible in the broil of earthly life, is only a construct of sensuality. That is your writer for you. But I myself cannot go on living because I have not lived, I have remained clay, I have not blown the spark into fire, but only used it to light up my corpse." It will be a strange burial: the writer, insubstantial as he is, consigning the old corpse, the longtime corpse, to the grave. I am enough of a writer to appreciate the scene with all my senses, or—and it is the same thing—to want to describe it with total self-forgetfulness—not alertness, but self-forgetfulness is the writer's first prerequisite. But there will be no more of such describing. But why am I talking of actual dying? It is just the same in life. I sit here in the comfortable posture of the writer, ready for all sorts of fine things, and must idly look on—for what can I do but write?—as my true ego, this wretched, defenseless ego, is nipped by the devil's pincers, cudgeled, and almost ground to pieces on a random pretext—a little trip to Georgental. [. . .] The existence of a writer is an argument against the existence of the soul, for the soul has obviously taken flight from the real ego, but not improved itself, only become a writer. Is it possible that separation from the ego can so weaken the soul? (I don't dare let this stand. Put this way it is also wrong.) Since I was not at home, what right have I to be alarmed when the house suddenly collapses. After all, I know what preceded the collapse. Did I not emigrate and leave the house to all the evil powers?

I wrote to Oskar yesterday, did mention my fear but promised to come. The letter has not yet been mailed. In the interval there was the night. Perhaps I will wait one more night; if I don't get through, I will have to cancel after all. This will mean that from now on I may not go out of Bohemia, next I will be confined to

Prague, then to my room, then to my bed, then to a certain position in bed, then to nothing more. Perhaps at that point I will be able to renounce the joy of writing voluntarily—voluntariness and joyousness are what count.

To underscore the whole story in terms of my writing —but I do not do the underscoring, the thing underscores itself—I must add that my fear of the journey is partly compounded by the thought that I will be kept away from the desk for at least several days. And this ridiculous thought is really the only legitimate one, since the existence of the writer is truly dependent upon his desk and if he wants to keep madness at bay he must never go far from his desk, he must hold on to it with his teeth.

The definition of a writer, of such a writer, and the explanation of his effectiveness, to the extent that he has any: He is the scapegoat of mankind. He makes it possible for men to enjoy sin without guilt, almost without guilt.

ERICH HELLER is Avalon Foundation Professor of the Humanities at Northwestern University. He is the author of, among other publications, *The Disinherited Mind*, *Thomas Mann: The Ironic German*, *The Artist's Journey into the Interior*, and *Franz Kafka*.

CLASSICS THAT WILL DELIGHT READERS OF EVERY AGE!

THE CALL OF THE WILD Jack London

A CHRISTMAS CAROL Charles Dickens

KON-TIKI Thor Heyerdahl

LES MISÉRABLES Victor Hugo

THE ODYSSEY Homer

PYGMALION George Bernard Shaw

THE RED BADGE OF COURAGE Stephen Crane

A TALE OF TWO CITIES Charles Dickens

WSP

Washington Square Press
Published by Pocket Books

743-05